TRUST

Michigan Studies in Political Analysis

Michigan Studies in Political Analysis promotes the development and dissemination of innovative scholarship in the field of methodology in political science and the social sciences in general. Methodology is defined to include statistical methods, mathematical modeling, measurement, research design, and other topics related to the conduct and development of analytical work. The series includes works that develop a new model or method applicable to social sciences, as well as those that, through innovative combination and presentation of current analytical tools, substantially extend the use of these tools by other researchers.

GENERAL EDITORS: John E. Jackson and Christopher H. Achen

Keith Krehbiel
Information and Legislative Organization

Donald R. Kinder and Thomas R. Palfrey, Editors
Experimental Foundations of Political Science

John Brehm
The Phantom Respondents: Opinion Surveys and Political Representation

William T. Bianco
Trust: Representatives and Constituents

TRUST

Representatives and Constituents

William T. Bianco

Ann Arbor

THE UNIVERSITY OF MICHIGAN PRESS

Copyright © by the University of Michigan 1994
All rights reserved
Published in the United States of America by
The University of Michigan Press
Manufactured in the United States of America
⊗ Printed on acid-free paper

1997   1996   1995   1994   4   3   2   1

*A CIP catalogue record for this book is available from the British
Library.*

Library of Congress Cataloging-in-Publication Data

Bianco, William T., 1960–
        Trust : representatives and constituents / William T. Bianco.
            p.   cm. — (Michigan studies in political analysis)
        Includes bibliographical references and index.
        ISBN 0-472-10510-8 (alk. paper). — ISBN 0-472-08267-1 (pbk. :
    alk. paper)
        1. Representative government and representation—United States—
    Public opinion.   2. Trust (Psychology)   3. United States.
    Congress—Public opinion.   4. Public opinion—United States.
    I. Title.   II. Series.
    JK1071.B5   1994
    328.73'073—dc20   94-6929
                                                                     CIP

To Regina Anne and Anna Cain,
with love, trust, and thanks

The aim of every political constitution is, or ought to be, first to obtain for rulers men who posess most wisdom to discern, and most virtue to pursue, the common good of society; and in the next place, to take the most effectual precautions for keeping them virtuous whilst they continue to hold the public trust. The elective mode of obtaining rulers is the characteristic policy of republican government. The means relied on in this form of government for preventing their degeneracy are numerous and various. The most effectual one is such a limitation of the term of appointment as will maintain a proper responsibility to the people.

—James Madison, *The Federalist* No. 57

Preface

Why do constituents sometimes defer to their representative's judgments about policy options? When does this sort of trust arise? These are narrow questions with broad implications. Any attempt to explain, predict, or evaluate behavior in legislatures such as the modern Congress is built on assumptions about trust. What is surprising is that contemporary theories of the legislative process are unable to explain the phenomena. Scholars know—or strongly suspect—that legislators' actions are shaped by their expectations about trust. Moreover, they suspect there is variation to explain: in some situations legislators appear to hold constituent trust, while in others they apparently do not. But scholars cannot account for this variation—they cannot say where trust comes from or predict when it will arise.

The aim of this book is to understand trust. Throughout the book, elected officials and ordinary citizens are described as rational actors, whose decisions vary with their goals, available information, and the actions taken by others. However, the book moves beyond the standard rational choice framework in three ways. First, it avoids narrow, unrealistic assumptions about motivations and information. Second, it attempts to show that many kinds of behavior that are not usually thought of as rational choices, such as voters' desire to be represented by "someone like them," are the product of a systematic, predictable calculus—moreover, a calculus aimed at securing favorable policy outcomes. Finally, the book exploits a unique data set, interviews with ninety-three members of the U.S. House of Representatives, to illustrate and motivate the abstract analysis and to test its predictions about trust.

Without implicating anyone as a supporter or critic, this book reflects comments from a number of colleagues, including John Aldrich, Douglas Arnold, David Austen-Smith, Jeffrey Banks, Robert Bates, John Brehm, David Canon, Roger Davidson, Richard Fenno, Morris Fiorina, Thomas Gilligan, Ruth Grant, Gary Jacobson, William Keech, James Lindsay, James Lietzel, Peter Ordeshook, Regina Smyth, John Wilkerson, and a number of anonymous referees. In particular, Aldrich, Arnold Lindsay, and Smyth read the entire manuscript providing invaluable suggestions about presentation and substance. Christine DeGregorio, Larry Evans, John Gilmour, Richard Hall, David Price, Burt Rockman, Steve Smith, and Joseph White gave much useful advice about the mysteries of fieldwork. Thanks are also due to my colleagues in the Department of Political Science at Duke University, particularly Allan Kornberg. R. Michael Alvarez, Mark Berger, William Bernhard, Tracy Hailey, Dean Lacy, Phillip Paolino, J. M. Patterson, and, especially, Matthew Schousen supplied expert research assistance. Joy Pickett and Carla St. John were, as always, the epitome of first-rate staff support. Funding for various aspects of the project was provided by the Pew Charitable Trust, the Ford Foundation, and the Duke University Research Council. Thomas Mann and his staff at the Brookings Institution provided a base of operations in Washington. Colin Day and his staff at the University of Michigan Press deserve my profound thanks for their efforts in guiding me through the publication process. Finally, I am extremely grateful to ninety-three members of the U.S. House, as well as a number of staffers and lobbyists, who graciously consented to interviews.

My greatest acknowledgment is to Regina Anne Smyth, whose insights and encouragement have spanned the professional and personal spheres. She shares the dedication with Anna Cain Bianco, whose arrival on May 20, 1993, provided the usual incentives for closure, as well as the beginning of a much more interesting enterprise.

Contents

CHAPTER 1

Introduction

First I want to know how you're going to use what I tell you. Because I can give
you political answers or I can tell you the truth.
                                                        —A Midwestern Democrat

Each time a representative faces a decision about policy, her constituents face
a decision about trust. Should they defer to their representative's judgment or
demand that she act as they think best? By virtue of their office, representatives are better informed about the policy process. They hold private information about the consequences of enacting policy proposals and the policy
implications of procedural choices. Put another way, the relationship between
legislators and constituents is one of asymmetric information. As a result,
legislators are often in a better position to judge whether a vote on a proposal,
an amendment, or a rule serves constituent interests. However, since legislators
hold policy concerns of their own and are often pressured by special interests
or their party, deference is not always appropriate. Constituents cannot accept
expertise as a blanket justification for actions that appear contrary to their
interests. They must develop criteria for making decisions about trust.

Assumptions about trust play a central, if sometimes unacknowledged,
role in theories of legislatorial behavior and theories of representation. Decisions about trust are implemented through evaluations of a legislator's past
behavior. To say that constituents trust their representative implies that she
will receive favorable evaluations regardless of how she votes. Without trust,
a representative receives favorable evaluations only if she acts as her constituents think best, even if she knows that her actions will not serve constituent
interests. Therefore, decisions about trust are a critical piece of the "electoral
connection" (Mayhew 1974) between legislators and their constituents—they
determine whether an action is politically beneficial or politically costly. If
scholars want to explain why legislators take some actions rather than others,
or if they want to understand how legislators mediate between the pursuit of
reelection and goals such as the desire to enact good public policy, they must
answer a simple question: when do constituents trust their representative, and
what is the basis of that trust?

Assumptions about trust also bear on a critical point in democratic theory: the expectation that the electoral connection creates, as Madison believed, a "proper responsibility" to constituent interests. In the modern era, many consider this expectation to be problematic, believing that asymmetric information leads constituents into two kinds of mistakes. Some argue that constituents force their representatives to vote in favor of inferior policies rather than allowing them to act in light of private information. Others say that constituents are all too quick to defer, enabling representatives to ignore constituent interests in favor of their personal views, or those of special interests, without being punished.

These accusations raise serious worries about democratic theory. In a world characterized by asymmetric information, to what extent is it possible to give elected officials the right incentive—the incentive to serve constituent interests? Moreover, what kinds of incentives do real-world constituents create? Put another way, how *should* constituents make decisions about trust? How *do* they make decisions about trust? The importance of these questions is matched by our ignorance about their answers. Analyses of the legislative process, as well as critiques of democratic theory, use a variety of assumptions about trust. Some of these assumptions are contradictory. None are based on a theory of how constituents should, or do, approach trust decisions.

This book is about trust. The premise is that trust is the product of rational calculation, albeit under asymmetric information. The first goal of the analysis is to understand how a rational constituent would approach trust decisions and how a rational legislator would act in anticipation of these decisions. The second goal is to show that real-world behavior conforms to this rational choice model. Throughout the book, the analytic focus is on trust decisions involving high-salience policy proposals. The empirical referent is the modern Congress.

A word on what this book does not do: it does not develop a general theory of representation, inasmuch as it examines only one aspect of this relationship, one type of action, and one legislature. However, decisions about trust are the nearest thing to a first principle in models of legislatorial behavior. Regardless of whether scholars are interested in predicting the behavior of individual representatives, predicting policy outcomes, or addressing larger questions about legislative institutions or performance, getting trust right is a necessary first step. Moreover, once we know how trust works in one context, it may be possible to generalize these findings to other kinds of actions and other legislatures.

Finally, a note on terminology. Throughout the book, female pronouns are used exclusively to refer to representatives, while male pronouns are reserved for constituents. This specification is made purely for expositional purposes, and in no way implies anything about the characteristics of either group. In addition, I use the terms *legislator*, *representative*, and *member of Congress* interchangeably.

The Plan of the Book

The next two chapters set up the analysis. Chapter 2 shows that assumptions about trust loom large in analyses of the legislative process and that most of these assumptions are problematic, or at best untested. Chapter 3 explains what it means to say that representatives and constituents are rational actors. Chapter 3 also describes—and defends—two key assumptions. The first assumption is that legislators' explanations are not a direct influence on their constituents' trust decisions. The second assumption is that constituents form beliefs about their representative using stereotypes: they reason from a representative's observed actions and attributes to form judgments about her unobserved policy goals.

Chapter 4 presents a two-player signaling game (labeled the evaluation game) intended to capture a single interaction involving a representative and her constituents. (The presentation in chapter 4 is informal; readers interested in the technical details should consult appendix 1.) One player, the representative, votes on a single high-salience policy proposal. After the vote, a second player, symbolizing constituents, makes a retrospective evaluation. The representative is motivated by two goals: reelection and the desire to enact good public policy. The constituent also holds policy goals, although these goals may differ from those held by the representative. The players are assumed to act under conditions of asymmetric information. The representative is fully aware of all factors relevant to her decision. The constituent, however, is unsure of two things: what policy outcome will follow from enacting the proposal in question and what kinds of policy goals the representative holds.

The analysis of this game shows, not surprisingly, that trust depends on perceptions of the act and the agent—what constituents know about the proposal being voted on and what they know about their representative. However, the analysis identifies the specific perceptions that drive trust decisions. Once some necessary conditions are satisfied, trust is a function of two perceptions: how much constituents know about a proposal and their estimate of the likelihood of a common interest. A common interest exists when the result (enactment or defeat of the proposal) that is consistent with a representative's interests is also consistent with the interests of her constituents. Beliefs about common interest are by far the most important factor in trust decisions. If constituents assess a low probability of common interest, they will never trust their representative, regardless of how uncertain they are. Conversely, if they believe the probability of common interest is high, they will always defer, even if their uncertainties are small.

Chapters 5 and 6 test these predictions using data drawn from interviews with 93 members of the U.S. House of Representatives. (For details on the data, see appendix 2.) Members of Congress were questioned about their votes on two proposals: the 1989 Ethics Reform Act and the repeal of the

1988 Medicare Catastrophic Coverage Act. These data are combined with contextual information ranging from election returns and committee assignments to financial disclosure forms. Analysis of these data confirms both the predictions drawn from game-theoretic analysis as well as the overall picture of trust and trust decisions. In particular, there is no sign that explanations generate trust. In addition, the analysis confirms that a representative's expectations about trust, and thus the forces acting on her decisions, can easily vary across proposals—perhaps even across amendments to the same proposal.

The substance of each proposal is easy to describe. The Ethics Act, which passed the House by a 252 to 174 vote on November 16, 1989, granted a 25 percent pay raise (approximately $25,000) to members of the House of Representatives and senior members of the executive branch and imposed a variety of ethics reforms on members and their staffs. Raise proposals are always controversial; most legislators want pay raises, and most constituents oppose them. For example, when describing their constituents' reaction to the raise proposed in late 1988 by the Quadrennial Commission, members used words like "vociferous," "visceral," "violent," "virulent," "vehement," and "vituperative" to describe the reaction. Constituents had the raise "shoved up their nose"; they were "stirred up," "inflamed," and "whipped into a frenzy"; they "sent letters with short, angry sentences and language I can't repeat." Small wonder that the recommendations were defeated by an overwhelming vote in both Houses (Hook 1989b; Wilkerson 1991, chap. 6). Yet a majority of House members cast recorded votes in favor of the Ethics Act. And, while many predicted that the Ethics vote would be a major issue in the 1990 election, it was not.[1] In fact, many of the representatives who voted for the Ethics Act believed that their constituents approved of their behavior, even though these constituents had earlier opposed the proposal. Where did this trust come from?

The repeal of Catastrophic Coverage suggests a different question. This program, which was enacted on June 2, 1988, expanded Medicare, the federal program that provides health care to senior citizens, to cover extended hospital stays.[2] More importantly, it was the first "pay-as-you-go" entitlement,

---

1. In early 1990, *Roll Call* ("The Newspaper of Congress") labeled the Ethics Act a "red-hot issue" (Winneker 1990), while *Congressional Quarterly*'s February, 1990, election outlook issue described it as one factor behind "potential volatility" in the upcoming election (Duncan 1990b). However, the vote was not mentioned in *Congressional Quarterly*'s October, 1990, pre-election report, and its postelection analyses noted it only in passing (Alston 1990; Duncan 1990a; Kaplan 1990). Scholarly accounts (e.g., Jacobson 1991) reached similar conclusions.

2. There were many other provisions, the most notable being that the federal government would pay for prescription drugs for seniors. Readers interested in the details of the program, or in the events leading up to its enactment and subsequent repeal, should consult the 1987, 1988, and 1989 editions of the Congressional Quarterly *Almanac*.

financed by a small increase in Medicare premiums and a special surtax imposed on beneficiaries. This surtax was based on ability to pay rather than risk: 40 percent of recipients would pay a surtax; an unfortunate 5.6 percent would pay the maximum: $800 per year for individuals, $1,600 for married couples. Even at the maximum rate, however, the insurance was arguably cheaper for seniors than equivalent programs offered by private sector firms. With all these features, it seemed no surprise that support for the program united both Democrats and Republicans in Congress, a Republican president, and many interest groups, including the largest senior citizen interest group, the American Association of Retired Persons (AARP). However, seniors did not respond favorably to Catastrophic Coverage. During interviews with this author, members of Congress would talk about the enormous numbers of letters they received against the program—six thousand, eight thousand, ten thousand, or even sixteen thousand—and then mention, almost as an aside, that they had also heard from six, or four, or two supporters. Moreover, despite the fact that many House members hold prosenior voting records and aggressively court support from seniors in their district, few expected to have trust on the repeal vote. As a result, little more than a year after it was enacted, Catastrophic Coverage was repealed—again by a nearly unanimous vote, with then-President Bush saying nothing and the AARP taking no position at all. Why the absence of trust?

Chapters 5 and 6 are not detailed case studies of the enactment of the Ethics Act and the repeal of Catastrophic Coverage. Readers interested in the machinations that brought these proposals to the floor of the House, set the procedures for voting on them, and determined their fate must look elsewhere. The reason is simple: questions about trust, or explanation, can be answered without investigating these larger questions. Of course, the answers to my questions may help to explain why these proposals were written as they were or explain procedural choices. Undoubtedly other readers will find chapters 5 and 6 filled with apparently extraneous material, particularly a large number of quotes. My intent is to give the reader a sense of the context within which House members developed expectations and made decisions. What did constituents want? What did members prefer? It seemed obvious that this context should be described in the members' own words. Moreover, the interviews provide a critical reality check: they suggest that the game-theoretic analysis, with all its restrictions, captures the essence of trust decisions.

Drawing on the game-theoretic and the empirical analyses, chapter 7 argues that constituent trust is a rational but extremely contextual phenomenon. We should expect that some representatives will be trusted more than others and that a representative's chances of being trusted will vary across proposals. We should expect that almost all representatives will find it extremely difficult to build the reputations necessary for trust. Some legislators, of course, may arrive in office with their reputations ready-made. Even these lucky individuals will constantly worry about damaging their positive reputations. This variation in trust, and the difficulty of reputation building, does not arise because constituents fail to appreciate the game they are playing. Rather, it occurs because constituents understand the game all too well. In the latter portion of chapter 7, I apply these findings in two areas. First, I critique existing models of legislatorial behavior and make some suggestions for improvement. Second, I evaluate various proposals for congressional reform, including measures that enhance congressional deliberation, measures that empower the congressional leadership, and the imposition of term limits. All these reforms are found to be wanting. The message seems to be that imperfect control is inherent in representative government.

Why Game Theory? Why Fieldwork?

The analysis presented here combines two very different research traditions: formal modeling and participant observation. The danger with this sort of enterprise is that it will offend everyone. Congressional scholars will worry that complex phenomena have been jammed into a spare and unrealistic framework. Formal theorists will worry that the analytic power of game theory has been subordinated to anecdotes and storytelling. Everyone will worry about the quality of the data. These are all valid concerns. However, given the nature of the questions asked here, this combination of approaches is the only option.

To begin with, game theory provides the only comprehensive statement of how people make decisions in light of goals and available information. In particular, games of asymmetric information are designed to reveal how well-informed players act in light of their opponents' uncertainties—and how uncertain players interpret the actions taken by a well-informed opponent. It is unclear how predictions about these phenomena could be developed except through game theory. Of course, skeptical readers will prefer empirical verification over my ascetic judgments. They will find comfort in chapter 4's frequent references to the substantive literature, in the empirical analyses in chapters 5 and 6, and in the interviews, which reveal that the details of the game analyzed here conform to the view of trust and trust decisions advanced by members of Congress.

After reading through the game-theoretic analysis in chapter 4, most readers will welcome the case studies in chapters 5 and 6. However, some will question the heavy reliance on interview data. The simple justification is that interviews seem the only way to gather the information needed to test predictions about trust and explanations. Alternate sources of data on constituent demands, legislators' policy preferences, or their expectations about trust simply do not exist. I am prepared to argue that legislators hold accurate beliefs about these factors. Certainly this is the conventional wisdom in congressional studies. And this conclusion is supported by the findings contained in chapters 5 and 6 and by a reliability analysis contained in appendix 2. Of course, even if legislators' perceptions were to some degree inaccurate or biased, there would still be merit in measuring these factors as they are seen "through the eyes of the representative" (Fenno 1978, xiii).

Part 1
A Theory of Trust

CHAPTER 2

Trust, Democratic Theory, and the Electoral Connection

There's something you can explain for me. When I was in college, I didn't take any political science because it seemed either too easy or irrelevant. Political scientists don't seem to know anything about street politics. For example, if you come in late to a meeting and right away you have to vote on an issue you know nothing about, how should you vote? Why, no, of course. Then you have the substance, plus all of the procedural questions, it's premature, untimely, not well thought out. Jesse Helms has made a career out of saying no. Political scientists don't know that kind of street politics.

—A border-state Democrat

This chapter sets out the context of trust decisions. It begins by describing constituents as policy-minded actors who make retrospective evaluations with the goal of controlling their representative's behavior and assessing her performance in office. Unfortunately, constituents are often ill informed about the policy process, a deficiency that makes the formation of accurate evaluations problematic. Elected officials, in contrast, are generally better informed about policy options. This asymmetry is what motivates constituents to consider trust—allowing their representative to use her judgment rather than forcing her to implement their demands. Unfortunately, while representatives want as much trust as they can get, deference is generally not a dominant strategy for constituents: a representative can use it to pursue her own interests at the expense of constituent welfare.

With this description in hand, the chapter examines the conventional wisdom on trust and trust decisions. Scholars agree that as long as a representative has some interest in reelection, expectations about trust can influence what she does and why she does it. Therefore, assumptions about trust should—and do—play a critical role in analyses of the legislative process. Unfortunately, there is no consensus on when trust exists, or on how constituents resolve trust decisions. Some analyses assume that trust is ubiquitous; some assume trust is rare or nonexistent. Others simply avoid the question. Intuitively, the answer lies somewhere in the middle: trust varies across representatives and across contexts. What is needed is a theory that can account for this variation.

Why Trust?

The essence of democracy is that citizens control government by choosing representatives and giving them the power to set public policy using majority rule. In the American political system, representatives are typically elected by geographically defined constituencies. What do constituents want from their representative? This book assumes that their preference is for a representative who behaves according to a criteria advanced by Pitkin:

> [Representing] means acting in the interests of the represented, in a manner responsive to them. . . . [The representative] must not be found persistently at odds with the wishes of the represented without good reason in terms of their interest, without a good explanation of why their wishes are not in accord with their interests. (1967, 209–10)

In other words, constituents want their representative to take actions that are consistent with their preferences across policy outcomes—their preferences with respect to results. (Such actions are labeled here as *fiduciary behavior*.) For example, when a representative votes on a policy proposal, her constituents want her to cast whatever vote produces the best possible policy outcome in light of their interests—their policy goals. For simplicity, this book makes the same auxiliary assumption as Pitkin: within a district, interests are homogenous. While it would be possible to account for the effects of heterogeneous interests, such a move would introduce considerable complication to no great advantage.

This definition of voter motivations is extremely broad. It is consistent with the idea that voters are selfish maximizers of economic well-being, as well as with the idea that voters want to achieve certain ideological goals, or even that they wish to implement policies consistent with a conception of the national interest. In addition, the definition does not imply that constituents ignore other aspects of their representative's behavior, such as her accessibility, personal attributes, or actions outside office. As Fenno notes,

> We shall have to consider the possibility that supportive constituents may want extrapolicy behavior from their representatives. They may want good access or the assurance of good access as much as they want good policy. They may want "a good man" or "a good woman," someone whose assurances they can trust, as much as they want good policy . . . the point is that we should not start our studies of representation by assuming [policy preferences] are the only basis for a representational relationship. They are not. (1978, 240–41)

To say that constituents are policy minded does not eliminate any of these complexities. Rather, it suggests an alternate interpretation of why these factors are salient: constituents care about access, appearance, or actions because taking account of these phenomena somehow helps them to secure favorable policy outcomes.

Pitkin's criterion also subsumes other conceptions of good representation. The most common alternate is that representatives should act in accordance with the national interest—the common good—even at the expense of their district.[1] This specification can be criticized on empirical grounds. Intuitively, a voter will favor implementation of his personal conception of the good and worry about the national interest only insofar as the two definitions coincide. However, a stronger counter-argument exists: most scholars who favor a common-interest definition of good representation argue that if representatives behaved in this way, all citizens would ultimately benefit, whatever their particular interests might be. If this argument is true, then the common-interest criterion merely restates Pitkin's criterion of actions consistent with constituent interests.

The problem constituents face is to ensure that their representative does what they want. Ideally, constituents could elect someone whose only goal was to implement their interests on all matters. Unfortunately, to paraphrase Madison, few representatives are angels. Therefore, constituents must look for ways to increase the chances that their representative will choose to act in their interests. In a democracy, the principal mechanism available to constituents is retrospective evaluations coupled with regular elections. The format of retrospective evaluations and their effect on a representative's behavior are discussed in the next section.

Retrospective Evaluations

Constituents make a retrospective evaluation when they rate or judge some aspect of their representative's performance in office, such as her vote on a policy proposal (Downs 1957; Fiorina 1981; Key 1966). In forming these evaluations, constituents ask the question: did our representative act in our interests? If constituents believe that their representative acted as a fiduciary, taking actions consistent with their interests, they will make a favorable evaluation. On the other hand, if constituents think their representative acted against their interests, they will make an unfavorable evaluation.

---

1. A classic statement is found in the comments of Melancton Smith, a noted Anti-Federalist, during the ratification debate in New York (reprinted in Storing 1981a). Storing (1981b) provides a useful summary of these arguments. For a contemporary advocate, see Maas 1983.

Vote decisions are a good example. Suppose constituents know, or believe, that they will be made better off if a certain proposal is enacted—they believe that the enactment of the proposal is consistent with their interests. Under these conditions, a yea vote constitutes fiduciary behavior, while a nay vote represents a deviation from constituent interests. Thus, constituents in this example would be expected to evaluate a yea vote favorably and evaluate a nay vote unfavorably.

Constituents make retrospective evaluations for two reasons. First, these evaluations are a convenient yardstick for assessing a representative's performance in office. With retrospective evaluations in hand, constituents can decide whether their incumbent should be reelected or replaced by a challenger. Intuitively, favorable evaluations increase a representative's chances of reelection; negative evaluations reduce it. In addition, retrospective evaluations—more specifically, the threat of unfavorable evaluations—can also function as a check on a representative's behavior. The idea is that if an incumbent wants to be reelected and expects that her behavior will be the focus of subsequent evaluations, she will cast votes that she expects will receive favorable evaluations. For example, if constituents believe that the enactment of a proposal will make them better off, their representative, anticipating future evaluations, will opt to vote yea, regardless of what she thinks about the resulting policy outcome.

This analysis takes a voter-level perspective on retrospective evaluations. That is, I speak of voters monitoring their representative's actions and making evaluations based on available information. An alternate assumption would be to say that monitoring is performed by district-level elites (i.e., potential challengers) who inform voters about an incumbent's behavior only if they observe that the incumbent has cast politically damaging votes.[2] This alternate assumption explains two apparently inconsistent regularities: while members of Congress anticipate retrospective evaluations when deciding how to vote, voters appear to know little about their representative's voting record. However, even if the assumption about elites is true, retrospective evaluations—more properly, the threat of unfavorable evaluations—remain a significant influence on incumbent behavior. Therefore, for the purposes of this analysis there is no need to choose between the two conceptions of retrospective evaluations.

There is considerable evidence that members of Congress take account of retrospective evaluations when deciding how to vote. Not surprisingly, this effect is most likely to occur when legislators vote on high-salience proposals (Arnold 1990; Fenno 1978; Fiorina 1981). Kingdon (1981, 45–47) defines issue salience in terms of whether the masses and the elites in a district are

---

2. I am indebted to John Zaller for this insight.

aware of an issue and care about its resolution. From a legislator's perspective, there are two types of high-salience proposals. One is a proposal, such as the Ethics Act, that attracts the attention of a large percentage of constituents and elites. The other is a proposal, such as Catastrophic Health Coverage, that is considered important by a smaller group of constituents who, along with their elites, happen to be extremely active in politics. (In the case of Catastrophic Coverage, the group consisted of senior citizens, who make up 10 to 20 percent of the population in most districts but have extremely high turnout and participation rates.) While these situations differ in terms of the number of constituents who will evaluate their legislator's vote, from the legislator's viewpoint there is no difference: in both cases, her vote will have significant political consequences, measured in terms of her probability of reelection. As Kingdon notes:

> . . . on high-salience issues the constituency is more important in the congressman's decision than it is on other issues. He subjectively considers constituents more important, and votes more in accordance with their wishes, to the point that the predictive capability of a constituency position is really quite remarkable. We have also seen that it apparently does not matter a great deal whether one is talking of low- or medium-salience issues. Once one leaves the exalted place of the high-salience issues, the constituency effects are similar. It is also important to note, however, that constituency still has a substantial impact even on low-salience votes. (1981, 44)

On the majority of votes, which involve low-salience proposals that are of interest to relatively few constituents, a legislator, even one who desires reelection, would be expected to favor her personal policy goals, ignoring the threat of unfavorable evaluations. (However, as later chapters will show, votes on low-salience proposals may also be influenced by reputational concerns.) The effects of salience both narrow and sharpen the problem facing a representative. Only rarely will her votes have large political consequences. However, precisely because most proposals do not attract the attention of constituents, "good" votes on those proposals will not offset the damage caused by "bad" votes on the small number of high-salience proposals.

High-salience issues may not involve questions that an objective observer would consider to be of great import. Consider the repeal of Catastrophic Coverage. From a senior's perspective, the introduction of catastrophic health insurance was a significant change, especially since coverage was essentially mandatory and, for some, costly. Thus, it makes sense that Catastrophic was a salient issue for senior citizens. But consider the Ethics Act. Clearly, the future of the Republic did not hinge on whether members of

Congress received a $25,000 raise in return for forgoing honoraria and outside income. Yet many constituents, for whatever reason, cared a great deal about the resolution of this proposal. As a result, legislators described the Ethics Act as a "hot button" issue, a "bell-ringer," where their vote would have immediate and significant political consequences, even though the proposal's effect on policy outcomes would be modest at best.

Recent trends in American politics have undoubtedly increased the influence of retrospective evaluations on legislators' behavior. As a result of the procedural reforms of the 1970s, members cast recorded votes on almost all major pieces of legislation and most important amendments (Oleszek 1989). Interest groups and the media have intensified their efforts to inform citizens about roll call votes (Schlozman and Tierney 1986). Changes in the electoral environment, such as the decline of presidential coattails, the erosion of party identification, and the rise of candidate-centered campaigns, have focused attention on a representative's behavior (Jacobson 1992). Thus, constituents are likely to know how their representative votes, at least on high-salience proposals. And if a legislator casts enough unpopular votes on these proposals, presidential popularity, a favorable party balance, or extensive casework will not save her from defeat.

Clearly, retrospective evaluations shape the political consequences of a representative's votes. However, they do not guarantee that a representative will behave as her constituents desire—even on high-salience proposals. A representative may deviate from constituent demands for a number of reasons: because she cares deeply about the resulting policy outcome, because she has little interest in reelection, because her actions are unlikely to become publicly known, or some combination. Thus, in making retrospective evaluations, constituents are doing everything they can to influence their representative's behavior. However, their efforts may not be enough to control their representative's actions—or, as the next section will show, enough to ensure fiduciary behavior.

The Problem: Citizen Misinformation

That citizens make retrospective evaluations seems clear. However, their efforts may not work as intended. The threat of unfavorable evaluations gives representatives the right incentives—incentives that promote fiduciary behavior—only if citizens are well informed about the policy process. Uncertainties or misperceptions do not preclude retrospective evaluations. The problem is that evaluations made under these conditions may have unintended, harmful effects. Citizens may be able to control who gets elected or determine the winner's behavior in office, but their efforts may not yield policy outcomes that are consistent with their goals.

Suppose, for example, constituents in some district believe, mistakenly, that they will be better off if some high-salience proposal is enacted. (The terms *demands* and *opinions* are used interchangeably to refer to these beliefs.) These beliefs imply that constituents should evaluate yea votes favorably and nay votes unfavorably, as a way of forcing their representative to vote for the proposal. And if the representative has a sufficient interest in reelection and expects these evaluations, she will do so. But a yea vote makes constituents *worse* off, not better. Put another way, a yea vote implements constituents' demands (or reflects their opinions), but it does not serve their interests. Even if the representative votes nay, there is a problem: constituents will infer, incorrectly, that she acted against their interests and might do so again in the future, thereby making them less likely to support the representative in the next election.

Alternately, constituents may be unaware of opportunities for sophisticated behavior—actions that exploit the sequential nature of legislative decision making.[3] For example, they may demand that their representative vote for an amendment designed to improve an already attractive proposal, not realizing that the unamended proposal will pass but that the amended version will be defeated. Again, if the legislator follows her constituents' demands, voting for the amendment, the result will be an inferior policy outcome. Constituent interests can be served only at the cost of an unfavorable evaluation, generated when the legislator votes against the amendment.

Such "responsiveness without responsibility" (Jacobson 1992, 216) is not an abstract problem. Decades of public opinion research have demonstrated that most citizens are ill informed about policy questions and that this ignorance has policy consequences. In their seminal article, Miller and Stokes conclude,

---

3. Suppose members of a legislature must decide among three alternatives: the status quo (S), a proposal (P), and an amended version of the proposal (A). Assume legislators will first choose between P and A, with the winner being voted on against S. Consider a legislator who rates A as the most attractive option, with P second and S last. Suppose she expects that P will win a majority of votes against S, but that S will beat A if the two alternatives are voted on together. Intuitively, since the legislator prefers A over P, she should vote for A when the two alternatives are considered together. This choice is *sincere behavior*, as it follows from her preferences across the two alternatives. However, the choice between P against A does not determine policy outcomes; rather, it sets up a subsequent choice. Insofar as the legislator cares about outcomes, her decision should reflect the ultimate rather than the immediate consequences of her vote. Recall that A will ultimately lose to S, while P will beat S. If so, a vote for A is really a vote for S, while a vote for P unambiguously yields P (McKelvey and Niemi 1978). By this logic, the legislator should vote for P over A, since she prefers P (the ultimate result if P wins initially) to S (the ultimate result if A wins). This vote constitutes *sophisticated behavior* (sometimes labeled strategic behavior), as it accounts for the ultimate effects of different actions rather than considering only their immediate effects.

Some of the more buoyant advocates of popular sovereignty have regarded the citizen as a kind of kibitzer who looks over the shoulder of his representative at the legislative game. Kibitzer and player may disagree as to which card should be played, but they were at least thought to share a common understanding of what the alternatives are.

No one familiar with the findings of research on mass electorates could accept this view of the citizen. Far from looking over the shoulder of their Congressman at the legislative game, most Americans are almost totally uninformed about legislative issues in Washington. At best the average citizen may be said to have some general ideas about how the country should be run, which he is able to use in responding to particular questions about what the government ought to do. (1963, 47)

Miller and Stokes's conclusion remains accurate today. In their recent study of public opinion, Page and Shapiro conclude,

it is undeniable that most Americans are, at best, fuzzy about the details of government structure and policy. They do not know with any precision how much money is being spent on the military, foreign aid, education, or food stamps. They have only a dim idea of what is going on in foreign countries or (in many cases) even where those countries are. They do not know much about monetary policy or economic regulation or labor relations or civil rights. Thus it would be unrealistic to expect the average American to hold well-worked out, firmly based preferences about a wide range of public policies. (1992, 13–14)

Page and Shapiro (1992), along with many other scholars (Arnold 1990; Krehbiel 1991), describe citizen ignorance in terms of the relationship between policy proposals and policy outcomes. Policy proposals are means; policy outcomes are ends. Citizens, it is said, are fully informed about ends, or the desirability of different policy outcomes, but are uncertain about which policy outcome will be produced by a particular policy proposal.[4] This description covers a range of possible beliefs. At one extreme, citizens have no idea—or only a vague idea—which proposal will produce a given outcome. At the other extreme, citizens are fairly sure about the relationship between proposals and outcomes. Two possibilities are consistent with the latter description. One is that the beliefs constituents hold are indeed accurate; the other is that they are wildly inaccurate.

---

4. Conceivably constituents might also be uncertain about the desirability of policy outcomes. Current theories do not allow for this possibility, although they could easily be modified to do so.

Where does this ignorance come from? In theory, since citizens will experience a proposal's effects following its enactment, they could simply forgo retrospective evaluations until they have full information. Unfortunately, it is difficult to envision circumstances where the passage of time is sufficient to resolve citizen uncertainty. For one thing, the marginal effects of a proposal may be hard to perceive. And, of course, constituents will never experience the effects of defeated proposals—or of the status quo in the case of proposals that are enacted.

The recent enactment of the North American Free Trade Agreement (NAFTA) illustrates these problems. At the time NAFTA was voted on, it would be no surprise to find (as many surveys did) that citizens were uncertain about the effect that the proposal would have on the state of the economy or on their personal well-being. The dynamics of international trade are poorly understood even by experts. Moreover, NAFTA's impact will be felt only in the long run, as firms and individuals adjust their behavior to the reduction in tariffs. The question is, will citizens be able to determine what difference NAFTA made, even in the long run? Can they determine what things would be like without NAFTA? It seems unlikely that the average citizen will be able to make these determinations. (One suspects that scholars will do little better.) If so, time will not resolve policy uncertainty. The citizens of tomorrow will be just as uncertain as those today about the virtues of NAFTA.

Alternately, citizens could judge policy proposals by listening to arguments presented by interest groups. Indeed, most theories of interest groups (e.g., Schlozman and Tierney 1986) posit an educational role for these groups. While acknowledging that many interest groups perform (or try to perform) this function, the overwhelming evidence from survey data is that their efforts do not produce a well-informed citizenry. (Whether their efforts are designed to produce this result is, of course, another question.)

In short, in order to become well informed about the policy process, citizens must trace out the relationship between proposals and outcomes. This is not an easy task, as Page and Shapiro note:[5]

> Events seldom speak for themselves. To work out the implications of an event for the costs and benefits of alternate public policies requires complex reasoning, involving knowledge or beliefs about what actually happened, and also ideas about what it means in terms of a set of goals and objectives and a view of how the world works (a system of beliefs about background facts and causal connections). It requires *interpretation* of the event. (1992, 340–41)

---

5. For a similar description, see Downs 1957, 215–16.

Given these costs, the question also arises whether becoming well informed is worth it. Popkin (1991, 44–45) argues that the benefits are low relative to the benefits people get from doing other things. Thus, citizen ignorance may be rational, even if it could be obviated and has unfavorable consequences.

Whatever the cause, many pundits argue that citizen ignorance leads to inferior policy outcomes. Politicians, it is said, want to be reelected and will do anything to secure this goal—including doing exactly what their constituents want, regardless of the consequences for public policy. Writing during the 1992 U.S. elections, Elizabeth Drew argues,

> It's not the processes that are the main problem now but the public's aversion to giving anything up, and our leaders' reluctance to lead. . . . The cry that the politicians are "out of touch" is mistaken: if anything, the elected politicians are all too in touch with the moods of their constituents, and extremely loath to get crossways with them. This is what lies behind the inability, or reluctance, to do anything difficult. (1992, 88)

A rationale for Drew's complaints is seen in the seminal work of Mayhew (1974). He argues that legislators pursue reelection by "position-taking," or taking actions that receive favorable evaluations (1974, 61–73). As a result, "The notion of members as seekers of effects needs a razor taken to it; the electoral payment is for positions, not effects" (Mayhew 1974, 146). Of course, Mayhew also says that reelection-oriented legislators will engage in "credit-claiming," or taking responsibility for particularized benefits received by people in their district (1974, 52–61).[6] Thus, the reelection goal provokes some interest in outcomes, but only in the narrow range of proposals that supply particularized benefits. Even in these cases, however, the need to take electorally advantageous positions remains. As a result, when constituents have an imperfect understanding of policy options, actions that help a representative get reelected can have extremely pernicious consequences for public policy. In effect, voters get what they ask for: a Congress that follows their opinions, even at the expense of their interests.

Other scholars, while acknowledging citizen uncertainty and myopia, have argued that it has the opposite effect, forcing citizens to abdicate all control over the policy process. Writing about the scholarly response to early survey data, Page and Shapiro provide a useful summary of this literature:

---

6. Particularized benefits are benefits given out to specific individuals or to geographic constituencies in an ad hoc fashion, such that a representative can credibly argue that she had some role in supplying the benefit (Mayhew 1974, 53–54).

The result was a wholesale revision of democratic theory. Schumpeter's weak procedural definition of democracy, in which elite leadership competes for voters' acquiescence but does not necessarily respond to their policy preferences ([1942] 1975, chap. 22), influenced more than a generation of scholars. Dahl (1956, chap. 2) cast doubt on the desirability of "populistic" democracy. Berelson et al. (1954) speculated that citizens' passivity might function as a useful buffer for system stability. (1992, 387)

Of course, Page and Shapiro (1992, 387), along with Arnold (1990, 37), note that most of the evidence used to support the abdication hypothesis is consistent with much higher levels of control. Arnold also cites the dangers of drawing conclusions about abdication from legislators' observed behavior:

If legislators consult the scholarly literature on congressional elections, they might conclude that they need not worry much about either the positions that they take or the effects that they produce because these are not the major determinants of electoral outcomes. This would be a dangerous conclusion. It would be equivalent to concluding that one need not fill out a tax return because the Internal Revenue Service prosecutes only a few thousand individuals each year for tax evasion. (1990, 37)

Still, the idea that uncertainty leads to abdication remains popular. A good example is found in Eulau's review of Converse and Pierce's (1986) book on representation in France, where he argues, "Except in the few instances, as in France in 1968, where at least some people's voices are so loud (or their feet so clattering) that they cannot be ignored, popular policy views may not exist at all or may be muted, or, when they can be heard, may be distorted by the elite's biased perceptions, rooted in the sociopolitical structure of the representational system" (1987, 204).[7] Similarly, Bernstein (1989) uses "The Myth of Constituency Control" as a subtitle for his book on representation.

These complaints are not new. Throughout the history of the United States, scholars and pundits alike have worried about citizen myopia and its effect on the policy process. Writing in *The Federalist* No. 63, James Madison argued that, ". . . there are particular moments in public affairs where the people, stimulated by some irregular passion, or some illicit advantage, or misled by the artful misrepresentations of interested men, may call for measures which they themselves will afterwards be the most ready to lament and condemn." Madison's concerns were shared by opponents of the Constitution.

---

7. For a similar view, see Wahlke 1971.

For example, Melancton Smith, a noted Anti-Federalist, argued during the ratification debate in New York that, ". . . the impulses of the multitude are inconsistent with systematic government. The people are frequently incompetent to deliberate discussion, and subject to errors and imprudencies" (quoted in Storing 1981a, 349).

Nor are these complaints unique to the American case. Writing about the role of legislatures in transitions to democratic rule, Blondel asks,

> How has an institution which is supposed to promote liberalism and democracy achieved apparently so little in the very countries in which liberalism is held to prevail? Why is the literature on the British, French, and American legislatures so full of complaints about inefficiency or uselessness? Why are legislatures so maladjusted to the very thing they are supposed to do? . . . Are they an unwieldy instrument, when left to work out freely the conditions of political life? Are they indecisive by their very nature and have they to be, not merely led, but in fact controlled and constantly guided? (1973, 1)

Blondel's comments suggest that the problems cited by Madison, by Smith, and by many others since then are not the product of U.S. history or political culture, or even recent changes in the nature of the political process; rather, they are endemic to legislatures given the nature of their accountability to the public at large and the public's lack of information about the policy process.

Retrospective Evaluations and Trust

If citizens are uncertain or misinformed, as they often are, retrospective evaluations may not work as intended. Bad policies will be enacted, good incumbents will be thrown out of office, or both. But to say that these problems are inevitable is at best premature. For citizens have an alternate strategy open to them, one that sidesteps their lack of information: instead of controlling their representative's behavior, they can allow her to act as she thinks best. That is, they can decide to trust their representative.

The rationale for trust is simple: compared to the average constituent, the average legislator has better information about the relationship between policy proposals and policy outcomes. Legislators get their information from hearings and floor debates, committee reports, caucus proceedings, and personal staff (Krehbiel 1991; Salisbury and Shepsle 1981). Game theorists (e.g., Rasmussen 1989) would say that elected officials have private information— they know things about policy proposals that constituents do not know and cannot learn without a prohibitive effort. Of course, legislators do not know everything all the time, but it seems safe to say that they often know more than the average constituent.

This book defines trust in terms of retrospective evaluations. Trust is said to exist when constituents evaluate (or are prepared to evaluate) their representative's vote favorably, regardless of whether they believe that the vote is consistent with their interests. Trust gives a representative *voting leeway,* allowing her to act as she thinks best in light of her private information, without fear that her vote will damage her chances of reelection. (The terms *trust* and *voting leeway* are used interchangeably throughout the book.) In contrast, trust is said to be absent under conditions where constituents issue (or are prepared to issue) a favorable evaluation only if their representative complies with their demands—that is, only if the representative casts the vote that constituents believe to be preferable given their interests and what they know about the relationship between proposals and outcomes. This definition of trust implies that at the time a legislator votes, her constituents have not made any decisions or evaluations. However, it is assumed that a legislator's vote decision is shaped by expectations about how constituents will react to different votes—including the likelihood that they will trust her judgment.

Of course, even when high-salience proposals are voted on, decisions about trust are not always a decisive influence on a representative's behavior. Even when a representative is sure that constituents will trust her judgment, she may choose to vote as constituents prefer, ignoring her private information. (The circumstances that give rise to this behavior will be detailed later.) And, of course, an intense interest in the policy outcomes at stake, or the lack of an interest in reelection, can lead a representative to act as her private information and policy goals dictate, even when she does not expect to be trusted. Even in a world where representatives uniformly desire reelection, the expectation that trust can be used to control a representative's use of private information is just that—an expectation, which holds sometimes but not all the time.

The concept of trust can also be described in terms of the well-known distinction between *delegates* and *trustees.* Many scholars see these *role orientations* as "patterns of expectations" or "norms of behavior" that guide a legislator's decisions (Jewell 1970; 1982). Delegates, it is said, follow the instructions of their constituents, while trustees act in light of their personal conception of the good (Wahlke et al. 1962, 272–76). The classic statement is from Edmund Burke, who argued that legislators should behave as trustees:

> Your representative owes you, not his industry only, but his judgement; and he betrays, instead of serving you, if he sacrifices it to your opinion. My worthy colleague says that his will ought to be subservient to yours. If that be all, the thing is innocent. If government was a matter of will

upon any side, yours, without question, ought to be superior. But government and legislation are matters of reason and judgement, and not of inclination; and what sort of reason is that in which the determination precedes the discussion, in which one set of men deliberate and another decide, and where those who form the conclusion are three hundred miles distant from those who hear the arguments? (Hoffman and Levack 1949, 115)

The delegate-trustee distinction has fallen into disrepute in recent years, largely because legislators' self-reported role orientations failed to explain any component of their behavior (Jewell 1970). However, the distinction is a useful way to describe the underlying forces that generate a legislator's action—does the legislator implement constituent demands (delegate) or use her judgment (trustee)? In this sense, a legislator could act as a delegate on one proposal and as a trustee on another.

Clearly, representatives want as much trust as often as they can get it. Trust enables a legislator to do what she thinks is right, rather than caving in to constituent demands because of a concern over reelection. Even if the representative is prepared to ignore her constituents in any case, trust lowers the political costs of doing so. For constituents, however, decisions about trust are problematic. On the one hand, deference can be seen as a sensible, rational decision, an attempt to tap a representative's intimate understanding of the policy process. So trust need not be irrational, or the result of disinterest, alienation, or false consciousness. The problem is that representatives hold interests of their own. Thus, constituents face a second problem, as Ferejohn notes:

> In choosing representatives, in delegating to them the authority to act on our behalf, we surrender to an enormous informational disadvantage. We will never be able to know enough about the choices faced by our leaders to be sure that they are always acting in our interests. As a result, we face the eternal problem of political control: how may we ensure that our chosen representatives act in our interest as well as in our names? (1990, 6)

Trust allows a representative to ignore constituent demands that are based on misinformation. However, it also allows her to disregard *all* demands, not just the inaccurate ones. Given trust, a policy-minded representative will implement constituent interests only if she happens to share them. Otherwise, she will favor her interests or policy goals at the expense of those held by constituents. Thus, while constituents undoubtedly prefer to have a representative they can trust, they must inevitably consider whether they should trust the one they have.

Trust and Models of the Legislative Process

How do constituents make decisions about trust? Without an answer, attempts to predict, explain, or evaluate the congressional process cannot go very far. The reason is simple: as long as representatives have some interest in reelection, expectations about trust fundamentally influence their behavior. Trust determines whether representatives are rewarded for using their judgment or for complying with constituent opinions—whether they are rewarded for behaving as trustees or as delegates. Clearly, in legislatures where the reelection goal is pervasive, such as the modern Congress, expectations about trust are likely to shape both individual behavior and overall outcomes and, presumably, the content of policy proposals and the procedures used to vote on them.

Congressional scholars recognize the importance of understanding trust. However, as this section will illustrate, they have been unable to answer two simple questions: When does trust exist? What factors drive trust decisions? This section illustrates the problem in two ways: first, by examining state-of-the-art theories of trust and trust decisions and, second, by surveying the assumptions about trust made in analyses of congressional behavior.

The Conventional Wisdom

Two concepts summarize what students of Congress know about trust: *traceability* (Arnold 1990) and *presentation of self* (Fenno 1978). The former suggests that trust decisions hinge on context; the latter, that trust follows from beliefs about a representative's goals and talents. Additional insight is supplied by a construct drawn from the economics literature: the principal-agent game (e.g., Ferejohn 1986). While this list of concepts may seem far too small, there is very little additional literature that provides substantial insight. As Arnold notes:

> To what extent are citizens able to control their government in a representative system? This is—or should be—one of the central questions in political science, one that should occupy the combined talents of democratic theorists and institutional specialists. All too often scholars avoid addressing the issue directly, hoping that their results will speak for themselves (they rarely do). (1990, 265)

Or, as Parker and Parker note in their recent paper, "Despite its significance, little if any effort has been devoted to constructing a reliable measure of

trust in the representative or in analyzing the antecedents of that trust"
(1993, 442).

What We Know

Writing about vote decisions, Arnold (1990, chap. 2) argues that constituents
are more likely to tolerate suspicious votes—votes that appear to make them
worse off—insofar as they are uncertain about the relationship between policy
proposals and policy outcomes. Thus, members of Congress who wish to vote
against their constituents will favor policy instruments and legislative procedures that minimize traceability—make it difficult for constituents to reason
from policy outcomes to the specific policy proposals that their representative
voted on (Arnold 1990, 47; see also Weaver 1988). Arnold's work makes an
explicit connection between retrospective evaluations and trust. To say that
members of Congress build trust by altering voters' beliefs about the relationship between votes and policy outcomes implies that trust decisions are made
retrospectively—constituents evaluate their representative's vote in light of
what they know about the options before her. Kingdon makes a similar point,
arguing that legislative procedures "sometimes provide congressmen with
graceful ways of getting off the hook" (1981, 51). That is, the complexities of
the legislative process—the committee system, closed rules, or the rules
governing votes on amendments—often serve as a justification for otherwise
suspicious votes.

   Presentation of self refers to a representative's efforts to alter her
reputation—what constituents think about her motivations, talents, and other
aspects of her character (Fenno 1978, chaps. 3–4). In part, presentation is
designed to engender the most general kind of favorable evaluation: "he's a
good man," or "she's a good woman" (Fenno 1978, 55). But in fact, says
Fenno, these efforts are aimed at building trust: "The ultimate response House
members seek is political support. But the instrumental response they seek is
trust. The presentation of self—that which is given in words and given off as a
person—will be calculated to win trust" (Fenno 1978, 56). Again, Fenno's
stress on reputations as a source of trust is consistent with a retrospective
specification. The impact of these reputations is felt only after a representative
casts an apparently suspicious vote—only then will constituents look to beliefs about the representative's motives to determine why she did what she did.

   Specifically, Fenno argues that trust is built by actions that stress a
representative's qualifications for office, her identification with constituent
interests, and empathy for constituent welfare (1978, 57–61). The idea that
qualifications matter is echoed by Eulau and Karps (1977), who suggest that
trust follows from the perception that a legislator holds expertise on policy
matters. Thus, the authors argue that legislators build trust by stressing their

qualifications, identification, and empathy, which in turn helps them achieve policy goals without sacrificing political support.

Finally, many scholars describe legislator-constituent interactions using a principal-agent game.[8] For example, Parker and Parker argue,

> We feel that constituents' loyalties to incumbents are sustained by a sense of personal trust in the legislator. If we place this issue in the context of the classic, economic principal-agent problem, we can understand the importance of a trustworthy representative to constituents. (1993, 443)

The essence of a principal-agent game is that one player, the principal, tries to induce a second player, the agent, to take actions that maximize the principal's payoff. All things being equal, the agent prefers to shirk—to take actions that maximize the agent's payoff at the principal's expense. Moreover, the principal's payoff is determined by a combination of the agent's actions, which the principal can observe, and additional factors that are known to the agent but not to the principal. Alternately, the principal observes outcomes but cannot observe the agent's actions. Either way, the "principal's problem" is to prevent shirking, given that the principal is unsure when it occurs.

Analysis of principal-agent games has revealed several ways for the principal to reduce—but generally not eliminate—shirking. Early work focused on the writing of binding contracts that made the agent's reward contingent on the principal's payoff. For example, the agent's reward might be a small fixed sum, plus a share of the principal's payoff. More recent work has shown that the principal's ability to control the agent can be enhanced by institutions that reduce or eliminate the agent's private information ("monitoring") and institutions that give agents (or potential agents) the incentive to reveal their type, and thus their propensity to shirk ("signaling," or "screening"). (For a review of this literature, see Rasmussen 1989.)

Most applications of principal-agent theory to legislator-constituent relations use the game as a metaphor for the problem facing constituents. An explicit application of the technology is provided by Ferejohn (1986). In his game, politicians—the incumbent and potential replacements—all have the same preferences and abilities (1986, 12). Specifically, they prefer to shirk—to act against constituent interests (Ferejohn 1986, 10). Constituents in the game evaluate their incumbent using a version of the strategy described above: they reelect the incumbent if policy outcomes are "good enough" in

---

8. This description is cast in general terms. Over the years, a wide variety of games has been given the principal-agent label, and it is impossible to write a description that covers them all. For a discussion of principal-agent games, see Rasmussen 1989, chaps. 6–8. For applications to representation, see Ferejohn 1986 and 1990, Kalt and Zupan 1990, and Kau and Rubin 1979.

light of their interests and replace her if outcomes fall short of this mark. The important result is that constituents can hold their incumbent to a higher standard, and receive better outcomes as well, insofar as the value of holding office is high (Ferejohn 1986, 17).

What We Don't Know

Taken together, these studies suggest a sensible intuition: trust decisions are based on perceptions of the agent and the act—what constituents know about their representative and what they know about the options open to her. Unfortunately, this intuition does not answer the questions raised earlier. What are the specific perceptions captured by traceability, or by qualification, identification, and empathy? What is the relative importance of these factors? Perceptions of the act may be the critical factor, with perceptions of the agent a residual influence. The reverse may be true. Both factors may be equally important. One or both may need to pass a certain critical level for trust to arise. We simply do not know.

Analyses based on principal-agent games have not improved on these insights. For one thing, these analyses can be criticized on empirical grounds: evidence cited earlier indicates that constituents evaluate their representatives largely on the basis of behavior, not policy outcomes. Whether constituents would do better if they focused on outcomes is a good question; the point is that they do not. Moreover, games such as Ferejohn's make unrealistic assumptions about the motives held by representatives and the beliefs that constituents have about these motives. For example, in Ferejohn's model, all incumbents prefer to shirk, and this fact is common knowledge to voters. In other words, voters know what their representative wants in terms of policy outcomes, and they know that her goals are antithetical to their own. Therefore, in Ferejohn's game, "the voter's problem is to police moral hazard [shirking] rather than to find and elect the more capable of benevolent officeholders" (1986, 12). These assumptions eliminate the possibility that trust decisions are shaped by perceptions of the agent. In fact, they appear to make trust an impossibility: why would constituents trust someone who always disagrees with them?

None of these criticisms imply that it is impossible to analyze trust using some sort of principal-agent game. The characterization of constituent strategies could easily be changed; representatives could be given a wider range of possible motivations; constituents could be assumed to hold beliefs about these motivations. Indeed, the game described in chapter 4 can be labeled a principal-agent game. The point is that contemporary applications of principal-agent technology do not supply much insight into the forces that underlie trust decisions.

An examination of the conventional wisdom about trust also reveals uncertainty about the level at which trust decisions are made. Many scholars (e.g., Parker and Parker 1993) argue that constituents make blanket—overarching—decisions about trust. Often these claims are illustrated using a quote from Fenno:

> When a constituent trusts a House member, the constituent is saying something like this, "I am willing to put myself in your hands temporarily; I know you will have opportunities to hurt me, although I may not know when these opportunities occur; I assume—and I will continue to assume until it is proven otherwise—that you will not hurt me; for the time being, then, I'm not going to worry about your behavior. (1978, 55–56)

While many scholars see this as a reasonable intuition, there is reason to think it suspect. Rather than closing off options, a rational constituent would prefer to make trust decisions as they come up. This suspicion is reinforced by interview data. Consider one legislator's initial comments about trust: "I don't need to poll my constituents to know what to do. The people don't have the information I have. They send you here to listen to the debate and make your own decision based on your judgment" [38].[9] This comment is consistent with the conventional wisdom. But consider what the legislator went on to say:

> But sometimes you get issues like [the Ethics Act and Catastrophic Coverage], where people depart from that rule. On most things they let you use your own best judgment. Sometimes newspapers pick out three or four votes and publish them along with the titles of the bills you voted on. People who read those kind of things have to base their judgment of you on the title of the bills. If it had "Pay Raise" in the title, they wouldn't want you to vote for it. It makes you wonder how much they know.

Comments along these lines suggest a different view, that trust decisions involving high-salience proposals are made one at a time rather than in some overarching manner. That is not to say that Fenno's description is incorrect. It may, for example, reflect behavior on low-salience proposals. For now, there is no way to tell.

In addition, the idea that trust decisions depend on perceptions of the agent raises a larger question: what do constituents know about their

---

9. The number in brackets refers to the interview that the quote was drawn from. For a description of the data, see appendix 2.

representative—what information is contained in a representative's reputation? Do constituents limit themselves to general evaluations—in Fenno's terms, "he's a good man," "she's a good woman,"—or are their decisions based on more detailed information? A complete characterization of legislators' reputations goes well beyond what is necessary to understand trust. However, a better theory of how trust decisions are made will help us to make sense of legislators' reputations, as well as their construction and maintenance.

Finally, there is the question whether constituents make good decisions about trust. Drew's (1992) portrayal of contemporary politics implies that constituents could generate better policy outcomes by relaxing their standards for trust, freeing representatives to use their private information. However, as Page and Shapiro (1992) indicate, other scholars argue that voters defer to elected officials all too much, suggesting that less trust would yield better policy outcomes. Without an explanation of where trust comes from, or a definition of when it exists, it is impossible to say which of these diagnoses is correct. The same information is needed to choose between alternate evaluations of the legislative process itself. Consider the charge that legislatures are unable to enact economically efficient, comprehensive, timely solutions to social problems. Drew's argument suggests that these inferior policy outcomes reflect the demands of myopic constituents. The scholars cited by Page and Shapiro (1992) suggest a different explanation: these outcomes occur because representatives are allowed to use their judgment and simply prefer policies that happen to be inefficient or because they exploit trust to further the goals held by special interests.

The Conventional Wisdom Applied

Most scholars who study Congress would agree that their analyses need to account for members' expectations about trust. Unfortunately, most analyses of congressional behavior rely on simple, unrealistic assumptions about trust, assumptions embedded in expectations about how members of Congress pursue reelection. To illustrate this point, this section examines assumptions about the electoral connection that appear in formal models of legislatorial behavior and in statistical analyses of the same phenomena.

Formal Models

A common assumption in formal models of legislatorial behavior is that the forces acting on a legislator's decisions—her goals, such as reelection, policy, etc.—can be expressed in terms of an ideal point, or an *induced ideal point*, in a multidimensional space that describes the range of possible policy outcomes:[10]

> In the positive theory of institutions, the public officials are almost always legislators who are assumed to be motivated by reelection. Their preferences over issues of policy and structure are induced by the preferences of other social actors, particularly in their constituencies, who are most relevant to their electoral popularity and success. What interest groups and constituents want, then, is incorporated in the ideal points of legislators as they go about their authoritative decisionmaking—and analyses that focus on legislators, even if they pay no attention to groups and constituents, see themselves as implicitly taking the latter into account. (Moe 1990, 27–28)

In fact, the specification usually works backward: analyses begin by positing that legislators act according to ideal points and then state that each legislator's ideal point, and her resulting preferences across policy outcomes, captures whatever goals she happens to hold. A similar assumption is often used to model voting on distributive programs: legislators are assumed to be single-minded seekers of reelection and therefore to act to maximize the net benefits flowing to their districts from government programs.[11]

In theory, induced ideal points are a simple, easily described summary indicator of a legislator's motivations. Moreover, the assumption also facilitates the application of results such as Black's (1958) Median Voter Theorem and Shepsle's (1979) concept of Structure-Induced Equilibria to the study of real-world legislatures. The assumption also simplifies empirical tests, as scholars can use Poole and Rosenthal's (1991) estimates of induced ideal points for all members of Congress from 1789 onward to test predictions about behavior, proposals, and outcomes.[12]

While the use of induced ideal points simplifies and facilitates the formal modeling enterprise, the appropriateness of this technique is open to question. As long as a multidimensional space is sufficient to describe policy outcomes, it seems reasonable that a representative's policy goals—or constituent interests—can be captured by an ideal point in this space. (In fact, chapter 4 contains several games in which outcomes and policy goals are specified in

---

10. Krehbiel (1991, chaps. 2–3) offers many examples of induced ideal points.

11. For examples, see Ferejohn 1984; Niou and Ordeshook 1985; Shepsle and Weingast 1981; Weingast 1979.

12. Kiewiet and McCubbins's (1991) analysis of the Appropriations Committee is built on these estimates. For other approaches to estimating induced ideal points, see Bartels 1991; Krehbiel 1986; Krehbiel and Rivers 1988.

this way.) But what about the reelection goal—or the combined influence of policy and reelection? The idea that legislators behave according to induced ideal points implies they are willing to take whatever actions are needed to move public policy toward a particular outcome. The problem is that legislators are evaluated on the basis of actions, not outcomes. Particularly when high-salience proposals are voted on, a legislator may have one set of preferences across policy outcomes (resulting from her policy goals, and perhaps her desire for particularized benefits), and a distinct set of preferences across actions (resulting from the factors mentioned earlier, combined with expectations about how constituents will react to each action). In these situations, a legislator's preferences across policy outcomes need not match her preferences across the actions needed to produce these outcomes. To say that these orderings are identical, as required by induced ideal points, is true only if one of two conditions are met. One is that the legislator's policy concerns invariably take precedence over her desire for reelection. The other is that the legislator always expects constituents to trust her judgment. Few advocates of induced ideal points would argue for the first condition—in fact, many of their analyses assume legislators are single-minded seekers of reelection. Therefore, the use of induced ideal points requires an extremely strong assumption about trust. Insofar as trust is a variable—across representatives and across contexts—then a legislator's induced ideal point, which captures her preferences across outcomes, will fail as a summary of her motivations or as a predictor of her actions.

A similar line of reasoning is advanced by Denzau, Riker, and Shepsle (1985), who argue that a legislator's interest in reelection can reduce or eliminate her incentive to cast sophisticated votes.[13] The problem, they say, is that constituents are ill informed about the congressional process and therefore are unaware of the opportunities for sophisticated behavior. As a result, sophisticated behavior, if it involves a vote against constituent demands, will generate unfavorable retrospective evaluations. The only way for representatives to avoid these costs is to comply with constituent demands, which requires that they behave sincerely, avoiding sophisticated actions. More generally, in situations in which constituents are uncertain or misinformed, a legislator might prefer a policy outcome over the status quo yet be unwilling to cast the (sophisticated) votes needed to produce the outcome. This situation can arise even when constituents themselves prefer the new outcome over the status quo.

Denzau, Riker, and Shepsle (1985) illustrate their argument using a well-known example: the case of voting on the Powell amendment. This case involved a bill designed to increase federal funding for school construction.

---

13. For a similar argument applied to vote trading, see Bianco 1989.

The Powell amendment prohibited funds from being sent to districts that segregated students according to race. The authors allege that a majority of legislators favored the unamended bill to the status quo but that a different majority preferred the status quo over the amended version. A key group, Northern Democrats, favored the amended bill first of all, then the unamended bill, then the status quo. Their constituents' preferences were the same. Intuitively, Northern Democrats should have voted against the Powell amendment: the amended bill was sure to fail, but the unamended bill would pass if placed against the status quo. In fact, many Northern Democrats voted for the Powell amendment—enough that it passed, and was followed by defeat of the amended proposal. Denzau, Riker, and Shepsle explain this anomaly by arguing that constituents in Northern Democrat districts refused to trust their representatives, not realizing that a (sophisticated) vote against the amendment would ultimately yield a preferable policy outcome. Faced with these constraints, many Northern Democrats voted for the amendment and for the amended bill, a strategy that satisfied their constituents' demands but produced the worst possible policy outcome for themselves and for their constituents.

Based on their analysis, Denzau, Riker, and Shepsle (1985, 1132) argue that formal models cannot assume that legislators are motivated solely by preferences across outcomes. Rather, they say, scholars must assume that legislators hold preferences across actions that take into account both the political and the policy consequences of their behavior. If this description is true, induced ideal points fail as a summary indicator of a legislator's motivations—they only account for her concern with policy consequences. However, the authors' analysis substitutes one problematic assumption for another. Saying that a desire for reelection precludes sophisticated behavior is just as unrealistic as saying that the goal never restricts sophistication. Put another way, Denzau, Riker, and Shepsle criticize models where trust is universal by saying trust never exists. Neither assumption seems tenable. This difficulty is highlighted by the fact that when the Powell amendment was voted on, some Northern Democrats voted as theories of sophisticated behavior would counsel: against the amendment and for the unamended aid proposal. Krehbiel and Rivers (1988) cite these votes to argue that the apparent lack of sophistication among the remaining Northern Democrats masks a deeper strategy: by voting for the Powell amendment, Northern Democrats who actually opposed school aid achieved their most favored policy outcome while complying with their constituents' demands. However, it is also possible that Northern Democrats generally supported aid, as Denzau, Riker, and Shepsle claim, but only some expected trust on the Powell amendment. If so, the apparent variation in sophisticated behavior among Northern Democrats is the product of variation in their expectations about trust.

Of course, the Denzau, Riker, and Shepsle (1985) analysis focuses on a single event—an event that is open to other interpretations. However, it is easy to construct examples that illustrate the problem with induced ideal points. Consider figure 1, which uses a single policy dimension to describe the ideal points held by a representative (R) and her constituent (C), as well as the location of the status quo outcome (s) and the outcomes that will result from the enactment of three proposals: α, β, and δ. Throughout this book, Greek letters denote proposals and the policy outcomes associated with them; constituent beliefs about a proposal are denoted with subscripted Roman letters. Thus, in figure 1, δ yields the outcome denoted by δ. However, C is unsure about δ. From C's viewpoint, there is some chance that δ yields outcome d_1, but there is also a chance that enactment yields outcome d_2. As is usual in these sorts of games, assume that given a choice between two outcomes, a player prefers the outcome that is closer to his or her ideal point. Consider a situation in which R votes on α, then on δ. Suppose C believes, correctly, that α yields the outcome denoted α in figure 1 and therefore demands a yea vote. Suppose R complies. Such a vote would be consistent with a range of ideal points near that of C. Suppose α fails to win passage. Now comes the vote on δ. Assume C has bad information about δ: C thinks that enacting the proposal will yield outcome d_1—the same as α—while in fact it will generate outcome d_2. Accordingly, suppose C demands a vote for δ, and R complies. The problem is, given the policy outcomes associated with α and δ, there is no ideal point that would compel a legislator to vote yea on both proposals. R casts these votes only because she follows C's demands on the two proposals, which in the case of δ are inaccurate. Under these conditions, it is not clear what induced ideal point can be imputed to R.

Consider a second situation. Again suppose R votes yea on α, and α is defeated. But now suppose R votes next on β. Without considering C's beliefs about β, suppose C is expected to trust R. If so, R will vote for β, since she prefers the policy outcome associated with this proposal over the status quo. Like in the previous example, there is no ideal point that is consistent with these two votes. However, the problem now is not C's uncertainties. Rather, it is that different goals drive R's behavior on each proposal: reelection in the case of α, policy in the case of β.

These anomalies raise fundamental questions about analyses that specify legislator's motivations in terms of induced ideal points. Consider Krehbiel's (1991) work on committee systems. Using a model in which legislators hold induced ideal points, he shows that legislators have reason to construct an informationally efficient committee system, one that provides them with detailed, accurate information about the link between policy proposals and policy outcomes. Yet the advantages of such a committee system rest on the

Fig. 1.   Ideal points in one dimension

assumption that legislators can use the information it provides. This assumption is trivial if legislators hold induced ideal points. Regardless of what a legislator learns, she can use this information to take actions in light of her induced ideal point, wherever that might be. It is as though constituents trust their legislator to use private information wisely. But what if the legislator's decisions are sometimes constrained by constituent demands—constrained to the point that she cannot use private information? If so, situations will arise in which the legislator cannot exploit information provided by an expert committee, critical though the information might be.[14] Thus, while Krehbiel's model highlights the abstract benefits of different institutional forms, it is not clear that these benefits can be captured under real-world conditions. The only way to be sure is to understand the conditions under which trust will arise.

A similar problem arises in models of distributive politics that use the net benefit maximizer assumption. Baron (1990) shows how procedural measures such as open rules can mitigate the pursuit of economically inefficient programs. However, in making their motivational assumption, Baron and others working in this tradition assume away the problems caused by constituent misperceptions: "The electorate and the legislators who represent them are assumed to be rational, to know the costs and benefits [of distributive proposals], and to understand the full consequences of their behavior" (1990, 58). But what if constituents fail to appreciate the costs and benefits of different proposals or the need for sophisticated voting on procedural questions? For example, constituents might demand votes against procedures that restrict inefficient pork barrel proposals, failing to see that these measures would make them better off. Under these conditions, only legislators who are trusted will act as Baron assumes. Legislators who do not expect trust are likely to comply with their constituents' demands and vote against restrictions.

The point is simple. Many formal analyses of legislative behavior rest on a strong, perhaps unrealistic, assumption about motivations—induced ideal points. Since scholars are unable to account for member expectations about trust, they cannot move beyond anecdotal criticism or justification for this technique. What is needed is a general explanation of how goals such as reelection and policy enter into a legislator's decisions and are reflected in her behavior.

---

14. Krehbiel (1991, 67) alludes to these problems but does not address them.

Statistical Analyses

Studies of congressional roll call voting are a canonical example of statistical analyses of legislatorial behavior.[15] These analyses typically posit that a legislator's votes are a function of goals such as reelection and the desire to enact good public policy. The influence of reelection is specified using one of two techniques. The first technique assumes that an interest in reelection motivates legislators to vote in accordance with constituent interests. For example, Kalt and Zupan assume that constituents are economic maximizers and "demographic variables provide suitable proxies for constituents' underlying economic interests" (1990, 110).[16] The second specification is consistent with the arguments made earlier: legislators pursue reelection by complying with constituent demands and opinions. Typically, measures of constituent demands are derived from survey data, although some authors use proxy variables here as well.[17]

To say that vote decisions are the product of policy concerns and political considerations seems reasonable. The question is, what weights should be assigned to each factor? To what extent do representatives vote according to their policy concerns, as opposed to casting votes that help them get reelected? Presumably the weights given to each goal vary with the salience of the proposal being voted on. However, they should also vary with a representative's expectations about trust. Thus, it seems obvious that models of roll call behavior should account for expectations about trust. In fact they do not. At best, analyses posit that "safe" representatives (those with high election margins) place a higher weight on policy concerns and a lower weight on reelection compared to "marginal" representatives (those with low election margins). While this specification appears plausible, there is no reason to think that a representative's election margin measures her constituents' willingness to trust her judgment, either in general or in the context of specific votes. Failing to control for expectations about trust is reasonable only if trust is a random variable, or if all members hold the same expectations. If trust varies systematically with context, and across legislators, analyses that ignore this variation are hopelessly biased.

---

15. The literature is far too large to review here. A recent study, Kalt and Zupan 1990, surveys models developed by economists. Bartels (1991) summarizes statistical analyses by political scientists; Krehbiel (1988) surveys the formal literature.

16. Carson and Oppenheimer (1984) assume that demographic variables proxy both economic and noneconomic interests.

17. Miller and Stokes 1963 is the seminal work. Bartels (1991) provides a recent example of survey-based measures of demands; Jackson and King (1989) measure demands using demographic variables.

The problem is not a consequence of assuming that legislators hold policy goals as well as an interest in reelection—it arises even if legislators are assumed to be single-minded seekers of reelection. Consider the techniques used to operationalize the reelection goal. The assumption that legislators pursue reelection by implementing constituent demands or opinions suggests that trust almost never exists. Conversely, in a world where constituents are uncertain about policy options, the idea that legislators get reelected by serving constituent interests implies that they are trusted almost all of the time. Intuitively, the truth lies somewhere in the middle—sometimes legislators incur benefits from their actions, sometimes from outcomes. Contemporary analyses are unable to account for this variation.

Similar problems arise in analyses that estimate a legislator's policy goals using her votes on other proposals (e.g., Kalt and Zupan 1990). Intuitively, since votes have policy consequences, vote decisions supply information about policy concerns. However, Jackson and Kingdon argue that this procedure amounts to a tautology—"explaining votes with votes" (1990, 7). It is easy to devise examples where this criticism is accurate. Suppose a representative did not expect trust and therefore complied with constituent demands. Under these conditions, the representative's vote would not contain any information about her policy concerns. But Jackson and Kingdon's criticisms are not always valid, even in a world where legislators put reelection first. Suppose a representative expected constituents to trust her judgment on a series of proposals, and therefore voted in accordance with her policy goals. These votes contain information about the legislator's policy concerns. The point is simple: votes can be used to estimate policy concerns—but only if scholars use the right votes, those where representatives have voting leeway. However, any conclusions about the validity of estimates constructed with this technique require an answer to the questions asked in chapter 1: when do constituents trust their representative, and what is the basis of that trust?

In sum, statistical analyses of roll-call behavior are subject to the same criticisms as formal models. They rely on simple, unrealistic assumptions about trust. Of course, this deficit is no surprise: simple assumptions were made because available theories did not support anything more complicated.

Summary

For students of the legislative process, the importance of understanding trust is matched by the difficulty of the task. Works by Arnold and Fenno provide important clues. And without saying so explicitly, most students of Congress would agree that there is variation to explain—in most situations, some legislators will be trusted while others will not. However, none of the works discussed here provide substantial insight into the forces that generate trust. And without an understanding of these forces, both formal and statistical analyses of the legislative process, as well as attempts to evaluate the process, hang by a thread, relying on simplistic and problematic assumptions about trust.

CHAPTER 3

Assumptions about Decisions and Beliefs

I could take you down the hall and introduce you to a member who just drips his district, from his shoes to his straw hat. You don't have to go to his district to know what it's like, you just have to look at him. That's why the House is so great. It's a bunch of different cultures, all in different districts. If I went to Long Island with my record, they'd laugh me out. Congress represents its districts because each member comes from his district much more so than because he tries to adapt his personal philosophy.

—A Midwest Republican

This chapter sets out three assumptions that underlie later analysis. The first, and fundamental, assumption is that representatives and constituents are rational actors who gather and use information in a systematic, predictable manner. The second assumption is that a representative's explanations—attempts to describe or rationalize her actions—have no effect on her constituents' trust decisions. The final assumption is that constituents use stereotypes to assess their representative's policy concerns.

Rational Actors and Rational Choice

Game-theoretic analyses are driven by the assumption of rational choice. The players in a game—politicians, voters, etc.—are assumed to behave purposively, taking actions designed to achieve their goals. Formally, when faced with a decision, a rational actor is said to evaluate the consequences of different actions in light of her goals, available information, and the actions taken by others. These consequences are measured in terms of a payoff that the player receives as a function of her actions and the actions taken by her opponents. Based on these calculations, the player takes the action that she expects will, on balance, generate what she regards as the most attractive set of consequences.

Models incorporating the rational choice assumption have provided insights into many aspects of the legislative process, including votes and vote decisions (e.g., Krehbiel 1988), legislative institutions and rules (e.g., Krehbiel 1991; Shepsle and Weingast 1987), and even "soft" phenomena such as persuasion and universalism (e.g., Austen-Smith 1990; Baron 1990). Other scholars have used the intuition of purposive behavior as a starting point for classic analyses of the legislative process, such as Fenno's (1973) book on congressional committees, his study of how members of Congress interact with constituents (1978), and Mayhew's (1974) essay on how legislators pursue reelection.

Given this heritage, there would seem little need to discuss the rationality assumption. However, many critics equate the assumption with an inaccurate, unrealistic model of human behavior. Specifically, they argue that rational actors are invariably motivated by economic self-interest—or, in the case of politicians, reelection—and fully informed about all factors relevant to their decisions. While these descriptions are consistent with the rationality assumption, they are in no way mandated by it. Rational actors can hold other goals, such as ideological concerns or the desire to enact good public policy. Rational actors can act on the basis of available information—beliefs that may be uncertain or wildly inaccurate. These complications play a critical role in later analysis. Therefore, before doing anything else, I will discuss what rationality implies about human behavior—and what it does not.

Critics of Rational Choice

Critics of rational choice argue that this perspective is problematic and "a view on the defensive" (Almond 1988, 833). The sharpest criticisms come from proponents of an alternate theory of human behavior, bounded rationality.[1] These scholars argue that people have at best a limited ability to compare alternatives and are motivated by a variety of hard-to-specify goals (Simon 1985). The rational choice approach, which is alleged to ignore these complications, is seen as an inadequate and inaccurate characterization of human behavior: ". . . what we observe in the world is inconsistent with the ways in which contemporary theories [rational choice] ask us to talk" (March and Olsen 1984, 747). Or, as Simon puts it, "Before we apply the methods of economic reasoning to political behavior, we must characterize the political situation, not as it appears 'objectively' to the analyst, but as it appears subjectively to the actors" (1985, 298).

Many political scientists agree with these criticisms. For example, in a review of Stewart's (1989) book on the late 1800s–era congressional appropriations process, Ruder argues that rational choice models of Congress are

---

1. Collections edited by Hogarth and Reder (1986), Cook and Levi (1990), and Kinder and Palfrey (1993) are superb introductions to this debate. Grafstein (1992) reviews the Cook and Levi volume, as well as other recent works. It should be noted that the bounded-rationality critique of rational choice is not the only objection raised in contemporary work. Most notably, Lowi (1992) criticizes rational choice models because of their alleged ideological character. Calvert (1993) provides an able response.

accurate only insofar as legislators are single-minded seekers of reelection: ". . . Stewart laboriously explains rational actor theory as applied to Congress. The motive force of that theory is, of course, the reelection imperative, an assumption much less applicable in the last century than in this one, as Stewart readily acknowledges but without altering his theory" (1990, 186).

Experimental psychologists have provided a justification for some of these criticisms. Tversky and Kahneman (1986) argue that an individual's evaluations of alternatives, and her choices among them, are influenced by the way that the alternatives are presented, or "framed." In one of their experiments, subjects were asked to indicate a preference between two sets of alternatives:

Decision (i). Choose between:
  A. a sure gain of $240.
  B. 25% chance to gain $1000 and a 75% chance to gain nothing.
Decision (ii). Choose between:
  C. a sure loss of $750.
  D. 75% chance to lose $1000 and a 25% chance to lose nothing.
    (1986, 71)

The authors found that 84 percent of their subjects preferred option A in Decision (i), while 87 percent preferred option D in Decision (ii). However, when the two decisions were combined—

A & D: 25% chance to win $240 and a 75% chance to lose $760.
B & C: 25% chance to win $250 and a 75% chance to lose $750.

—the B & C combination was "invariably chosen" (Tversky and Kahneman 1986, 72). The B & C combination is also the dominant portfolio—a rational choice for a wealth-maximizing individual. But this combination is only chosen by only 3 percent of the subjects when the decisions are presented separately. Thus, Tversky and Kahneman conclude, people are not simple rational actors; something more complicated is going on: ". . . the logic of [rational] choice does not provide an adequate foundation for a descriptive theory of decision making. We argue that the deviations of actual behavior from the normative model [rational choice] are too widespread to be ignored, too systematic to be dismissed as random error, and too fundamental to be accommodated by relaxing the normative system" (1986, 68).

In light of these findings, advocates of bounded rationality propose that human behavior must be understood in terms of a limited search for alternatives, a cursory assessment of consequences, and a heavy reliance on standard operating procedures (Simon 1985, 295; Tversky and Kahneman 1986, 88–

89). In addition, they argue, models of human behavior must allow for a wider range of motivations: "Although self-interest undoubtedly permeates politics, action is often more based on discovering the normatively appropriate behavior than on calculating the return expected from alternate choices" (March and Olsen 1984, 744).

These criticisms are directed more at models of mass behavior rather than models of elites. For example, the typical analysis of legislatorial behavior focuses on decisions for which the stakes are relatively high—the decision to run for office, the structure of legislative institutions, the choice of policy instruments, or votes on important proposals. Faced with these situations, legislators have a considerable incentive to gather all the information they can, and to act only after making a systematic comparison of the consequences of different choices. Moreover, at least in the modern Congress, staff (Salisbury and Shepsle 1981), legislative institutions (Krehbiel 1991), and party caucuses (Rohde 1991) are organized to supply them with information. To say that they are "rational actors" under these conditions seems a modest claim— although questions remain about the nature of their motivations and the quality of their beliefs. The problem arises when analyzing mass behavior. Consider retrospective evaluations. Most constituents are poorly informed about the legislative process. They know little about policy proposals. They know little about their representative. Whether citizens could become well informed if they wanted to is irrelevant—they are not. Under these conditions, are retrospective evaluations—and trust—the product of rational choices? Bounded rationality? Or are these decisions impossible to model?

In Defense of Rational Choice

The bounded-rationality critique of rational choice models deserves attention. All too often, rational choice analyses oversimplify the political process, sacrificing important behavioral and institutional nuances to construct a tractable —analyzable—model. In the real world, information is scarce and goals are complex, yet many believers in rational choice appear to see these complications as irrelevant. However, the criticisms raised above go further, suggesting that the problem lies with the rationality assumption itself rather than its implementation. Such a general criticism is overdrawn. Critics who make these arguments have focused on a narrow range of experimental evidence and have ignored current applications of rational choice, which typically use more complex assumptions about information and motivations than were the standard a generation ago.

Consider the experimental evidence. While agreeing that some experiments designed to test rational choice assumptions have yielded disturbing results, Plott (1986) notes that many other experiments confirm the tenets of rational choice.[2] In addition, Gigerenzer (n.d.) shows that many experimental anomalies can be explained as the product of "surplus structure"—information available to the subjects in an experiment that is overlooked when developing predictions about their behavior. For example, in the Tversky-Kahneman experiments, the definition of rational behavior depends on whether subjects are assumed to make decisions simultaneously or sequentially. Anomalous responses may also result from the fact that in many experiments, including the one described above, subjects are asked to express a preference rather than making a choice that would have an actual effect on their welfare.[3]

As to the complexity of rational choice models, Plott (1986) notes that the intuitions that underlie these conditions are quite simple. Moreover, models derived from principles of bounded rationality wind up looking just as complicated. For example, Herstein (1981; reprinted in Kinder and Palfrey 1993) models vote decisions using a bounded-rationality model. In the model, a voter first determines whether he holds negative evaluations of any candidate. If so, he votes against that candidate. If not, the voter "compare[s] candidates on a few salient particular items and choose[s] the one favored on these items" (Herstein 1981, 854). At first glance the model is simple. But this simplicity is illusionary—it has been achieved by focusing on the last step in a voter's decision process. How does a voter pick the "few salient particular items" and compare candidates in light of his choice? Rational choice models appear complex because they describe how these decisions are made. At best, Herstein's model is incomplete. A fully specified version would be subject to the same criticisms he levels at rational choice.

The second critique, that rational choice models cannot account for the effects of uncertainty and misperceptions, is easier to put to rest. In making this argument, critics have conflated two assumptions, one about information, the other about choice. *Assuming that people make rational, purposive choices says nothing about the quality or quantity of information available to them.* The tenets of rational choice apply as equally to situations in which players have a complete, accurate understanding of the consequences of their decisions as they do to situations characterized by incomplete information,

---

2. Kinder (1993) offers a second line of defense: the rational choice assumption may be useful as a predictor of behavior, even if its accuracy is in question. "It would be foolish to throw away a useful theory in light of evidence that its assumptions are, under some circumstances, violated. Unrealistic, even heroic, assumptions about individual behavior may serve the development of theory about aggregate behavior well—and sometimes better than more 'realistic' ones" (Kinder 1993, 120).

3. For similar arguments, see Hogarth and Reder 1986; Kinder 1993.

where players are unsure or misinformed about the consequences of their actions. People do not need full information to make rational choices; they act rationally in light of what they know.

The confusion about rationality and information probably stems from the fact that early applications of rational choice modeled behavior under conditions of full information. Downs's (1957) model of elections is an archetypal example. He assumes that party leaders know the distribution of voters' policy goals; citizens in turn know what policies will be implemented if a given party wins control of government. Under these conditions, each party chooses a platform that maximizes their chances of winning election given the platform chosen by their opponent; citizens decide who to vote for by comparing party platforms. These assumptions yield the well-known prediction of party convergence: leaving other concerns aside, both parties will advocate the policies desired by the median voter.

Full-information assumptions reflect a sensible strategy: once individual goals are specified, analysis can focus on characteristics of the situation that do not vary with the identity of the participants. As a description of human behavior, however, the full-information assumption is problematic. In most situations, it is reasonable to say that people know something about the games they are playing, but problematic to say that they know everything. Fortunately, advances in game theory permit a more realistic characterization: rather than being fully informed, players are assumed to act under conditions of incomplete information.[4] The term *belief* is used to describe what a player knows about a factor that she is unsure of. (In this analysis, the terms *beliefs, judgments, assessments, inferences,* and *perceptions* are used interchangeably.) *There is no expectation that beliefs are accurate or even sensible.* Typically, the focus is on games of asymmetric information, in which players are differentially informed about the strategic situation they face. Information known to only one player is labeled her "private information." Players are assumed to revise their beliefs in light of any new information—such as actions taken by their opponents—but there are no restrictions on the beliefs that players bring to these games.

The game analyzed in later chapters is a typical asymmetric information game. Constituents in the game are uncertain about the relationship between policy proposals and policy outcomes. They have beliefs about the proposal their representative votes on—they know what outcomes the proposal might produce and know whether a given outcome is likely or unlikely. But they do not know for sure what the proposal will do if it is enacted—what outcome will follow from enactment. Constituents are similarly uncertain about their

---

4. For a lucid introduction to games of incomplete information, see Rasmussen 1989. Gilligan and Krehbiel 1990 and Krehbiel 1991 are superb applications of this technology.

representative's policy goals. The representative, in contrast, is fully informed about all aspects of the game—she has private information about the policy proposal and about her policy goals. The latter assumption is admittedly unrealistic, but it simplifies the analysis while maintaining the asymmetry of information between the players.

The introduction of beliefs changes the definition of what it means to be rational. Put simply, in a game of incomplete information, a rational actor will do what seems best, given what she knows. As in a full-information game, choices will be shaped by evaluations of the consequences of different actions and expectations about the actions of opponents. The only difference is that these evaluations and expectations are based on beliefs that may be uncertain or inaccurate. These principles are captured in the technique that is typically used to derive predictions from games of incomplete information, sequential equilibria (Kreps and Wilson 1982a, 1982b). When applied to an incomplete-information game, this technique defines an equilibrium, or prediction about behavior, for each set of beliefs that constituents might conceivably hold. Thus, in the game constructed in chapter 4, predictions about trust are expressed as a function of constituents' beliefs: when constituents hold certain beliefs, they will trust their representative; when they believe otherwise, they will not. (The representative's beliefs need not be considered, as she is assumed to act under full information.) Forecasts of the representative's vote decision are couched in similar terms.

The introduction of beliefs, uncertainty, and asymmetric information resolves many of the problems and anomalies cited by critics of the rational choice enterprise. For one thing, it introduces the possibility of mistakes. Under full information, actions have known consequences. Therefore, it is sensible to speak of a player taking the action that maximizes her utility or welfare. Under incomplete information, however, actions may have unanticipated consequences. A rational actor allows for this possibility by taking the action that she expects will make her best off given her beliefs. But there is no guarantee that a player's rational choices will "maximize utility"—yield the most attractive set of consequences in light of her goals. Rationality implies only that a player will try to achieve this end; it does not guarantee that her efforts will be successful.

Thus, with the introduction of beliefs, the principles of rational choice are entirely consistent with the allegation that individuals are susceptible to "distortion and error" (Quattrone and Tversky 1988). Even impeccably rational actors will make mistakes if they are misinformed about the strategic situation they face. The idea that people make rational choices under uncertainty is also consistent with evidence that they fail to consider all possible actions or do not fully and completely analyze the consequences of each one. Both strategies could follow from appropriately constructed beliefs about what factors were relevant to a decision. (They could also arise because gathering additional information is costly, a possibility that is not considered here.)

Moreover, as later chapters will show, the idea that people make rational choices under uncertainty has an additional attraction: it mirrors the view held by members of Congress. As one legislator noted, "You have to understand, the perception about facts is reality. That's how politics works, that's how life works." Members of Congress do not expect that their constituents will know everything. What members expect is that constituents will act systematically, and predictably, based on what they know.

Finally, the argument that rational choice models incorporate a narrow, inaccurate specification of motivations is similarly time bound. In Olson's (1967) analysis of interest groups, for example, individuals are assumed to be motivated by economic well-being. In a similar vein, scholars who modeled the legislative process were at one time content to assume that members of Congress were single-minded seekers of reelection. *There is nothing inevitable about these assumptions.* Most contemporary analyses begin with a richer, more accurate specification. In the next chapter's analysis, for example, the representative is motivated by reelection and the desire to enact good public policy. Thus, while she might cast votes designed to facilitate her career in politics, she can also act out of ideology, civic-mindedness, or a concern with the national interest. Moreover, as noted in chapter 4, the representative's policy concerns can also be seen as reflecting her desire to please special interests, party leaders, or the president. This specification may not capture all possible motivations, but it is closer to reality than those used a generation ago.

Testing Game-Theoretic Models: The Problem of Beliefs

One of the central themes in analyses of rational choice under uncertainty is the importance of information: to predict what a rational actor will do, you need to specify her beliefs. Specifically, predictions require information about prior beliefs—the beliefs each player brings to a game. As Kreps and Wilson conclude,

> We have carried out a game-theoretic analysis of *one* very simple incomplete information formulation. We have therefore avoided *ad hoc* assumptions about the entrant's behavior. But we have made *ad hoc* assumptions about their information, and we have found that small changes in these assumptions greatly influence the play of the game. So at some

level, analysis of this sort of situation may require *ad hoc* assumptions. (1982a, 277)

This conclusion is derived from analysis of interactions between a monopolist firm and a series of competitors. In the game, competitors are unsure whether the monopolist will fight to preserve its dominant position—start a price war—or will acquiesce to the entry of new firms. At the beginning of the game, all competitors hold the same beliefs about the monopolist's type. Competitors who face the monopolist later in the game revise their beliefs in light of the monopolist's reaction to early entrants. Even so, the competitors' prior beliefs remain a critical influence on their behavior throughout the game. In fact, predictions about competitor behavior are expressed as a function of their priors. As a result, attempts to use this game to predict competitor behavior in the real world require additional information, or "ad hoc assumptions," that describe the prior beliefs of these individuals. Without this information, the only prediction one can make is that anything can happen. As the authors say in an earlier part of their paper,

> The reader may suspect that something more is true: By cleverly choosing the nature of that small uncertainty [the entrants' prior beliefs], one can get out of a game-theoretic analysis whatever one wishes. We have no formal proposition of this sort to present at this time, but we certainly share these suspicions. If this is so, then the game-theoretic analysis of this type of game comes down eventually to how one picks the initial incomplete information. And nothing in the *theory* of games will help one to do this. (1982a, 276)

The problem is a general one. Game theory predicts behavior as a function of beliefs. While it can account for changes in beliefs as a game is played, or as a real-world situation unfolds, it says nothing about the beliefs that players, or people, bring to a game. By definition, these beliefs lie outside the range of phenomena that game theory can account for.

The techniques used to analyze games of incomplete information raise two problems for the analysis here. For one thing, the predictions developed in chapter 4 will be expressed as a function of constituents' prior beliefs. Tests of these predictions require a technique to specify the beliefs held by real-world constituents. Should the game be expanded to model the process of belief formation? Even if this expansion were possible, predictions would still be cast in terms of some set of prior beliefs. Moreover, expanding the game would push back the point in time at which these beliefs were relevant, making them even harder to specify. Something outside the game itself is needed.

Political scientists have done little better in specifying the source of voter beliefs. Arnold (1990, chap. 2, nos. 1 and 5) argues that no one has developed a full and complete theory of belief formation. While acknowledging the essential truth of Arnold's claim, two exceptions bear emphasis. First, Zaller (1992) argues that voters get their beliefs by looking to elites who share their ideological predispositions. Members of Congress would likely agree: several argued that constituent perceptions of the proposals analyzed here were shaped by factors such as interest-group endorsements, statements made by talk show hosts, and, in the case of the Ethics Act, the endorsement of the proposal by Representative Newt Gingrich, the Republican Minority Whip. Even so, using Zaller's theory to specify constituent beliefs about the Ethics Act and Catastrophic Coverage—or to account for variation in beliefs across constituents or across districts—requires detailed information about elite positions, voter exposure to these positions, and voter perceptions of the motives held by elites. Such information is simply unavailable. Therefore, while Zaller's work provides insight into the process of belief formation, his theory does not solve the problem here.

The second exception to Arnold's claim comes from the literature on representation. Numerous studies have found that legislators expend considerable time and energy explaining their behavior to constituents (Fenno 1978; Jewell 1982; Kingdon 1981). Do explanations alter constituent beliefs, leading them to trust their representative in situations where they otherwise would not? Most congressional scholars would agree. If they are right, the game constructed later must include a stage or move where the representative communicates with her constituents. But this modification would introduce vast complications into the analysis—and, as will be seen later, there is good reason to doubt this bit of conventional wisdom.

The remainder of this chapter outlines the techniques used in later chapters to specify voter beliefs. To begin with, comments made by members of Congress are used to justify a critical assumption: while explanations are politically beneficial, they are not a mechanism for persuasion—they do not generate trust. (This assumption will be tested in later chapters.) Of course, this assumption only highlights the problem of specifying beliefs. In the empirical chapters, this problem is solved using two techniques—one simple, the other more complicated. First of all, constituent beliefs about policy proposals will be coded from the interview transcripts. Unfortunately, the interviews do not provide sufficient information to code constituent assessments of a representative's policy goals. Happily, there is a well-developed theory of where these assessments come from: the theory of stereotyping. Therefore, after the section on explanations, the chapter turns to a discussion of stereotyping, and explains how constituents are expected to use stereotypes to form beliefs about their representative.

Beliefs and Explanations

It is well known that legislators spend considerable time and energy offering explanations to their constituents. To paraphrase Fenno (1978, 141), explanations involve descriptions, interpretations, and justifications of behavior. They are designed to generate political support, to increase an incumbent's chances of reelection. They occur during face-to-face interactions, such as speeches or question-and-answer sessions with constituents, and through indirect means, such as media coverage or newsletters.

The conventional wisdom is that explanations are a mechanism for persuasion—they alter what constituents think about legislative proposals or about their representative's policy concerns. For example, Parker argues that "incumbent congressmen make a point of explaining their votes and policy positions to their constituents when they are called upon to do so. . . . Explanations can be used by members to gain some leeway in their pursuits in Washington" (1989, 23). Austen-Smith's game-theoretic analysis of explanations and trust makes the link explicit: "Legislators' voting decisions are influenced by the need to justify Washington behavior to home constituents. An inability to offer a satisfactory explanation for some particular vote is perceived as jeopardizing an incumbent's chances of reelection" (1992, 68). Both statements convey the idea that explanations are a mechanism for persuasion or conversion. The negative aspect is emphasized: representatives take care to avoid unexplainable votes, votes that will anger constituents regardless of how they are rationalized. But there is a positive angle as well: explanations are thought to be a mechanism that gives representatives room to maneuver, the freedom to deviate from constituent demands without fear of political consequences.

How Members of Congress View Explanations

The interviews conducted for this study confirm some of the conventional wisdom about explanations. Legislators expect to be asked to explain their votes and give considerable thought to how different votes can be explained. However, the interviews also reveal a serious problem: *in the main, members of Congress do not think of explanations as a mechanism for persuasion.* During the interviews, a considerable number dismissed questions along these lines as the product of foolish academic notions, completely out of touch with the exigencies of real-world politics. In the first place, legislators say, explanations reach only a few constituents. Moreover, constituents who hear an explanation are likely to ignore it.

On the difficulties involved in contacting constituents, consider what two senior members of Congress said when they were asked if they could explain a vote against the repeal of Catastrophic Coverage:

> It would be difficult. It has to do with my district: because of the low density, I'd have to go to 23 media markets and deal with each community on its own. [19]

> I've got fifty thousand retirees in my district. How do I consult fifty thousand people? It's hard to talk with all those who are affected by a program. It's not that easy. We each represent five hundred thousand people, and we don't have the opportunity to talk with each of them. [70]

A junior representative was asked a similar question about voting for the Ethics Act:

> No, no way. Districts are so huge today, just by sheer logistics there's no way. My district is 180 miles north-south and 250 miles east-west. I go home and spend four days traveling around. But there's no way to come into contact with all those people, even if that's the only issue to talk about. [43]

The term *explaining* suggests a forum where constituents assemble to hear their representative. However, congressional districts contain over a half million individuals, often scattered across a large area. Even with a maximum effort—sending out newsletters, aggressively courting print and electronic media, speaking before every group who will listen—only a minority of constituents are likely to be exposed to an explanation. This finding is consistent with other analyses. As Fenno notes, "The more one observes members of Congress at work in their districts, the more impressed one is by the simple fact that people are hard to find" (1978, 234). Working from a survey of state legislators, Jewell (1982, chap. 3) concludes that constituents in rural areas are too spread out to contact effectively, while legislators in urban areas cannot get media access when they need it.

Moreover, contact is only the first step in persuasion. Constituents also have to believe what they are told. However, the message from the interviews is that constituents are reluctant to accept their representative's explanations, however well informed they believe her to be. For example, when asked how his constituents would react to an attempt to explain a vote in favor of the Ethics Act, a senior legislator replied, "No one but the mothers of members of Congress think that members of Congress would vote for ethics as the objective rather than a pay raise. You have to have a friendly judge to believe that" [41]. In fact, a substantial number of legislators argued that attempts at persuasion only make constituents angry. As one freshman put it,

I learned during my [first] month in the district not to take on the task of educating the public about the intricacies of an issue like Catastrophic. If you start explaining issues, you have to deal with numerous perspectives and issues. Seniors had been fed a lot of misinformation. Some had rational reasons for opposing Catastrophic, but on the whole if you tried to go down the list and explain, they were so antagonistic that their response was that you were trying to defend it. . . . Trying to analyze it for them so they could make an informed decision put you in hotter water, even though you were doing what they wanted. [94]

Faced with these problems, many representatives apparently steer clear of anything that sounds like persuasion:

I could tell them that if I vote yea the sun will come up, and if I vote no pestilence will descend. But my biases come in if I do that. So I try to provide them with as much information as I can. Sometimes I say, "look I'm biased but here's what I think." I go back home and talk with people, figure out where they are. I try to tell them about some questions they should be asking, answers they should look for. Legislators who try to tell people what the world is about wind up telling more about themselves than about the world. [9]

Thus, while it appears that members of Congress offer explanations, they do not try to persuade, nor do they expect that constituents will be persuaded. Again, this view finds support in the substantive literature. Fenno argues that when representatives offer explanations, they do not spend much time trying to educate—persuade—their constituents about policy matters:

. . . we think of education as an effort to persuade people to change their attitudes when the effort itself cannot be seen, in the short run anyway, as electorally beneficial. Education is something you do to your supporters —not your nonsupporters. Education involves the willingness to spend electoral capital—votes, even some trust—in an attempt to alter supporter attitudes about member activity in Washington. Few members would deny the importance of "educating your constituents" in the abstract. . . . But if education is a home activity that by definition has to *hurt a little*, then I did not see a great deal of it. (1978, 162)

This excerpt suggests that when reading *Home Style* many scholars have focused on the term *explanation* without considering what Fenno meant by it.

To a game theorist, it is not surprising that constituents view explanations with suspicion. In the main, explanations are "cheap talk": there is no cost to lying. And as the label implies, rational actors usually disregard cheap talk

(Banks 1991). The reasoning is simple. An explanation designed to persuade is likely to cite information that cannot be verified—private information. In the case of the Ethics Act, for example, a legislator could argue that passage of the act would reduce ethical infractions and encourage middle-class people to run for Congress. Yet even if the Ethics Act became law, constituents would never know whether these claims are true. Many ethics violations are never discovered. The factors driving candidacy decisions are poorly understood. It is also impossible to tell what would have happened if the proposal had been defeated. In sum, when making claims about the Ethics Act, a representative may be telling the truth, but it is also possible that she just wants a raise and is willing to say anything to get it. There is no way for constituents to be sure.

Again, Fenno's discussion of explanations confirms that constituents are suspicious of cheap talk and that legislators are well aware of this fact (1978, 55):

> . . . [House members] believe that what they say, their verbal expression, is an integral part of their "self." But, with Goffman, they place special emphasis on the nonverbal, "contextual" elements of their presentation. At the least, the nonverbal aspects must be consistent with the verbal ones. At the most, the expressions "given off" will become the basis for constituent judgement. Like Goffman, members of Congress are willing to emphasize the latter because, with him, they believe that their constituents will apply a heavier discount to what they say than to how they say it or how they act in the context in which they say it.

How constituents form beliefs about their representative will be discussed shortly. One thing seems clear: a representative's statements have at best an indirect effect on these perceptions.

Of course, it is possible to construct a game in which explanations are not cheap talk. The problem is that these analyses rely on ad hoc assumptions to render explanations informative. An example is Austen-Smith (1992). In his game, a representative's explanations are statements about her policy goals. A representative is punished if voters determine that she misrepresented her preferences. When the cost of being caught in a lie is high enough— relative to the value of staying in office—the representative will tell the truth, and constituents can believe what she says.[5] While this construction allows rational constituents to take their representative's communications seriously, it raises at least two substantive questions. For one thing, most explanations will involve claims about a representative's private information. The question is,

---

5. For a similar analysis, see Harrington 1988.

will constituents even be in a position to evaluate the veracity of their representative's claims? Insofar as a representative's private information remains private—and the discussion in chapter 2 suggests it often does—such evaluations are impossible. The second problem is to motivate the assumption that lying is costly. Austen-Smith gives a single-sentence justification: "Such a cost could arise, for example, from public vilification in the press, or from lost opportunities for advancement, or private sector appointments after leaving office, due to a diminished reputation, and so forth" (1992, 70). Austen-Smith's game also omits the problems associated with contact. In sum, his analysis does not provide a compelling rationale for the assumption that explanations constitute persuasion.

It must be emphasized that the legislators interviewed for this study *did not* claim that explanations are valueless. Rather, their comments were consistent with Fenno's (1978, 131–35) argument that members of Congress try to appear accessible to their constituents. At a minimum, explanations, regardless of who hears them or how they react, appear to be aimed at strengthening this perception. As one Midwestern Democrat put it,

> On any issue where a member votes contrary to a large vocal group, he has to have political capital, a sense of understanding that enables him to cast tough votes. If you explain and make yourself available, you can minimize the damage. The mistake members make when they cast a controversial vote is that they try to hide it. Voters can't relate to a politician who hides. They want to tell you off to your face. You need to defend your position. If you give a rational and reasonable answer, they'll say, "I disagree with your vote, but I understand why you did it, and I don't hold it against you." [3]

Perhaps representatives are rewarded simply for going home and reporting on their actions or for responding to constituent queries. Explanations might be a mechanism for position taking (Mayhew 1974, 61). Alternately, ducking queries about a vote may signal that a representative has something to hide, something worse than a vote against constituent interests. Whatever the reasons, explanations appear to have political value, even if they are not a mechanism for persuasion.

The Explanation Hypothesis

The conventional wisdom is that legislators use explanations to persuade, to shape their constituents' opinions and demands. However, the interviews conducted for this study suggest a different view: when legislators ask, "is this vote explainable?" they are not referring to the act of persuasion at all.

Rather, an explainable vote is one that constituents will approve of, for whatever reasons. The only persuasion occurs inside constituents' heads, as they assess their representative's action in light of their beliefs. Legislators certainly offer explanations, but their efforts do not seem to influence trust decisions. Therefore, it makes sense to exclude explanations from this analysis.

Some readers will favor an alternate strategy of modeling the problems of contact and cheap talk, on grounds that a simple exclusion of explanations is likely to be inaccurate some of the time. Admittedly, situations are likely to arise where representatives can get around the problem of contact. And under the right conditions, explanation might be taken seriously—perhaps because they can be verified, or because constituents have confidence in their representative's veracity. Unfortunately, it is not clear how to capture these exceptions within the confines of a game. Moreover, these possibilities must be placed against evidence that they do not often arise—and the goal of keeping the analysis simple enough to test.

Because this assumption about explanations cuts against the conventional wisdom, it will be treated as a hypothesis and tested in the empirical chapters. During the interviews, representatives were asked about the amount of explaining they did concerning their votes on the Ethics Act and on Catastrophic Coverage. The hypothesis developed here about the purpose of explanations suggests that two patterns will be observed. First, on each proposal, representatives who were trusted and who voted against constituent demands should report a low rate of explanation. Confirmation of this prediction would provide strong evidence for the hypothesis: explanations cannot be the source of trust if few individuals who reported (and exploited) trust did any explaining.[6]

Of course, representatives might report substantial amounts of explaining that are unrelated to trust, such as if constituents asked questions about their vote during town meetings or if they mentioned the vote as part of a general discussion of their work in Washington. This possibility suggests a second, weaker prediction: the amount of explaining reported by representatives who vote against their constituents' demands and were trusted should be similar to the amount reported by representatives who did not have trust and who complied with constituent demands. Similar amounts of explaining would suggest that this activity was not a vehicle for converting constituents

---

6. In principle, this test should include all legislators who reported trust, rather than only those who deviated from constituent demands. However, legislators in the latter category presumably hold accurate perceptions of whether they were trusted, as they had experienced their constituents' response to their vote. The perceptions of legislators who complied are open to question, since they might be wrong about how their constituents would react if they had deviated.

and gaining their trust; rather, it was undertaken for entirely different reasons and had entirely different effects. However, this implication is weaker than the first: while contrary evidence would falsify the explanation hypothesis, confirming it does not provide strong support. Even if legislators in the two groups are found to do similar amounts of explaining, it may be that those in the first group built trust by saying different things or said the same things but were taken seriously.

Stereotyping

Game theorists want to know where beliefs come from—beliefs that shape decisions. Theories of stereotyping begin with a similar question: how do people form impressions that ". . . define the situation, enabling others to know in advance what [an individual] will expect of them, and what they may expect of him" (Goffman 1959, 1). The answer is that judgments are formed using stereotypes, beliefs about the relationship between visible attributes that a person might have, or actions that she might have taken, and her unobserved interests, talents, or motivations.[7] In everyday discourse, stereotypes take the form of common wisdom, or truisms, as Lippman describes:

> . . .modern life is hurried and multifarious, above all physical distance separates men who are often in vital contact with each other, such as employer and employee, official and voter. There is neither time nor opportunity for intimate acquaintance. Instead we notice a trait which marks a well-known type, and fill in the rest of the picture by means of the stereotypes we carry about in our heads. He is an agitator. That much we notice, or are told. Well, an agitator is this sort of person, and so *he* is this sort of person. He is an intellectual. He is a plutocrat. He is a foreigner. He is a "Southern European." He is from Back Bay. He is a Harvard Man. How different from the statement: he is a Yale Man. He is a regular fellow. He is a West Pointer. He is an old army sergeant. He is a Greenwich Villager: what don't we know about him, then, and about her? (1922, 89)

Stereotyping can occur in two ways. First, learning something about an individual may cue or trigger a stereotype, resulting in an evaluation that is stored for future use, in a more or less automatic process. Alternately, stereotyping may occur on the fly, as a person searches for stereotypes that will allow her to reason from what she knows about an individual to certain judgments which she desires to make. The expectation in the stereotyping literature appears to

---

7. For a recent review of the stereotyping literature, see Sherman, Judd, and Park 1989.

be that the latter mechanism predominates—being cognitive misers, people will not form judgments until forced to do so.

Theories of stereotyping emphasize that this activity does not occur willy-nilly. In particular, actions are discounted if they appear to be the product of calculation. As Goffman puts it, ". . . when an individual appears in the presence of others, there will usually be some reason for him to mobilize his activity so that it will convey an impression to others which is in his interest to convey" (1959, 4). As a result, Goffman (1959, 7) argues, people focus on expressions that a person gives off, rather than the expressions she gives. He provides an apt example:

> . . . in Shetland Isle one crofter's wife, in serving native dishes to a visitor from the mainland of Britain, would listen with a polite smile to his polite claims of liking what he is eating; at the same time she would take note of the rapidity with which the visitor lifted his fork or spoon to his mouth, the eagerness with which he passed food into his mouth, and the gusto expressed in chewing his food, using these signs as a check on the stated feelings of the eater. (1959, 7)

Goffman argues that the crofter's wife is following a simple rule: she focuses on cues that are difficult to manipulate. In particular, she ignores verbal assertions, believing that her guest would profess that he enjoyed his dinner regardless of his true feelings. As a substitute, the crofter's wife examines other aspects of her guest's behavior—facial expressions, unconscious gestures, and, presumably, whether he asks for seconds—as an indirect, but more accurate, measure of his true feelings. (This rule is similar to the logic behind disregarding cheap talk.)

Stereotypes and Game Theory

The principles of stereotyping are not cast in game-theoretic language, but they are entirely consistent with the intuitions of rational choice. Consider an example that is often used to illustrate the concept of sequential equilibria, Kreps's game of beer and quiche:

> Party A is one of two types; either he is a wimp or he is surly. A knows which type he is; B assesses (at the outset) probability .9 that A is surly. Eventually, B must decide whether to challenge A to a duel. If A is indeed a wimp, then B will profit by challenging A, but if A is surly, B will lose by issuing the challenge. Regardless of whether A is a wimp or is surly, A prefers not to duel.
>
> But before B must decide whether to duel, B first gets to see a signal

that may be informative about A's type. To wit, B observes what A has for breakfast. There are two possible breakfasts, beer and quiche. If A is surly, then A prefers the beer. If A is a wimp, A prefers quiche. But in both cases, the cost to A of having the less preferred breakfast is less than the cost of having to engage in the duel. (1983, 4)

In this game, player A's choice is a signal or indication of his type. That is, knowing that wimps prefer quiche and surly individuals prefer beer, player B can sometimes reason from player A's choice to a new, updated belief about player A's type. Sequential equilibrium analysis shows that this process of updating occurs under some but not all conditions. One situation where updating will occur is if player A was willing to face a duel if this is necessary to eat his preferred breakfast. If so, player A would always choose his preferred breakfast in equilibrium—and player B could read player A's choice as a signal of A's type. However, in Kreps's game, player A's preferences are reversed: he would rather avoid a duel than eat what he wants for breakfast. Therefore, his equilibrium strategy is to drink beer for breakfast, regardless of whether he is a wimp or is surly. This strategy enables player A to mask his type from player B. From player B's perspective, player A may be surly and enjoying his beer or be a wimp and drinking beer only to avoid a duel. The choice tells him nothing. As a result, player B is reduced to making his decision on the basis of his prior beliefs—A is surly with probability .9. Based on that information, player B's best choice is to avoid a challenge.

In the language of stereotyping, the beer-quiche game has player B making a judgment about an unknown factor, player A's type, based on an observable action, what player A eats for breakfast. It is as though player B has two stereotypes in mind, one saying that wimps eat quiche, the other saying that surly individuals drink beer. In the game as described here, the assumption that player A wants to avoid a duel at all costs implies that his breakfast choice is a cue that can be manipulated at low cost. Therefore, the principles of stereotyping would lead to the same prediction as sequential equilibrium analysis. Player A, wanting to avoid a duel, would drink beer regardless of his true preference. Expecting this, player B would ignore the choice—refuse to apply stereotypes—on grounds that the decision says nothing about player A's type. If, however, player A was willing to duel in order to eat his preferred breakfast, the theory would predict that player B would stereotype player A on the basis of his breakfast choice—the same prediction made by sequential equilibrium analysis.

From this discussion, it should be apparent that the two theories, game theory and stereotyping, are quite compatible. The principal difference between the two approaches is that stereotyping focuses on how people form beliefs, while game theory focuses on how people act on beliefs. Neither approach is complete. Game theory does not explain where priors come from. Similarly, the theory of stereotyping does not explain how stereotypes arise (Taylor et al. 1978, 792). These questions are not ignored completely— Lippman, for example, argues, "The subtlest and most pervasive of all influences are those which create and maintain the repertory of stereotypes" (1922, 89–90). Just as rational actors are assumed to do what seems best given what they know, the theory of stereotyping assumes that people make judgments about others based on preexisting stereotypes. Questions about the origin of stereotypes remain unanswered.

Political Stereotypes

That stereotypes are used to make sense of politics is so basic that it can escape notice. But they are. Consider the 1992 edition of *Politics in America* (Duncan 1991), a 1,600-page guide to the membership of the 102d Congress. It is hard to find a page that does not contain a stereotype. Representative Lee Hamilton (D-Ind.) is described as "Middle American to his core" (Duncan 1991, 513); Representative Robert Walker (R-Pa.) is the "quintessential legislative outsider" (1991, 1302). In some cases, legislators themselves do the stereotyping: Representative Joe Moakley (D-Mass.) is quoted as saying, "I'd like to be a Tip O'Neil-type guy if I could" (1991, 704). These labels are not chosen by accident. They are political shorthand, used because of the images and impressions they evoke.

Voters use stereotypes too. Popkin (1991) argues that voters want to acquire information about candidates' policy stands, values, and expertise to cast a reasoned, well-informed vote but are unwilling to spend the time and energy needed to obtain this information. Stereotypes—in Popkin's terms, "low-information reasoning"—provide a low-cost alternative. For example, Popkin argues that voters stereotype presidential candidates using a wide variety of actions and attributes, ranging from those that are explicitly political, such as past votes, policy stands, or party affiliation, to ostensibly nonpolitical actions, such as religious beliefs. The fact that voters use actions and attributes in this way explains the political significance of events and actions that seem far removed from the political sphere:

> In 1976, when President Ford tried to eat an unshucked tamale, he committed a faux pas far more serious than spilling mustard on his tie or ice cream on his shirt. To Hispanic voters in Texas, he betrayed an unfamiliarity with their food which suggested a lack of familiarity with their whole culture. Further, tamales were a way of projecting from the personal to the political, of assuming that personal familiarity with a

culture and the acceptability of a candidate's policies to a group were linked. (Popkin 1991, 111)

Popkin concludes, ". . . low-information reasoning is by no means devoid of substantive content, and is instead a process that economically incorporates learning and information from past experiences, daily life, the media, and political campaigns" (1991, 212). Similar positions are taken by Conover and Feldman (1986, 1989), Fiske (1990), King and Gelman (1992), and Rahn et al (1990).

Politicians are well aware of stereotypes too. Fenno's idea that members of Congress "present themselves" to constituents is drawn directly from Goffman's work. His work suggests that members of Congress know about stereotyping, expect to be stereotyped, and take actions with stereotyping in mind.[8] Representatives don't visit country fairs (or urban greenmarkets) and sample the local cuisine just because they're hungry—they are trying to get voters to infer shared values and interests. The message is almost audible: "if we do the same things, we must think the same way, and have similar interests." These efforts gain a new urgency in an era where politicians rank below used car salesmen on surveys of public attitudes. Absent any other information, voters will form beliefs about their representative based on the one bit of information they have: that she is a politician, an incumbent, and presumably unworthy of their support.

Stereotyping Representatives

The theory of stereotyping confirms what students of politics have believed all along: an elected official's actions and personal attributes are imbued with political significance. But this regularity does not arise because citizens deviate from rational calculation. Rather, stereotyping is a sensible, rational, predictable response to the problem of assessing unobserved aspects of an elected official's character. Thus, stereotypes offer at least a partial answer to the question, how do constituents form beliefs about their representative? or, equivalently, the question, where do reputations come from? Put simply, we should expect to see these beliefs vary with a representative's attributes and her record of past actions. Representatives with similar actions and attributes will be seen as having similar goals or talents; those whose actions and attributes differ will be thought to hold different goals or talents.

---

8. Fenno limits his attention to legislators' behavior while in office. However, many would-be politicians are worried about their image long before they decide to enter public life. Consider Bill Clinton's decision to register for the draft: he believed that failing to register would destroy any chance he might have for a career in politics.

In the abstract, it is difficult to identify the specific actions and attributes that constituents will use to assess a specific policy concern, such as their representative's feelings about abortion or deficit reduction—or congressional pay raises. In general, the answer will depend on which of a representative's actions and attributes are known to constituents and on the content of the stereotypes available to them. At the present time these matters must be considered to be empirical questions and are treated as such in later chapters. Happily, interviews with legislators provide a great deal of information about these questions, so the inability to specify these factors in advance is not much of a problem.

The theory of stereotyping does, however, provide two hints about how the process works in the context of trust decisions. First, the set of relevant actions and attributes is likely to vary across proposals, representatives, and time. Faced with a trust decision involving a specific proposal, constituents will focus their attention on a narrow set of actions and attributes—those that signal goals that would motivate a legislator to support or oppose the proposal at hand. It is possible that the same actions or attributes will provide sharp, clear inferences across a range of proposals. However, insofar as proposals address different policy questions, it would be no surprise to find that the actions or attributes that help constituents to assess one set of policy goals are no help on the next. (This expectation is confirmed in later chapters.) In addition, the content of politically relevant stereotypes—and thus the set of relevant actions and attributes—could easily vary across representatives, depending on where their districts are located. A candidate's tamale-eating ability might not be politically salient in the Midwest, even though Hispanic voters in south Texas see it as critical. Finally, the set of politically relevant actions and attributes is likely to vary over time as voters learn new stereotypes and discard old ones. A generation ago, divorce or past use of illegal drugs equaled political death for a would-be candidate. Nowadays, absent unusual circumstances, such revelations are no longer politically relevant— or, in the language of stereotyping, these actions no longer provide sharp inferences about an individual's character. During the same time, the increased activity of evangelical groups in politics may have provided voters with new actions, such as membership in the Moral Majority, that can be used for stereotyping.[9]

Second, while it may be hard to identify in advance which actions and attributes will be used for stereotyping in a particular situation, it is easy to identify a set of actions that are unlikely choices, regardless of where constituents live or what they are trying to infer. These are politically beneficial actions—actions designed to increase a legislator's chances of getting

9. For anecdotal evidence that supports this assertion, see Hershey 1984.

reelected or actions taken to build a favorable reputation. (More precisely, constituents must believe that an action was aimed at one of these goals.) For example, suppose a legislator voted for a proposal, believing that constituents would be angered by a nay vote, or voted yea to demonstrate that she agreed with her constituents' concerns. Either way, policy goals played no role in the legislator's decision. While the vote may have had policy consequences, it cannot be used to assess the member's policy goals. The only conclusion constituents can draw is that their representative was willing to sacrifice her policy concerns for political ends—the pursuit of reelection or reputation building.[10]

This caveat applies only to actions that are politically beneficial. Actions that are politically damaging, such as actions that are contrary to constituent demands or beliefs, provide a basis for stereotyping. To continue the example raised above, suppose the representative voted nay over her constituents' objections. This action suggests that she holds certain policy interests, and holds them intensely enough that she will accept costs—negative evaluations and a damaged reputation—in order to achieve them. Constituents could draw similar inferences from actions that, while politically popular, force a representative to incur personal or policy costs that outweigh whatever political benefits the action may generate. Moreover, this reasoning implies that legislators have two reasons to avoid casting votes that will anger their constituents. Not only are the votes damaging in terms of retrospective evaluations, they also signal disagreement with constituent interests.

This argument suggests that in a legislature such as the modern Congress, where the reelection goal is ubiquitous, many of a representative's actions are useless for stereotyping. Of course, many of a representative's actions in office will go unnoticed by her constituents. The problem goes deeper than that, however. Consider vote decisions. In general, an interest in reelection will lead a representative to cast votes that are received favorably back home—votes that are the product of political factors, not policy concerns.[11] If so, a representative's voting record, or any transformation of these votes, may not contain any information about her policy goals. This suggestion is consistent with the work of Fenno (1978), who finds that when legislators interact with constituents, they spend a great deal of time describing their personal characteristics and their efforts as policy entrepreneurs but give short shrift to their voting record. Along the same lines, Popkin (1991) finds that

---

10. Barber (1985) makes a similar point in arguing that judgments about a presidential candidate's character must be based on the candidate's behavior in early life and during her "first independent political success"—that is, on actions taken before the candidate became concerned with maintaining a politically beneficial public image.

11. As shown in chapter 4, this incentive exists, albeit in a reduced form, even if a representative expects that constituents will trust her judgment.

during presidential campaigns, voters focus on a candidate's personal attributes to the exclusion of her record in political life. It may be that information about attributes is less costly to acquire and process, as Popkin argues. But voters may also focus on attributes because they cannot be the product of calculation and therefore provide a clearer signal of a candidate's policy concerns.

Insofar as constituents stereotype legislators on the basis of actions, we should expect them to focus on actions that are difficult to undo. This finding is echoed by Rahn (1993), who finds that voters stereotype candidates on the basis of partisan affiliation. In one sense this result is a surprise. Given that the Republican and Democrat candidate pools are heterogenous, a candidate's party affiliation may not supply precise inferences about her goals. Moreover affiliation decisions are probably skewed by political considerations. However, the decision is not completely strategic. A candidate cannot alter his party affiliation in order to suit the circumstances of a particular election. At a minimum, party switching is costly. Thus, as long as policy concerns play some role in affiliation decisions—a reasonable assumption—it makes sense that these decisions function as policy signals, even if the inferences they allow are necessarily vague.

Just as voters' stereotypes are likely to vary over time, so will the set of actions that are considered political. For example, in the early twentieth century, when members of Congress had limited travel and office budgets and voters usually cast party-line votes, taking frequent trips home or having a district office probably signaled that a member of Congress wanted to be accessible and attentive to constituents. Since the personal cost of these actions was high and the reelection benefits low, they were taken only by legislators who genuinely desired to be accessible and attentive. In the modern era, the cost of these actions is much lower, since legislators have substantial office allotments and travel money. Moreover, in an era when elections are candidate centered, appearing indifferent to district concerns is politically fatal. Thus, legislators who desire to be attentive or accessible still take the actions, but other legislators, those who care little about their constituents but desire reelection, do the same. Accordingly, present-day voters are likely to interpret these actions as a signal of their representative's interest in reelection rather than an indication of her desire to keep in touch. This reasoning is supported by Jacobson's analysis of postwar congressional elections: ". . . it is striking that the steep increase in [congressional] staff, travel, and communications allowances during the 1960s and 1970s failed to produce any net improvement in incumbents' reelection prospects at the time they were occurring" (1992, 43). Of course not; once everyone saw that frequent contact was politically beneficial, they all started doing it, thereby changing the inference that could be drawn from these actions.

CHAPTER 4

The Leeway Hypothesis

First I want to know what you're trying to prove. No one writes a book without trying to prove something. I know that, I wrote a book once. [Aide: "That's right, sir, you wrote a book once."] You say you just want to know what's going on, but only journalists do that. So what are you trying to prove?
—A senior Democrat

In this chapter I construct a game, the Evaluation game, and use it to develop predictions about trust. These predictions are summarized by a hypothesis— the leeway hypothesis. In addition, I use the game to evaluate the concept of induced ideal points. This test confirms the doubts raised in chapter 2: while legislators sometimes behave as though they held induced ideal points, this assertion does not hold true in general.

A note about terminology. In order to distinguish statements about players in the Evaluation game from statements about real-world representatives and constituents, the players are always referred to as R, meaning the representative or legislator, and C, meaning the constituent. Thus, references to how R behaves, or what C thinks, are to the game itself. Statements that use the unabbreviated terms—representative and constituent—refer to real-world representatives and constituents. In addition, continuing the earlier pattern, female pronouns are used to refer to R, or to representatives, while male pronouns are used to refer to C, or to constituents.

Aside from frequent allusions to R, C, and β (the proposal that R votes on), the Evaluation game and its predictions are described informally. More-over, the particulars of the game are justified by references to the empirical literature on legislatures, usually citing works on the U.S. Congress. The intent is to give nonspecialists a sense of the techniques used in the analysis and to reassure them that the analysis builds on, or is at least consistent with, well-known and well-accepted precepts about the legislative process. Appen-dix 1 contains the technical version of the Evaluation game, as well as the characterization of equilibrium behavior that underlies the leeway hypothesis.

The Evaluation Game

The Evaluation game captures a single interaction involving R and her constit-uents. R votes on a policy proposal (β) that, if enacted, will produce a new policy outcome. Afterward, C evaluates R's action. As noted in chapter 2, player C is a stand-in for the set of constituents in R's district who are prepared to make retrospective evaluations of R's vote on β. Since β is considered to be a high-salience issue, this set includes either a high percentage of R's constituents or a smaller but politically significant group.

The structure of the Evaluation game reflects the circumstances described in chapter 2. Each player wants to enact the best possible policy outcome given her policy goal. R also wants to be reelected and considers this goal to be more important than securing good policy. The players pursue these goals under conditions of asymmetric information. R is fully aware of all factors relevant to her decision. C is similarly well informed about most facets of the game, but he does not know two things: what policy outcome will be produced if β is enacted and the content of R's policy goals. Formally, C has beliefs about these factors—beliefs that may be uncertain or inaccurate.

Overall Structure

The Evaluation game models trust in the context of vote decisions, specifically a single vote. Of course, decisions about trust might involve other kinds of actions, such as the provision of constituent services.[1] However, vote decisions seem the obvious place to begin an analysis of trust. In any event, insofar as constituents use similar criteria to resolve trust decisions across a variety of legislatorial actions—which seems likely—analyzing trust in the context of vote decisions will reveal more general results.

The analysis focuses on a single vote decision because this combination is the fundamental unit of analysis. Consider: a representative votes on one proposal at a time. While she can vote the same way on a number of proposals, or apply the same decision rule across a number of vote decisions, in principle she faces a series of independent choices. Similarly, while constituents might make a blanket decision to trust their representative's judgment in different areas, they need not do so. In both cases, absent transaction costs or some other constraint, a rational actor would not make a series of decisions all at once when she could make them one at a time. Moreover, even if representatives and constituents make decisions at some level of aggregation, an analysis of the singleton case is needed to explain why they choose to make decisions in bunches. The drawback with confining the analysis to a single vote is that this construction excludes reputational effects—the possibility that a representative would avoid casting certain votes because of the inferences constituents would draw from them. However, as later discussion will show, even the one-vote case provides some information about this phenomena.

---

1. For a discussion of the various possibilities, see Eulau and Karps 1977.

Others will take exception to the focus on high-salience policy proposals. Taken literally, this assumption limits the applicability of the analysis to the few hot-button, bell-ringer issues that capture public attention each year. However, this focus has several virtues. Once we understand how expectations about trust influence behavior on high-salience issues, it is fairly easy to explain the low-salience case. The assumption also facilitates empirical analysis. On high-salience votes, trust is likely to have a direct, observable effect on a representative's actions. High salience also guarantees that citizens face the largest possible incentive to make the right decision about trust. Finally, the assumption directs attention to votes that settle controversial debates or make large changes in government policy. These are the actions that citizens would most like to control and, not coincidentally, the actions that scholars would most like to explain.

The assumption that R is the pivotal voter in the legislature means that her vote determines whether β is enacted or defeated. This assumption simplifies the analysis by making policy outcomes contingent on R's vote. Focusing on the pivotal legislator is also a standard tactic used to simplify models of legislatorial behavior (e.g., Gilligan and Krehbiel 1990). However, neither the structure of the Evaluation game nor the results derived from it would change if R was assumed to be a member of a pivotal coalition, or if there was only a chance that R was the pivotal voter. Some combination of these alternate interpretations covers most real-world situations that the Evaluation game might be applied to.

Finally, the focus on a game with a small number of players is a standard tactic in the application of asymmetric information technology to political phenomena.[2] Insofar as district preferences or perceptions are heterogeneous, this construction captures only a portion of the constituency. However, it would be difficult to solve a game with a large number of players. This dilemma is not unique to game-theoretic models of representation. Empirical analyses of representation typically estimate a regression equation in which a legislator's voting behavior (a single vote or an index such as a voting score) is the dependent variable, and voter demands are captured by independent variables that measure demographic data for the legislator's district or, in a few cases, aggregated survey data.[3] Regardless of the number of variables, the intent is to arrive at a single measure or referent, label it *the constituency,* and assume that if representatives respond to anything, they respond to this indicator. Spatial models of elections incorporate similar assumptions (Enelow and

---

2. For example, all the models discussed in Krehbiel's (1991) book on legislative organization contain either two or, occasionally, three players. Similarly, Austen-Smith's (1992) analysis of explanations uses a two-player game.

3. Recent examples include Bartels 1991, Bernstein 1991, Kalt and Zupan 1984 and 1990, and Krehbiel and Rivers 1988.

Hinich 1984). Happily, later chapters will show that members of Congress make much the same simplification when they talk about their constituents. Thus, assuming a unitary constituency, while fundamentally inaccurate, may capture the political world as representatives see it.

Strategies and Trust

In the Evaluation game, a strategy for R specifies her vote, yea or nay, as a function of her policy goals and information about β. R is pivotal, so if she votes yea, β is enacted and a new policy outcome goes into effect. If R votes nay, β is defeated and the status quo outcome prevails. C's strategy tells how he will evaluate different votes by R: favorably or unfavorably. Thus, he has four options: issue favorable evaluations regardless of how R votes, issue favorable evaluations only if R votes yea, issue favorable evaluations only if R votes nay, and issue unfavorable evaluations regardless of how R votes.[4]

Together with the assumptions about sequence, these assumptions reflect the idea that trust is expressed in terms of retrospective evaluations— evaluations that are made only after R votes. R is assumed to move first, with C issuing retrospective evaluations only after he sees R's vote. However, because C is a rational actor and because R is informed about C's policy goals and beliefs, R knows how C will respond to different votes and takes these expectations into account when deciding how to vote. Trust, or voting leeway, is said to exist if C will issue a favorable evaluation regardless of how R votes. Trust does not exist if C will evaluate R's vote favorably only if it is consistent with his demands or opinions.

An example may prove helpful. Suppose C believes that enacting β will make him better off. Given these beliefs, C's demand, or his idea about what is best, is that β should be enacted. Therefore trust exists when C, given his beliefs about β, would issue a favorable retrospective evaluation regardless of whether R voted yea or voted nay. That C would approve of a yea vote in this example is no surprise—after all, he thinks enacting β is preferable. However, the approval of a nay vote makes sense only if C believes that R has private information about β, information that indicates, contrary to C's beliefs, that the status quo is preferable given his interests. To say that C decides

---

4. The last strategy does not receive much attention. The idea that C cares about policy outcomes implies that if he cannot trust R's judgment about outcomes, surely he will attempt to use retrospective evaluations to enforce fiduciary behavior. If so, the only situation in which a strategy of unilateral punishment might be preferable is if the chances of ever being able to trust R are so low that C prefers to elect a new representative at the next possible opportunity. Even then, chances are good that C will still try to control R's behavior, rather than accepting a string of inferior policy outcomes until the next election. These intuitions are borne out in appendix 1.

against trust in this example implies that he will evaluate yea votes favorably and nay votes unfavorably. That is, C will approve of R's vote only if it appears to generate the best possible policy outcome for him.

While this conception of trust is consistent with theories of retrospective evaluation (e.g., Fiorina 1981; Key 1966), the reader might argue that constituents can issue threats and make demands before their representative votes on a legislative proposal. If this assertion were true, the Evaluation game should allow constituents to choose a strategy before their representative votes, not after. This change would undoubtedly increase C's control over outcomes in the Evaluation game: in general, the ability to precommit has this effect.[5] However, it seems unreasonable to think that constituents, even one at a time, can make commitments about how they will react to a vote. Rather, it should be assumed that constituents make whatever evaluation seems best when they are forced to make one—after their representative votes, not before. Given this assumption, trust, or its absence, must be defined in the terms used here.

Information, Asymmetric Information, and Beliefs

The Evaluation game uses a standard technique to generate asymmetric information: choices by a nonstrategic player, Nature (Harsanyi 1967). At the beginning of the game, before R and C choose their strategies, Nature determines which outcome will be produced by enacting β. Specifically, Nature chooses a policy outcome from a set of two possible outcomes. At the same time, Nature decides whether R shares C's policy goal or holds a policy goal that differs from C's. R learns about Nature's choices immediately— informally, she knows what she wants and knows how to get it. C, however, is informed only after he evaluates R's vote. When C acts, he knows the likelihood that Nature made each possible choice, but he does not know which choices were actually made. Both players are fully informed about all other features of the game, such as what outcome will result if β is defeated, that R values reelection over policy, that R has private information, and the content of C's policy goals.

While these assumptions may seem unrealistic, they reflect the essence of the conventional wisdom presented in chapter 2: legislators know the game they are playing; constituents do not. Of course, the assumption that constituents know very little about politics will not distress many readers. The problem is to justify the assumption that legislators are fully informed. Readers familiar with Krehbiel's book on legislative organization will note that the Evaluation game violates his Uncertainty Postulate: "Legislators are often

---

5. For an example, see Aldrich and Bianco 1992.

uncertain about the relationship between politics and their outcomes" (1991, 20). The easy response is that the Evaluation game assumes that mechanisms such as those described by Krehbiel (e.g., the congressional committee system) have already functioned and supplied R with information about β. In addition, as noted below in the introduction to part 2, there is reason to expect that legislators hold accurate beliefs about the game they are playing. Finally, it is almost certainly true that all the results described here would hold in a more general version of the Evaluation game, in which R had some uncertainty about β's effects but was less uncertain than C.

The structure of the Evaluation game implements the standard policy proposal–policy outcome distinction used in signaling games that model the political process (e.g., Krehbiel 1991). Using this terminology, β is a policy proposal. If enacted, it will produce a new policy outcome, a move from the status quo. (If β is defeated, the status quo policy outcome prevails.) One of Nature's choices determines which policy outcome will follow from β's enactment—informally, the choice determines what the proposal will do if enacted.

The idea that Nature determines certain parameters of the game should not be taken literally. Nature is simply a mechanism for ensuring that R has private (and full) information about her policy goals and about β. The effect is to replicate the essence of the problem faced by real-world constituents: C knows what his interests are but does not know whether his interests are best served by the enactment or the defeat of β. That is, he knows what he wants but not how to get it. Moreover, while C knows what policy goals R might hold, he is unsure what her motivations actually are. Analytically, the mechanism allows C's beliefs about β and about R to be specified in terms of the probability of Nature making different moves. By varying these probabilities, it is possible to analyze how constituents will act under a range of conditions, including high uncertainty, when they know very little about a proposal or about their representative; low uncertainty, when they are (or think they are) well informed about these factors; or any combination in between. Finally, the definition of Nature's moves also ensures that the Evaluation game satisfies a necessary condition for trust, the *private information* condition. Intuitively, constituents will never trust their representative unless there is some chance that she knows something about the proposal that they do not. In the Evaluation game, C is sure that R has private information about β.

Figure 2 illustrates the situation that C faces in light of these assumptions about asymmetric information. The figure shows a version of the Evaluation game in which policy outcomes and policy goals are specified as points on a single policy dimension. In this game, C knows two things for sure: the location of his ideal point (C) and the location of the status quo outcome (b_2). However, C is uncertain about two things. The first is the location of b_y, or the

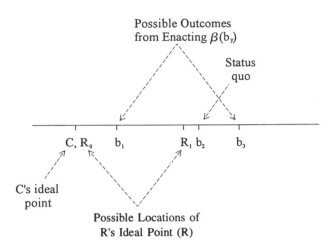

Fig. 2. **Asymmetric information in the Evaluation game**

outcome that results from enacting β. From C's viewpoint there are two possibilities: b_y can be at point b_1 or at point b_3. C is also unsure of the location of R's ideal point (R). Again, there are two possibilities: R can be at R_0 or at R_1. Given these uncertainties, C can be playing one of four games, as illustrated in figure 3. *The problem is, C does not know which game he is playing—but R does.* Does enacting β make C better off (that is, yield an outcome that is closer to his ideal point than the status quo), as in the first and third diagrams, or does it make him worse off, as in the second and fourth? Does R share C's policy concerns, as in the top two diagrams, or does she hold different concerns, as in the bottom two? R knows which diagram in figure 3 describes the situation she and C are in. Thus, she chooses a strategy under full information. C does not. Because of his lack of information, C must make his evaluations based on beliefs about which game he is playing— which diagrams are likely to be accurate and which are not.

Payoffs and Motivations

In the Evaluation game, R is motivated by two goals: enacting good public policy and getting reelected. Her policy goal implies that she likes some policy outcomes more than others. That is, these concerns give her preferences across ends—the effects of governmental action. Formally, R's policy concerns can be described in terms of a preference ordering, or ranking, of feasible policy outcomes. These preferences, combined with information about what policy outcome β will produce if enacted, determine whether R prefers to enact β or to defeat it. To stress, because of her policy goal, R

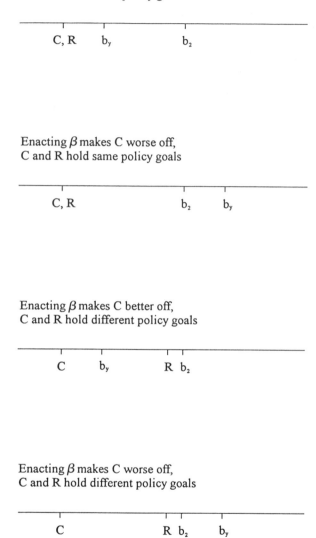

Fig. 3. The impact of asymmetric information: What game is C playing?

prefers some policy outcomes over others; these preferences determine whether she prefers to enact the policy proposal β, which would yield a new policy outcome, or to defeat β, which would preserve the status quo policy outcome. The impact of R's second goal, reelection, is easier to specify: R wants her votes to receive favorable evaluations. Furthermore, since R ranks reelection over policy, she always prefers to cast a vote that receives favorable evaluations over one that yields a preferable policy. Thus, that R favors the enactment of β does not imply that she is willing to vote for the proposal. The question is, how will C evaluate a yea vote?

This specification is intended to capture the motivations that a typical career-oriented member of Congress holds when voting on a high-salience policy proposal. That representatives want to be reelected is a stylized fact with considerable support: even in the 1992 elections, few legislators voluntarily retired unless they were faced with scandal, redistricting, or the advent of their golden years. But reelection is not the whole story. Even representatives who see reelection as an overriding concern are likely to have an opinion, however marginal, about the merits of a policy proposal. Thus, it makes sense to assume that their decisions are shaped by policy concerns as well as the desire to be reelected. Some readers will argue that members of Congress hold additional goals, such as progressive ambition, a desire for internal influence, or a preference for accommodating the wishes of party leaders. Without dismissing these arguments, it is clear that policy and reelection constitute the principal motivations for most representatives on most proposals. Moreover, insofar as other goals are relevant, they can be seen as factors that influence the content of a representative's preferences across policy outcomes. Thus, the simple two-goal specification used here may capture some portion of the effect of other goals.

Objections might also be raised to the assumption that R's interest in reelection takes precedence over her policy concerns. Admittedly, it is easy to think of exceptions. A representative might care little about reelection, perhaps because she is nearing retirement or was elected under a system of term limits. A proposal might tap policy concerns that a legislator regards as supremely important. Constituents may be indifferent about a proposal. Given any of these exceptions, policy concerns, even if they are marginal, will override political considerations. But when high-salience proposals come up, it seems safe to assume that most legislators will sacrifice good policy on the altar of political expedience, if this sacrifice is required to keep constituents happy. Arnold, for example, argues:

> [My] theory assumes that members of Congress care intensely about reelection. Although they are not single-minded seekers of reelection, reelection is their dominant goal. This simply means that legislators will

do nothing to advance their other goals if such activities threaten their principal goal. If reelection is not at risk, they are free to pursue other goals, including enacting their own visions of good public policy or achieving influence within Congress. (1990, 5)

The structure of the Evaluation game is consistent with Arnold's expectation. However, a discussion of policy-minded representatives will be included later in this analysis.

A few scholars will argue for a narrower specification of goals, claiming that most legislators are interested in reelection to the near exclusion of policy concerns. Arguments along these lines are usually justified by a Darwinist rationale: in the long run, legislators who care about policy will likely be defeated by legislators who are willing to subordinate everything to the pursuit of reelection. There are three responses. The first is intuitive: virtually everyone, including legislators, has policy preferences of some kind, even if these preferences are extremely weak. The critical question is what priority is assigned to these concerns. Here the Evaluation game makes an assumption that critics can agree with: on high-salience issues, policy concerns usually—but not inevitably—take second place to the reelection goal. The second defense of including policy concerns is empirical: few students of Congress would argue that representatives are completely indifferent to the content of public policy, even after controlling for the impact that policy outcomes have on their chances of reelection. As Sinclair notes,

Much legislative strategy cannot be understood without an understanding of members' multiple goals and the score of circumstances that allow them or force them to place priority on one or the other. . . . Assuming the single goal of reelection makes for easier theory-building, but that is not sufficient justification for adopting an assumption that leads to disastrously distorted predictions. (1992, 4)

A final rationale is suggested by the nature of the analysis. Insofar as constituents are policy-minded, they may prefer a legislator who holds policy goals and therefore cares about the consequences of her votes over one who does not.

C is motivated by a single goal, enacting good policy. Like R, this goal is specified as an ordering across feasible policy outcomes. And, in light of this ordering and his beliefs about β, C has an idea, or a guess, whether enacting β will produce a policy outcome that he will prefer over the status quo outcome. This estimate is referred to as C's *demand* or *opinion* about β. Because C is not sure which policy outcome will be produced by enacting β, there is some chance that his demand is inconsistent with his interests—he may think that the proposal will produce an outcome preferable to the status quo when that is not the case. This characterization of constituent goals is consistent with the idea that constituents are fundamentally self-interested: they want their representative to cast votes that are consistent with their long-term, discounted interests. However, the Evaluation game does not restrict the content of constituents' interests. The characterization of C's preferences is consistent with a variety of interpretations, including the idea that constituents prefer outcomes that are consistent with the national interest, or that constituents want the interests of poor people to take precedence over their own welfare.

The assumption of a unitary constituency may create some confusion at this point. This assumption does not imply that R achieves reelection by implementing an abstract social-welfare function or some collective preference. On the contrary, R's actions are governed by how she expects C to respond to different votes. In a more complicated version of the Evaluation game, where the unitary constituency assumption was relaxed, R would consider how multiple constituents, or different groups in her constituency, would respond.

C's policy goal also implies that he wants to make an accurate evaluation of R's vote. There are two kinds of accurate evaluations: favorable evaluations of votes that yield the best possible outcomes for C and unfavorable evaluations of votes that do not. If C always makes accurate evaluations, R will be rewarded for behaving as a fiduciary and punished if she deviates. This assumption reflects the conventional wisdom about retrospective evaluations (Fiorina 1981; Key 1966). At the margin, favorable evaluations increase an incumbent's chances of reelection. Thus, accurate evaluations are desirable, since they further the preservation of good incumbents (those who act according to constituent interests) and the removal of bad ones (those who deviate). The value of accurate evaluations persists even if vote decisions are sensitive to other factors, such as judgments about other aspects of incumbent behavior, party identification, etc.

C's beliefs about β in the Evaluation game are assumed to satisfy a second necessary condition for leeway, the *lottery condition*. This condition reflects the intuition that C will consider trust only if he is unsure whether enacting β is consistent with his interests.[6] If, despite his uncertainties, C was sure that β would improve on the status quo (produce a policy outcome that is ranked higher in his ordering than the status quo is), he would have no incentive to allow R any discretion. The same would be true if C was sure that the status quo was preferable to any outcome that β might produce.

---

6. Formally, b_2 is the status quo, and b_1 and b_3 are the two policies that could result from enacting β. C's ordering of the three policies, which satisfies the lottery condition, is b_1 p b_2 p b_3. The only other ordering of the three policies that satisfies this condition is b_3 p b_2 p b_1.

The Conditions for Trust: Common Interest and Policy Uncertainty

Proposition 1 in appendix 1 gives the formal game-theoretic predictions about behavior in the Evaluation game. Given this characterization, there is little need to continue to focus on players R and C. Instead, drawing on appendix 1, this section describes the conditions under which rational constituents will trust their representative and shows how expectations about trust enter into a representative's vote decision.

Where Does Trust Come From?

Before defining the conditions under which trust arises, it is necessary to describe the factors that shape vote decisions and trust decisions. The forces shaping constituent behavior will be described first: while a representative moves first, her decision is based on expectations about how different votes will be evaluated.

Constituents

After their representative votes, constituents must decide how to evaluate her action. Proposition 1 shows that once the private information and lottery conditions are met, two factors drive trust decisions: how much constituents know about the proposal—their *policy uncertainty*—and the likelihood that they and the representative have a common interest on the proposal.

Measuring constituent uncertainty about a proposal is straightforward. Saying constituents know a lot about a proposal, or have low uncertainty, means they can predict with high confidence what kind of policy outcome the proposal will produce if enacted. Along the same lines, saying they know little about a proposal, or have high uncertainty, means they have only a vague idea what the proposal will do once enacted. To illustrate this concept, suppose constituents, like C in the Evaluation game, know that a proposal will produce one of two outcomes if enacted. They are highly uncertain when they believe that the outcomes are equally likely—from their viewpoint, each could occur with probability .5. Their uncertainty is smaller insofar as they think one outcome is more likely to result than the other if the proposal is enacted. For example, constituents might believe that there is a 75 percent chance of realizing one outcome, and a 25 percent chance of realizing the other. At the extreme, where constituents think that one outcome is the near-certain product of enacting the proposal, their uncertainty is low—they are confident that they know what will happen if the proposal is enacted. This characterization would be true if, for example, constituents believed that one outcome was 99 percent likely, while the chance of seeing the other outcome was only 1 percent.

The effect of policy uncertainty on constituent behavior is simple. Constituents who are confident, who think they know what a proposal will do, have little reason to defer to their representative. Increased uncertainty creates a rationale for deference, as a means of tapping the representative's private information. At the margin, then, constituents should be more likely to trust their representative when they are highly uncertain about a proposal compared to when their uncertainties are small.

The concept of a common interest is somewhat harder to describe. Formally, given the status quo policy outcome and whichever policy outcome will be produced by enacting a proposal, a common interest exists if the two outcomes are ranked the same way in the preference orderings of a representative and her constituents.[7] (Recall that these orderings are determined by the individuals' policy goals.) Common interest requires only the same relative ranking. The individuals may disagree about the absolute desirability of one or both policies, but they must agree on which policy is relatively better than the other. Thus, when a common interest exists, the players agree whether a proposal should be enacted or defeated. Under these conditions, a representative can be trusted to act in the interests of her constituents—not out of altruism but because her policy goals are such that she will do exactly what her constituents would want, if they knew what she knows. Similarly, the absence of a common interest implies that a representative and her constituents disagree on what should be done with a particular proposal. Under these conditions, the representative wants to cast a vote (secure a policy outcome) that is harmful to interests held by constituents—the vote will produce an outcome that constituents consider inferior to the status quo. Therefore, if constituents believe that a common interest does not exist, they should refuse to trust their representative. Of course, insofar as constituents are unsure about their representative's motivations or about a proposal's effect, they are unlikely to know for sure whether a common interest exists or not. However, as appendix 1 shows, constituents can use beliefs about these factors to estimate the likelihood of a common interest and use this probability to guide their trust decision.

Figure 4 illustrates the concept of common interest by classifying the four games in figure 3 according to the locations of the players' ideal points and the existence of a common interest. In the top two diagrams, the players have the same ideal point. Therefore, the players always have a common interest: regardless of what β will do if it is enacted, they can agree on the

---

7. For example, if enacting β yields b_1, while b_2 is the status quo, a common interest exists if R and C both prefer b_1 to b_2, or the reverse.

Same policy goals, common interest

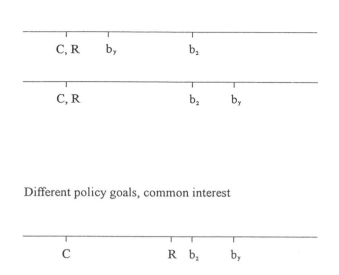

Different policy goals, common interest

Different policy goals, no common interest

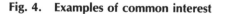
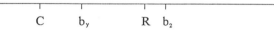

Fig. 4.   Examples of common interest

proposal's fate. For example, in the top diagram, the players agree that enacting β improves on the status quo: compared to the status quo outcome (b_2) β's outcome (b_y) lies closer to both player's ideal points. In the second diagram, b_y lies further from the players' common ideal point than does the status quo. In this case, the players again have a common interest, since they both prefer to defeat β. As Proposition 1 shows, these diagrams illustrate a general principle: when players have the same ideal point—have identical policy goals—a common interest always exists, regardless of where b_y and b_2 are located.

The third and fourth diagrams are more complicated. The third diagram illustrates a situation in which the players' ideal points—their policy concerns—are obviously different: R's ideal point lies well to the right of the ideal point held by C. Yet the players have a common interest: both prefer the status quo over the outcome generated by β. Thus, they can agree on the defeat of β. A common interest does not exist in the fourth diagram. Again, the players' ideal points are obviously different. Moreover, R prefers to defeat β, as the status quo (b_2) is closer to her ideal point compared to the product of β, b_y. C has the opposite preference: he wants to enact β because he prefers b_y over b_2. Thus, the players do not have a common interest.

Figure 4 shows that conclusions about common interest require information about the outcomes associated with enacting or defeating a proposal, as well as information about the policy goals that a representative and her constituents hold. The obvious response is that C does not know some of this information—he does not know which of the four diagrams in figure 4 describes the game he is playing. What a rational individual would do in this situation is to use what he knows—the likelihood that each of the diagrams given above reflects the actual game he is playing—to assess the likelihood of common interest. In this example, C knows that a common interest exists in all but one situation, that given by the fourth diagram. Insofar as he thinks this situation is unlikely, he will assess a high probability of common interest. Insofar as he believes the situation is likely, he will assess a low probability.

Figure 4 also shows that common policy goals are sufficient, but not necessary, for common interest. In the top two diagrams, the players have common policy goals and a common interest. From these diagrams, it should be clear that regardless of where b_y was located—what β will do if enacted—the players would have a common interest. The third diagram in figure 4 shows a situation where a common interest exists even though the players' ideal points are different. However, given a divergence of ideal points, common interest requires a particular configuration of policy effects. To see this, note that the players' ideal points are the same in the bottom two diagrams. However, the shift in b_y makes a common interest impossible.

The Ethics Act provides a substantive example of the conditions for common interest. This act gave members of Congress a pay raise and, by raising pay and implementing ethics reforms, was supposed to improve congressional responsiveness to the interests of average citizens. Suppose a constituent holds the following interests: he wants improved responsiveness and opposes a raise in congressional pay but would support a proposal that has both effects.[8] Regarding the Ethics Act, suppose the constituent is sure that the proposal will raise pay but thinks there is a small chance that it will improve responsiveness as well. Given these interests and perceptions, sup-

---

8. As chapter 5 notes, this ordering was fairly typical.

pose the constituent knows that his representative favors a pay increase but is indifferent to ethics reform.[9] If so, the constituent can be almost certain that a common interest does not exist. The representative would prefer to pass the Ethics Act regardless of whether it improves responsiveness, whereas the constituent favors the proposal only if it does. Therefore, a common interest exists only in the unlikely event that the Ethics Act improves both pay and responsiveness. If, as the constituent fears, the act amounts to a camouflaged pay raise, the representative will exploit trust by voting yea and enacting the proposal, a result that is consistent with the representative's interests but contrary to those of the constituent. Thus, given the representative's policy goals in this example, the constituent should refuse to grant leeway.

In contrast, suppose the constituent holds the same interests and beliefs about the Ethics Act but believes that the representative favors both a pay raise and ethics reform, that the representative prefers to defeat a proposal that has one effect but not the other. Note that the players have different policy goals: while they agree on the desirability of ethics reform, the representative favors pay raises and the constituent opposes them. Despite this disagreement and the constituent's uncertainty about the proposal, he can be sure that a common interest exists. The reason is that both players prefer the status quo over the outcome where only the raise takes effect, and both consider the status quo to be inferior to an outcome in which both congressional salaries and congressional responsiveness are improved. Given her revised motivations, the representative will respond to leeway by casting a vote that, taking into account her information about the Ethics Act, satisfies *both* players' interests. If the representative votes nay, the constituent will infer that his suspicions about the act were correct—it was just a pay raise bill. However, if the representative votes yea, the constituent will infer that he was wrong—the Ethics Act will improve responsiveness as well as pay.

The concept of common interest captures exactly what policy-minded constituents should worry about: if they let their representative act as a free agent, what are the chances that she will act in their interest? This question would not be asked in the abstract. Rather, it will be cast in terms of the policy proposal at hand. Nor would constituents be concerned about policy goals their representative might hold that have nothing to do with the proposal at hand. Rather, they should focus on the specific decision the representative has made and the motives she had (or might have had) for making it. This focus makes sense from the perspective of a cognitive miser, but it also makes sense given the nature of trust decisions. To make this decision, constituents do not need to know all of their representative's policy goals. They need only con-

---

9. As noted above, constituents are often unsure of their representative's motives. This complication is ignored to simplify the example.

sider the goals that might have given her a reason to vote one way or the other. And they need not worry if the representative's policy goals differ from their own, as long as it appears that she had no reason to vote against their interests on the proposal at hand.

Representatives

Looking at one proposal at a time, the Evaluation game suggests that a representative's vote decision is essentially a choice of which goal to maximize, policy or reelection, conditioned on her expectations about trust. A representative who anticipates trust will cast whatever vote secures her preferred policy outcome. If she prefers the status quo to the outcome that will result from enacting a proposal, she will vote nay; if her preference is reversed, she will vote yea. Intuitively, once the representative knows that she will receive favorable evaluations regardless of what she does, policy considerations are the only force driving her decision.

There is one qualification. As shown in chapter 3, votes can function as signals of a representative's policy concerns. A career-minded representative will take these reputational considerations into account when deciding how to vote given trust. The arguments presented in chapter 3 suggest that votes that are consistent with constituent demands may enhance a legislator's reputation—strengthen beliefs about common interest—while votes that run contrary to these demands will certainly cause damage—weaken beliefs about common interest. Thus, taking advantage of trust now reduces the chance of being trusted in the future, but failing to exploit trust may not produce any reputational benefit. These costs arise even if constituents are prepared to trust their representative and the representative expects them to do so. With these considerations in mind, career-minded representatives may prefer to act according to their constituents' demands or opinions, even though they expect trust.

Now consider a representative who believes that constituents are not inclined to grant leeway. Under the conditions assumed thus far, where reelection takes precedence over policy, the representative will vote as her constituents desire. If constituents believe that the proposal should be enacted, she will vote yea; if they believe defeat is preferable, she will vote nay. (Of course, these votes may coincidentally serve the representative's policy goals.) Aside from signaling the representative's willingness to comply with constituent demands, these votes will not have any reputational consequences. They are political votes, uncolored by policy considerations. Thus, constituents, regardless of whether they are stereotype mavens or judicious consumers of signals, should not use votes cast in the absence of trust as a source of information about the member's policy concerns.

What if the representative's political concerns take second place to her interest in good policy? This statement implies that the representative is willing to accept the cost of unfavorable evaluations plus any additional damage the vote causes to her reputation. Under these conditions, constituents lose all influence over their representative's actions. They will continue to make retrospective evaluations, as these judgments help them to assess the representative's performance in office. Moreover, votes cast under these conditions provide a clear signal of the representative's policy concerns. This result is consistent with theories of stereotyping and signaling: insofar as constituents use votes to assess policy concerns, they will focus on low-salience proposals, where the political consequences are minimal, and on the occasional act of political courage, where a legislator's concerns with public policy overrides her interest in getting reelected.

The Conditions for Trust

The next step is to make predictions about trust. This task requires a characterization of equilibria to the Evaluation game—predictions about how the representative and the constituent will behave in light of their goals and available information. This characterization is stated in Proposition 1, which the interested reader will find in appendix 1. Figure 5 translates these predictions into the terms discussed in the previous section. The horizontal axis in figure 5 measures constituent uncertainty about the proposal on a 0 to 1 scale.[10] On the left-hand side, constituents are highly uncertain. Moving rightward, their uncertainty decreases until, at the right-hand edge, they, just like the representative, are fully informed. The vertical axis measures the likelihood of a common interest. At the top, constituents are certain that a common interest exists. Moving downward, the likelihood declines until at the bottom constituents are sure that a common interest does not exist. (The points labeled α, β, δ, and ε will be discussed later.)

Proposition 1 reveals that the existence of trust varies across the two regions separated by a dotted line in figure 5. In the top triangle in figure 5, the likelihood of a common interest is high relative to the amount that constituents know about the proposal. Under these conditions, constituents do best by trusting their representative. This decision may not always yield the best possible policy outcome for constituents, but refusing trust—forcing the representative to vote as constituents think best—is less likely to do so. Thus, given what constituents know, trust is the preferable choice. Under these conditions, the representative's optimal response—again, ignoring reputation effects—is to act as a trustee, voting in line with her policy interests. She will do this regardless of whether policy or reelection ranks first among her con-

---

10. See appendix 1 for details on the construction of this scale.

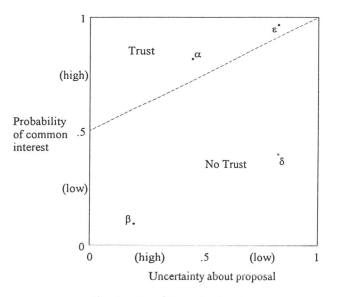

Fig. 5. Conditions for trust

cerns. Such a vote will reveal some of the representative's private information to constituents, both about the proposal and about her goals.[11]

The shape of the area where trust exists in figure 5 indicates that the likelihood of common interest needed to generate trust increases as constituents learn more about a proposal. When constituents are poorly informed, they are willing to take a chance and trust their representative, even when the probability that she shares their concerns is only slightly better than .5. When constituents are well informed, they can be picky about whom they trust and will defer only if they are fairly sure that their representative shares their interests. However, even when constituents are all but certain about a proposal's effects (the upper right-hand corner of the top region), they will grant leeway if the probability of common interests is high enough.

A member's description of his vote against the repeal of Catastrophic Coverage illustrates the conditions for trust depicted in the figure:

> ***What did your constituents want?*** Originally my constituents were for repeal. . . . [Now] when I tell them what I did they say, "you're absolutely right."

---

11. In the parlance of game theory, Region 1 conditions yield semi-separating equilibria: the representative's vote depends on the content of her private information. Or, in terms of stereotyping, since policy goals drive the representative's vote, constituents can use the vote to develop or to refine their beliefs about her policy goals.

> *Why did they change their minds?* First, my poll results indicate that I was and remain enormously popular with senior citizens. I spend time on issues that concern them, we send lots of mail to them, and we are constantly in touch with them. Of my strong supporters, they are the strongest, and they also vote. This vote did nothing to hurt my support. . . . *They sense that I'm on their side on most things.* Also I tell them that I won't cut their Social Security, though I do say that I'll vote for taxing it. [62]

As the member tells it, even though his senior-citizen constituents favored repeal, they approved of his vote to preserve the program. Their change of heart was based on their belief that the representative would vote for Catastrophic Coverage only if he thought it made seniors better off. Seniors did not believe that the representative agreed with them on all issues, such as taxing Social Security benefits. But they perceived agreement on Catastrophic Coverage and reasoned that since the representative voted against repeal, the program must be worth saving. Accordingly, they deferred to their representative's judgment and made a favorable evaluation of her vote against repeal.

In the region below the dotted line in figure 5, the likelihood of common interest is low relative to constituent uncertainty about the proposal. Thus, compared to the top region, constituents have less of a reason to defer to their representative, and deference is less likely to produce favorable results. (Note that this difference is relative—constituents can still be highly uncertain about the proposal's effects.) Proposition 1 predicts that under these conditions, constituents will refuse to trust their representative, leaving her the choice of behaving as a delegate or incurring the costs associated with unfavorable evaluations. Assuming a representative values reelection over policy, she will anticipate this response and comply with her constituents' demands. Of course, the representative's vote may happen to serve her own policy concerns as well as those held by constituents. In addition, votes cast under these conditions will not be read as signals of the representative's private information. [12] The only thing constituents learn is that the representative is willing to sacrifice good policy in the pursuit of favorable evaluations. (Of course, if the representative's goals are reversed, she will behave as a trustee under these conditions. Her vote will then signal private information just like in the top region. Even with this information, however, constituents will punish deviations from their demands.)

A real-world example of behavior under these conditions is seen in a legislator's comments about his vote against the Ethics Act:

---

12. Game theorists would label Region 2 behavior as a pooling equilibrium—the representative does what constituents want, regardless of what she knows about the proposal or what she thinks is best.

I said it's the right thing to do, but because of my inability to convey that to my constituents or the members of my delegation I decided to vote no. I cast a vote which was not in the interests of good public policy. . . . my constituents understood I had made a political decision. [26]

As the legislator tells it, he cast a "political vote"—he did what his constituents wanted, to avoid the political damage that would ensue if he did otherwise. However, there is no hint that the vote had a favorable impact on his reputation. Apparently constituents saw the vote as a response to their demands, not as a signal of their representative's personal concerns. This asymmetry reflects the principle discussed in chapter 3: while politically harmful votes influence a legislator's reputation, politically attractive votes often do not. Of course, as long as a representative values reelection over policy, as did the legislator quoted here, she will avoid casting such votes in the first place.

Table 1 uses a one-dimensional version of the Evaluation game to illustrate these predictions about trust. These examples are specified for the Evaluation game depicted in figure 6 where R's ideal point is at 9, C's ideal point is

Table 1. Interpreting Proposition 1: Four Examples

Proposal	True Outcome	C's Beliefs about		
		Possible Outcomes	Likelihood of Outcome	Common Interest
α	11	$a_1 = 7$	.3	.8
		$a_2 = 11$	.7	
β	6	$b_1 = 6$	.4	.1
		$b_2 = 14$	.6	
δ	4	$d_1 = 4$	.9	.4
		$d_2 = 12$	.1	
ε	4	$e_1 = 4$	.9	.98
		$e_2 = 12$	.1	

Fig. 6.   The Evaluation game in one dimension

at 0, and the status quo policy outcome, s, is at 10. (Due to space limitations, the figure only depicts ideal points, the status quo, and the range of possible outcomes for proposal α.)

Consider proposal α. This proposal, if enacted, will produce a new outcome, $\alpha = 11$. C believes that α will produce outcome $a_1 = 7$ with probability .3, and outcome $a_2 = 11$ with probability .7. Thus, on a scale of 0 to 1, C's level of uncertainty is .4. (For details on the construction of this index, see appendix 1.) C also assesses the probability that he has a common interest with R on proposal α at .8.[13] Thus, the point labeled α is located in the top-middle area of figure 5. Now suppose R votes on α. According to Proposition 1, the probability of a common interest on α is sufficiently high and C knows sufficiently little about α that C will trust R. Expecting this choice and preferring the status quo (10) to the result of enacting α (11), R will vote nay on α.

In contrast, C believes that enacting β is (slightly) more likely to move policy outcomes away from his ideal point than it is to move outcomes closer.[14] However, his estimate is based on relatively little information: he places a fairly high probability on each possible outcome. Reflecting this, C's level of uncertainty on β is only .2, which is why the point labeled β is located fairly close to the left-hand side of figure 5. Even so, the probability of common interest (.1) is quite low—note that β is also located near the bottom of figure 5. Given these beliefs, Proposition 1 shows that C's optimal strategy is to refuse trust, instead using a strategy of evaluating nay votes favorably and yea votes unfavorably. Expecting these evaluations, R will vote nay, since she values reelection over policy.

The final two proposals, δ and ε, illustrate the importance of common-interest perceptions. C has the same beliefs about what the two proposals might do if enacted but different beliefs about common interest. According to table 1, C knows a lot about both of these proposals: note that both points are located near the right-hand side of figure 5. Thus, when δ is voted on, C will refuse trust since the probability of common interest is only .4. In light of C's

---

13. For simplicity, this example specifies common-interest perceptions exogenously—without considering how C arrived at them.

14. As shown in table 1, C believes that β is more likely to produce $b_2 = 14$ than $b_1 = 6$. Formally, the probabilities C associates with the two outcomes are .6 and .4, respectively. Therefore, given a status quo of 10 and an ideal point of 0, β is more likely to harm C than to help him.

beliefs, which imply that δ is more likely to yield a policy preferable to the status quo, R will vote yea. But consider ε, where the probability of common interest equals .98. Under these conditions, even though C is fairly sure what ε will do if it is enacted, he will opt to trust R, who will in turn vote yea.

Discussion

When does trust exist? The Evaluation game suggests an answer in the form of a hypothesis, the leeway hypothesis. Under the conditions captured by the Evaluation game, trust is the product of two factors: how uncertain constituents are about a proposal's effects and their beliefs about common interest. (Of course, trust also requires that the lottery and private information conditions be satisfied.) The analysis shows that perceptions of common interest are by far the most important factor in trust decisions. Constituents will always trust their representative if they are sure that a common interest exists. If constituents are suspicious about common interest, they will grant leeway only if they are sufficiently uncertain about a proposal's effects. Below a certain point (in the Evaluation game, a fifty-fifty chance of common interest), constituents will never trust their representative, even if they know very little about a proposal. Thus, trust can arise even when constituents know a lot about a proposal; it can be absent even when constituents know almost nothing. Moreover, deference may be the preferable option even when constituents are certain that their representative's policy goals differ from their own, as long as they think their interests coincide on the proposal at hand.

The analysis also shows that retrospective evaluations are insufficient to guarantee delegate behavior—behavior consistent with constituent demands. The threat of unfavorable evaluations has this effect only when a representative's interest in reelection outweighs her policy concerns. When only a few constituents care about a proposal, or when a proposal taps one of a representative's core values, constituents are unlikely to have any real influence over her actions. She may do what they want, but only if there is a coincidence between their demands and her policy goals. Conversely, trust does not guarantee trusteeship—it does not ensure that a representative will use her judgment and vote on the basis of private information. Constituents can only offer the opportunity; representatives decide whether to take advantage of it. Even if a representative expects trust, she may decide to behave as a delegate because doing otherwise would damage her reputation and her chances of trust on future proposals. This consideration looms largest when a representative votes on a high-salience proposal, where the reputational consequences of the vote are presumably high. A representative is more likely to take advantage of trust when voting on a low-salience proposal, a proposal that taps an area of high concern for her, or if she cares little for reelection in any case. Of course, all these conditions make trustee behavior more likely in any case, regardless of the decision constituents make about trust.

Finally, the analysis shows how constituents can learn from their representative even when they ignore—or never hear—any of her statements about the policy process. A representative's vote can reveal some of her private information. This transmission occurs in situations in which a representative expects trust and ignores reputational concerns and in situations where she ignores the political consequences of her actions. No information is revealed, however, if a representative complies with constituent demands, either to gain favorable evaluations or to avoid reputational damage. Thus, a representative can educate constituents, but only by ignoring the political and reputational consequences of her actions. And constituents can induce, but not guarantee, education only by deciding in favor of trust.

Combined with chapter 3's findings about stereotyping, the leeway hypothesis implies that when a proposal is voted on, certain actions or attributes will separate representatives who are trusted from those who are not. The set of relevant actions and attributes will be the ones that constituents take to be signals of common interest in light of their stereotypes, what they know about their representative, and their beliefs about the proposal. In the case of the Ethics Act, for example, legislators should be more likely to report trust insofar as they hold actions or attributes that signal their indifference or opposition to a pay raise or their unwillingness to vote for a measure that raised pay without improving congressional ethics. Moreover, these actions and attributes should be more likely to generate trust insofar as a legislator's constituents are unsure about the Ethics Act—and should have no effect in districts where the private information or lottery conditions are not met. Representatives who have the misfortune to come from districts where these conditions do not hold, or who lack the right actions or attributes, should not report trust, even if they spend much time and energy proclaiming their sympathy to constituent interests.

The results given in Proposition 1 also identify two distinct circumstances under which trust will arise. The first possibility is that constituents believe their representative's policy goal in some area is identical to their own. Rational constituents would trust such a representative whenever she votes on a proposal that sets policy in this area. The reason is simple: regardless of what the representative knows about these proposals, she has no incentive to deviate from fiduciary behavior—votes that yield the representative's preferred outcomes do the same for constituents. Under these conditions, trust will exist as long as the necessary conditions (the private information and lottery conditions) are satisfied, regardless of how much or how little constituents know about a proposal. Amendments, complex voting procedures, or arcane policy instruments may alter constituent beliefs about what the proposal might do if it is enacted but will not shake their judgment that the representative will act in their mutual interests.

However, trust can also arise when constituents know that their representative's policy goals in some area differ from their own or are unsure about her goals. Even under these conditions, it is easy to envision combinations of beliefs—beliefs about the proposal and beliefs about a representative's goals—that generate a relatively high probability of common interest and make trust the preferred option. (Of course, the beliefs also have to satisfy the private information and lottery conditions.) But this trust is highly conditional. It exists only in light of what constituents think the proposal might do—and how uncertain they are. Given different beliefs about the proposal, or more information about its effects, their decision could easily be reversed. More generally, in situations in which constituents are not sure that their representative shares their policy concerns, the prospects for trust depend on how a proposal is packaged and voted on.

Evidence from the contemporary Congress suggests that conditional trust is the norm. Many studies have shown how the judicious markup of policy proposals, coupled with the selection of procedures used to vote on them, generates voting leeway. Bach and Smith (1988), for example, show that in the mid-1980s, congressional Democrats used procedures such as "king of the mountain" to enable representatives elected from conservative-leaning districts to vote in favor of Democratic proposals without angering their constituents.[15] If trust was for the most part unconditional, there would be no reason to choose such complex procedures. The fact that these procedures are increasingly common suggests that for many legislators, the prospects for trust depend on context—not just with a proposal's true effects but with the procedures that structure voting.

Moreover, while the Evaluation game deals with only one proposal, its results imply that variation in trust may also occur across policy areas. It would be no surprise to find that constituents deferred to their representative in one area but not another—across a series of Evaluation games—based on their beliefs about the representative's policy goals in each area. Such varia-

---

15. The "king of the mountain" procedure "provides for votes on a series of alternate versions of a measure; but if a majority votes for more than one of the alternatives, only the last of them wins" (Bach and Smith 1988, 74). For example, when votes were taken in 1987 for funding of the Strategic Defense Initiative (SDI), four amendments were voted on in order (this account is drawn from Rohde 1991, 118): one to increase funding, one to dismantle the program, one to implement a modest cut in the program's budget, and the last, offered by Charles Bennett (D-Fla.), to cut funding by $400 million. Under this procedure, anti-SDI Democrats from pro-SDI districts could vote in favor of increases in the program's budget or for modest cuts, knowing that they could reverse these outcomes with a later vote in favor of the Bennett amendment. Presumably this procedure increased constituents' uncertainty about what different votes would do, thereby increasing legislators' chances of leeway.

tion would be mitigated if constituents used a single action or attribute, such as party affiliation, to determine whether their representative shared their concerns in a variety of policy areas. But if the factors used to stereotype representatives vary across policy areas, the representatives' chances of being trusted may vary as well. Thus, in moving to empirical analysis in the next two chapters, we should expect to see a great deal of variation in trust, both across representatives and across proposals.

Finally, these results unify the disparate findings about trust described in chapter 2. Each of these theories appears to highlight one, but only one, of the factors that shape trust decisions. For example, Eulau and Karps (1977) emphasize the importance of private information: constituents must believe that their representative knows more than they do. The analysis presented here shows that asymmetric information is a necessary but not a sufficient condition. Without it, constituents will never defer. However, rational constituents may decide against deference even if they are sure that their representative has private information.

Similarly, Arnold (1990) suggests that trust is more likely insofar as constituents are unsure what a proposal will do if it is enacted. Kingdon (1981) takes a similar perspective: deference is more likely when proposals are voted on using complex parliamentary procedures. Proposition 1 identifies constituent uncertainty as an influence on trust decisions. However, minimizing traceability, to use Arnold's term, is not enough. Constituents can be well aware of their ignorance yet refuse to grant leeway because they do not think their representative shares their interests. Fenno (1978) emphasizes the latter perception. But unless constituents are sure that a common interest exists, their willingness to grant leeway also depends on how much they know about the proposal being voted on. And, contrary to the arguments advanced by Downs (1957, chap. 12), trust can exist even though constituents are sure that their representative's policy goals differ from their own. Agreement on general principles, or even the perception of such an agreement, is not a precondition for trust.

In addition, the leeway hypothesis mirrors Fenno's (1978, 57–61) description of qualification, identification, and empathy. Qualification—in Fenno's terms, "I understand the job"—is analogous to the private information condition: constituents will defer only if they believe that their representative knows more than they do. Identification—"I am one of you"—captures the importance of beliefs about a representative's policy concerns. Of course, the analysis suggests that identification may be defined in terms of common interest, not common policy goals. Again, this finding resonates with Fenno, who argues that some representatives build trust by stressing common interests rather than common goals: "You can trust me because—although I am not one of you—I understand you." Finally, empathy—"I can see the world the way you do"—seems to tap the quality of a legislator's information about constituent interests. This factor was assumed away in the Evaluation game, but it is a small stretch to see that it plays a critical role in real-world trust decisions.

Induced Ideal Points

The discussion of induced ideal points in chapter 2 ended with a question: does this technique capture the forces that generate a legislator's behavior? This question can be addressed using the Evaluation game. As the figures in this chapter indicate, it is easy to specify a version of the game in which policy outcomes and policy goals are specified as points in a one-dimensional policy space. Proposition 1 can then be used to predict R's vote on a series of policy proposals. The question is, are these predictions consistent with a point or set of points on the policy dimension, consistent in the sense that if R voted as though one of these points was her ideal point and this ideal point was the only factor behind her decisions, she would vote as predicted by Proposition 1? If the proponents of induced ideal points are right, then for every combination of policy goals, beliefs, and proposals, there should exist at least one point that is consistent with the game's predictions. A finding that consistent points do not exist for some combinations suggests that under these conditions, any induced ideal point we might impute to the legislator would fail to capture some of the forces driving her behavior and fail to generate accurate predictions about her behavior.

This section examines predictions about R's votes on combinations of the four proposals (α, β, δ, and ε) described earlier in table 1 and figure 5.[16] Table 2 gives the policy outcome associated with each proposal, C's strategy choice, and R's vote decision. Recall that these predictions are made in a situation where R's ideal point is at 9, C's ideal point is at 0, and the status quo policy outcome, s, is at 10.

In the first example presented here, R votes on α and δ. These votes can be explained in terms of a sensible induced ideal point. By table 2, R will vote nay on α and yea on δ. Given these votes and the true effects of each proposal, R's votes are consistent with any ideal point that is less than 7. That is, anyone

---

16. Proposals are assumed to be voted on in a particular sequence in order to conform to the Evaluation game's assumption that both players know the location of the status quo. If, for example, R first voted yes on δ, thereby enacting it, C would have to make his next trust decision without full information about the status quo. Thus, any examples where R votes on δ must have this proposal voted on last in the sequence. This assumption does not appear to place any restrictions on the conclusions developed here. If anything, the introduction of additional uncertainties for C would make the existence of a consistent point even more problematic.

Table 2. Predictions about Votes, Predictions about Trust

Proposal	True Outcome	R's Vote	C's Decision
α	11	Nay	Trust
β	6	Nay	Reward nay, punish yea
δ	4	Yea	Reward yea, punish nay
ε	4	Nay	Trust

who held an ideal point in this region would vote against α and for δ.[17] In other words, R's induced ideal point can be placed anywhere within this range and still generate accurate predictions about her behavior. We could, for example, say that R's induced ideal point was equal to C's ideal point, 0.

Now for some problems. Suppose R votes on α and ε. Table 2 shows that C will trust R on both proposals, and R will cast two nay votes. Again, these votes are consistent with a range of possible induced ideal points: points that are greater than 7 and less than 10.5. When compared with the first example, however, this one shows that the location of an induced ideal point depends on the existence or nonexistence of trust. The only difference between δ and ε is C's beliefs about common interest. Yet this change is enough to alter C's decision about trust as well as R's vote on the proposal and thereby generate a completely different range of possible induced ideal points. Moreover, given this new range, we cannot impute C's ideal point of 0 to R; this point is now inconsistent with R's behavior. We could, however, say that R behaved according to her own ideal point, 9.

A second and more serious problem arises when R votes on β and δ—by table 2, nay on β and yea on δ. *No ideal point is consistent with these votes.* Given β yields an outcome of 6, a nay vote is consistent with ideal points greater than 8. Similarly, δ puts the outcome at 4, so a yea vote on δ is

---

17. Given that α yields an outcome of 11, an actor with an ideal point less than 10.5 would prefer to defeat α and preserve the status quo, 10. Assuming α fails, an actor with an ideal point less than 7 would prefer to enact δ, which produces an outcome of 4, rather than keep the status quo of 10 in place. Taken together, the two votes are consistent with any ideal point that is 7 or less.

consistent with ideal points that are less than 7. Thus, no ideal point is consistent with the two votes; equivalently, no ideal point would motivate a player to vote nay on β and yea on δ. In this situation, any ideal point that might be imputed to R would fail to capture the forces driving her vote decisions or to yield accurate predictions about her behavior.

A final anomaly can be generated with some changes in table 2. Assume, first, that C's beliefs about α are reversed: enacting α yields $a_1 = 7$ with probability .7 and $a_2 = 11$ with probability .3. (Note that α actually sets policy at 11.) This change in beliefs will not change C's trust decision on α, but it will lead him to change his strategy: now he will evaluate yea votes favorably and nay votes unfavorably. Accordingly, R will switch to voting yea on α. Next, suppose that C's beliefs about β remain the same but that β's true effect is switched from 6 to 14. This change will not alter C's strategy or R's vote. Given these revisions, suppose R first votes on β followed by a vote on α. Given the change in β's true effects, these votes are consistent with ideal points that are between 10.5 and 12.[18] Unfortunately, this range does not lie between the player's ideal points.

These examples show that it is problematic to characterize legislators' motivations in terms of induced ideal points. While legislators will sometimes behave as though they held induced ideal points, this assertion is not always true. Moreover, it is possible to construct examples where the set of possible induced ideal points lies outside the area bounded by the ideal points of a representative and her constituents. Thus, even if policy outcomes are realized in a simple one-dimensional space and the policy goals a representative and her constituents hold can be expressed in terms of ideal points in this space, it may not be possible to specify a legislator's motivations in terms of an induced ideal point.

Two mechanisms appear to generate these problems. First, legislators pursue reelection by taking actions, not securing outcomes. When constituents are poorly informed, their demands expressed vote by vote may not be congruent with their policy goals or any conceivable policy goal. Second, a legislator's incentive to take account of constituent demands varies across proposals—if nothing else, with her expectations about trust. Given this variation, some of a legislator's votes will reflect one set of interests—her own—while others will reflect constituent demands. The latter demands may reflect constituent interests, or they may not. Either way, this variation is simply too complicated to be captured in terms of an ideal point and associated preferences across outcomes.

---

18. Since β yields 14 and the status quo is at 10, a nay vote is consistent with ideal points that are less than 12. Similarly, given that α yields 11, a yea vote is consistent with ideal points that are greater than 10.5.

Part 2
The Theory Applied

Introduction to Part 2

Chapters 5 and 6 turn to the real world of congressional politics, testing the leeway and explanation hypotheses by examining two cases: the passage of the Ethics Act of 1989 and the late-1989 repeal of the Medicare Catastrophic Coverage Act. In particular, these tests exploit variables coded from interviews with members of Congress, along with additional contextual data. The interviews are also used to operationalize the leeway hypothesis, particularly its assumptions about stereotyping.

Why these proposals? The decision to examine only two proposals was mandated by the expectation (later proven accurate) that representatives would at best allow a fifteen- to thirty-minute interview. The two proposals were selected by examining media coverage of the first session of the 101st Congress, with the aim of finding proposals where expectations about trust were likely to have played some role in vote decisions. For one thing, both proposals were highly salient—*Congressional Quarterly* listed them among the dozen or so "key votes" for the first session of the 101st Congress. Moreover, a substantial number of representatives disagreed with their constituents about the merits of these proposals. Thus, the conventional wisdom that most legislators "just reflect where they come from" (Kingdon 1981, 47) does not apply here. Given these factors, it seems safe to assume that when these proposals were voted on, trust was neither automatic nor inevitable. It also seems safe to assume that most representatives made conscious, considered decisions about how they would vote.

As described in appendix 2, a simple random sampling technique was used to select potential interviewees. Though this tactic produced a sample that is broadly representative of the entire House, it created some problems as well. Most notably, the sample contains only a small percentage of members who expected trust on the vote to repeal Catastrophic Coverage. The obvious question is why I did not oversample legislators who voted against repeal. The reason is that I planned to ask questions about other proposals as well. My worry was that a sampling design that increased variance on Catastrophic Coverage might reduce variance on other proposals. Plus, deviations from a simple random sample could be seen as an attempt to stack the deck in favor of my hypotheses.

The use of interview data is consistent with a reemerging conventional wisdom in the subfield of legislative politics. For example, in a recent review,

Jackson and Kingdon argue that interviews are essential for studying members' votes and vote decisions:

> The main point is that we need more intensive types of observation than publicly available sources allow. [Interviews have] been used to probe the questions of interest here, and such designs can be used in future research as well. We need to devise methods that get at the values, preferences, and beliefs of politicians, as opposed to using indicators that meld various influences (e.g., constituency, party, interest group pressure, as well as their own ideology) into a public behavior. Publicly available sources nearly always involve such melding. . . . In addition to exploring politicians' ideologies directly, interviewing and personal observation can also help us to understand how politicians process information about constituent preferences and economic impacts. (1990, 17–18)

Or, as Sinclair notes, "There is no substitute for some first-hand contact with members of Congress and some close-up observation of the legislative process for congressional scholars." (1992, 5)

These comments aside, the heavy reliance on interview data raises three concerns, all of which are the subject of detailed analysis in appendix 2. The first is the problem of truthful revelation. For example, when representatives talked about their personal policy preferences, did they reveal their preferences accurately, or were they biased against mentioning any disagreement with their constituents? Put another way, why would a legislator give potentially damaging information to an academic that she had never met before and was unlikely to meet again? Thankfully, it appears that legislators were truthful. If nothing else, a glance at chapters 5 and 6 shows that representatives were not reluctant to disagree with their constituents, even when their private position conflicted with their public statements or their votes.

The second problem is that of interpretation. To what extent can interviews be translated into variables? Coding the interviews did not prove to be much of a problem. Appendix 2 shows that the variables generally have high measures of intercoder reliability.

The third, and biggest, problem, is the question of accuracy. Do representatives have a good idea of their constituents' demands? Do they hold accurate expectations about trust? Insofar as they do not, variables constructed from interview data may generate a kind of self-fulfilling prophecy, as legislators reverse-engineer from their behavior to a consistent, but inaccurate, definition of their constituents' beliefs and decisions. A final concern is even more worrisome: do representatives understand the game they are playing? For example, it is clear from the interviews that members of Congress believe their motives are assessed using stereotypes. Their comments about stereotyping play a critical role in the analyses contained in the next two chapters. As a result, the quality of the conclusions rests on the claim that legislators know what they are talking about.

As appendix 2 shows, questions about accuracy are difficult to resolve. The problem is that there are few alternate sources of data that could be used to evaluate variables coded from the interviews. (Indeed, this deficit is one of the principal rationales for doing interviews.) This problem is especially acute for variables that measure a legislator's policy preferences or the existence of trust. It might be argued that survey data could be used to develop measures of constituent demands or beliefs. Unfortunately, there are no surveys with reasonable district *N*s that ask the right questions about the Ethics Act or Catastrophic Coverage, or indeed any other high-salience proposal. Another possibility would be to estimate these opinions using demographic data. Tests that use this technique are contained in appendix 2. While these tests support the claim that legislator's perceptions are both accurate and revealed truthfully, in the absence of a theory that predicts district opinion about pay raises or health insurance—or anything—as a function of demographics, these tests cannot be seen as definitive.

The position taken here is simple. Insofar as representatives appear to reveal information truthfully, I am prepared to assume that they will do so accurately as well. Most congressional scholars would agree that members of Congress are well-informed about their constituents' demands, beliefs, and willingness to grant leeway. Arnold, for example, claims,

> . . . legislators use a form of political intuition that comes with experience. They talk with and listen to their constituents, they read their mail, they watch how past issues develop over time, they look for clues about salience and intensity, they consider who might have an incentive to arouse public opinion, they learn from one another and from others' mistakes. (1990, 11–12)

In an era in which members of Congress are professional politicians and pay close attention to their constituents—making frequent trips home, reading the mail, commissioning polls, etc.—it seems reasonable to assume that they know what is going on in their districts. Moreover, the interviews conducted for this study were performed several months after members had voted on the two proposals, allowing them time to discover whether their perceptions were indeed accurate.

Finally, by confirming the leeway and explanation hypotheses, the empirical results presented in the next two chapters provide indirect evidence about the quality of the interview data. The analyses show, for example, that members' reports about trust are not random. On the contrary, their statements are consistent with a game-theoretic model that predicts trust as a function of legislators' characteristics. Of course, this confirmation cannot be taken too far: one cannot use the data to test the theory and the theory to validate the data. Still, skeptics should take some comfort in the tight fit between the two.

Scholars who consider these rationales inadequate may be comforted by a final point. Even if representatives' beliefs and expectations about their constituents are to some degree biased or inaccurate, they still bear examination. Accurate predictions or explanations of legislators' actions will be possible only insofar as we understand how they view their constituents. Moreover, any conclusions about the quality of legislators' beliefs and expectations must begin with information about what these factors actually look like. Interviews may not tell the whole story, but it is hard to support a claim that they do not provide valuable insights.

CHAPTER 5

Raising Pay without Losing Office:
The Ethics Act of 1989

In the end, people ought to see it. People are moving off the bench, out of Congress. It's the guys who are 45, who have kids in college. You give up a great deal to be in public service, but you draw the line when it comes to your children. You sacrifice to be here, but you don't want them to. So there are a lot of reasons why Congress should be paid decently. And then there are the expenses. Housing in Washington is awful—my house here could fit in the living room of my house back home. But all that's rational. To the average coal miner in Virginia or pig farmer in Iowa, ninety-six thousand sounds like a lot of money.

—A freshman Democrat

The focus of this chapter is HR 3660, the Ethics Act of 1989. To many observers, the surprising thing about the Ethics Act was that anyone voted for it, much less a majority. Since the Founding, public opposition to pay raises has been nearly uniform (Davidson 1980; Fisher 1980; Wilkerson 1991). Not surprisingly, elected officials disagree with their constituents about the need to raise their pay. As a result, they face the problem of finding a way to raise their pay without being thrown from office. Over the last 200 years, members of Congress have used a variety of markup and parliamentary tactics to camouflage pay raises (Wilkerson 1991). Even so, legislators usually describe pay raise votes as the political equivalent of root-canal surgery. However, a majority of House members cast recorded votes for the Ethics Act. Moreover, in a surprising number of districts, constituents apparently deferred to their representatives' judgments about the Ethics Act despite earlier opposition to the idea of raising pay.

Interviews with ninety-three members of Congress confirm that almost a majority had leeway when they voted on the Ethics Act. And if these representatives are to be believed, trust arose from policy uncertainty and perceptions of common interest. Attributes such as personal wealth and actions such as refusing the raise were interpreted as signals that monetary self-interest did not factor into a member's vote decision. With this motive removed, constituents apparently inferred that their representative was motivated by an interest they shared, that of improving congressional ethics and responsiveness.

99

Statistical analysis confirms this finding, even with controls for electoral vulnerability.

Besides confirming the leeway hypothesis, the analysis also explains why the Ethics Act was enacted with only a minimal amount of political controversy: the proposal was constructed to enhance the prospects for trust. With a significant portion of the House able to vote for the proposal without angering their constituents, the remainder of a majority coalition was formed by members whose interest in increasing congressional pay overrode their interest in reelection.

The data also support the explanation hypothesis. In almost all cases, members who reported trust on the Ethics Act did little or no explaining of their vote. In general, members who did a lot of explaining also received unfavorable evaluations from constituents. This finding supports the idea that constituents use actions and attributes, not words, to assess motive and effect. Finally, various anecdotes are used to show how votes on the Ethics Act were colored by reputational concerns.

Setting the Stage:
Constituent Demands and Legislatorial Preferences

At first glance, interview data confirm the conventional wisdom about pay raises: the typical member of Congress supported the Ethics Act because they wanted higher pay but represented constituents who opposed it. (As defined here, a representative's support or opposition to the Ethics Act reflects her personal evaluation of the proposal—not her vote, public position, or assessment of constituent demands.) However, a nontrivial percentage of members claimed they opposed the act. Moreover, contrary to the expectation of Bartlett (1979) among others, monetary self-interest was not the only factor driving members' preferences. Some representatives focused on the ethics provisions. Others viewed pay levels as a way to alter the mix of people who run for Congress.

Members' comments also confirm that most constituents opposed the Ethics Act. However, support for the act was the prevailing sentiment in some districts. And, in a few districts, constituents apparently had no opinion about the proposal. The data also reveal two categories of opposition: districts where constituents opposed a pay raise under any circumstances (strong opponents) and districts where constituents were prepared to accept a raise under certain conditions (qualified opponents).

The distribution of legislators' evaluations of the Ethics Act and their assessments of district sentiment is summarized in table 3. Almost 80 percent (seventy-three of ninety-two) of representatives expressed support for the Ethics Act. Only a few supporters (fourteen, or 15.2 percent) reported that their constituents supported the act or had no opinion (these two categories are combined in subsequent discussion). Fully 84.8 percent (seventy-eight) of the legislators in the sample represented districts where constituents opposed the Ethics Act. However, relatively few legislators (thirteen, or 14.1 percent) were faced with strong opposition.

Representatives

In the main, representatives who supported the Ethics Act cited financial pressures as their reason for wanting higher pay, such as this junior Democrat:

> The leadership felt that the raise was necessary to keep regular people in Congress. A guy like me, without much wealth, not much net worth, couldn't afford to maintain two households without it. There's a tremendous amount of start-up costs. You need to buy new furniture, dining room sets, new plates, a new toaster. I had to buy a new set of suits for down here. So you're either well-off, or you struggle. [25]

It seems that many representatives are, as one lobbyist put it, "just living beyond their means"—their congressional salary was outstripped by the obli-

Table 3. The Ethics Act: Constituent Demands and Legislatorial Preference

Legislator Preference	Constituent Demands				Row Total and *n*
	No Opinion	Support	Oppose	Strong Oppose	
Support	4.3 (4)	10.9 (10)	54.3 (50)	9.8 (9)	79.3 (73)
Oppose	0 (0)	0 (0)	16.3 (15)	4.3 (4)	20.6 (19)
Column total and *n*	4.3 (4)	10.9 (10)	70.6 (65)	14.1 (13)	

Note: In each cell, the top number is the cell percentage, the bottom number is the cell *n*, with column and row totals along the bottom and the right-hand side. Total percents do not always add up to 100 due to rounding. Table $N = 92$, with one case omitted because of missing data.

gations of "a house here and something back home," college tuition, and other accoutrements of an upper middle-class lifestyle. These members described how their spouses were pressuring them to vote for a raise and complained that they could not afford to send their children to private universities. Economic self-interest drove their support for the proposal.

Other members explained that they supported a raise because it would have a favorable impact on the composition and performance of the House:[1]

> [The raise] gives members of Congress more time to tend to their congressional business, and be less beholden to the special interests. Not that they're bought, but if they're flown first class to a beach resort, put in a luxury hotel, have their greens fees paid, and treated like they're special, it develops a personal relationship that arguably makes them less independent. . . . I didn't want Congress to become a body for rich people. [20]

Readers may be suspicious about comments indicating disinterest in a $25,000 increment. Yet this member probably was sincere. His net worth is in the millions, and the honoraria and outside income that he lost because of the Ethics Act more than offset his raise.

Opponents of the raise also cited financial incentives. However, they argued that strengthening these incentives was wrong in principle, that pay should be kept low to increase congressional turnover: "Before I came here I was a partner in a law firm. If I was paid my market wage, I'd be making a lot more than I do now. It's not like I don't need the money; I rent in both places and I had to take a loan out to pay my taxes. But government is public service, or it's supposed to be" [36]. These arguments were usually made by junior Republicans and are consistent with the conventional wisdom that they favor a chamber composed of mid-career, short-term members over the largely careerist post war Congress. A few representatives also opposed the raise on grounds that it was inappropriate in a time of economic troubles and high deficits.

Members' reported evaluations of the ethics provisions were much less intense. A few legislators said the reforms were worthwhile, like one who practiced medicine before his election to Congress:

> When I speak on medical matters I see nothing wrong with honoraria. But it's way too complicated to write an honoraria restriction to limit talks to things you know about. On the other side, I had lunch with three

---

1. For a discussion of how financial incentives influence candidacy decisions, see Lazear and Rosen 1980.

lobbyists and when I got up, there was an honoraria, an envelope with a thousand dollars in it. I gave it back, but that's bullshit. But I'm on Commerce, so they call me and ask if I want to have lunch and get an honoraria for talking with them. It's hard to shut that out, so we have to blanket it. [77]

A small minority, like this Southern Democrat, argued that attempts to legislate ethical behavior were futile and inappropriate:

I don't need rules to tell me how to be ethical. I know the difference between right and wrong; I learned it at the end of my daddy's belt. You can't write down the difference between right and wrong. It's like when you pay for something at a store and get too much change back. You know what you should do. If you need rules to be ethical you have a big problem—a personal ethics problem. [31]

However, most representatives either had no opinion about the ethics provisions or saw them only as a vehicle for enacting a pay raise: "Ethics was a snare and an illusion as always. . . . The thought up here was, if we have all this ethics stuff that doesn't matter, we can get a pay raise through. It lets you make a speech where you say that the raise was tough to swallow, but we needed it to get the ethics reforms through" [36]. This argument has some validity, but it must be qualified: while bundling pay with ethics reduced the political risks associated with voting for a raise, it was undoubtedly the only way to get the votes needed to enact a ban on honoraria and restrictions on outside income. As one Democrat put it,

I felt if they take away my ability to make outside income, they had to supplement my salary. I'm not a rich guy, I spend every nickel I make. I couldn't survive without outside income, but as long as the bill put me in the same ballpark I was content to support it. But I couldn't vote for one without the other: ethics reforms without a pay raise. [47]

Perhaps because of these sentiments, a provision of the Ethics Act states that if the raise is ever repealed, the ban on honoraria and restrictions on outside income are void as well.

Constituents

District sentiment about the Ethics Act fell into four categories: districts where constituents strongly opposed the proposal, districts where opposition was qualified, districts where constituents supported the proposal, and a small

number of districts where constituents apparently had no opinion. The justification for this aggregate, four-category specification of constituent demands
is simple: members of Congress described it that way. Admittedly, few
claimed that constituent demands were completely homogeneous. Rather,
their statements should be read as political assessments of their district's
central tendency. While a finer classification of district sentiments might be
possible given survey data about constituent attitudes or more extensive interviews, the four-category variable appears to capture most of the variation. In
addition, appropriate survey data do not exist.

Strong opposition districts were characterized by intense opposition to
any kind of pay raise and indifference or opposition to ethics reform. Consider
the comments of two representatives:

> [Pay raises] are just the biggest fishhook issue around. Clay and his
> colleagues tried to get a raise and they were booted out. It's a no-win
> issue, a revolving door issue. . . . It's just a lose, lose, lose issue. They
> equate it with the salary they make and the problems the nation has, and
> they resent the hell out of it. [78]

> The average man on the street doesn't give a rat's ass what it costs to live
> here, or what we could make on the outside. It's just a raise in pay, he's
> opposed, and that's all. . . . most of the people in my district don't
> know what an honoraria is. It takes a fairly sophisticated constituent to
> understand that we gave up outside income as a trade for a pay raise to
> obviate any special interests from trying to persuade you. [58]

Another legislator from a strong opposition district commented, "[My constit-
uents] are not going to give accolades for eliminating behavior that shouldn't
be entered into in any event" [53].

In sum, it appears that constituents in strong opposition districts opposed
the Ethics Act to the point that they were virtually certain that defeat was
preferable. From their viewpoint, there was only a small (or nonexistent)
chance that enactment of the proposal would yield an outcome preferable to
the status quo.

The second category, qualified opposition, contains districts where constituents opposed the Ethics Act but where their opposition was less intense or
mediated by support for the ethics proposals. Two members from such districts described their constituents' feelings as follows:

> The mail volume was 9-1 against [the Quadrennial proposal and the
> Ethics Act], but the volume was less for the second. The perception was
> that you may have voted for it, but not at midnight, whispering behind a

tree. I don't think they're ever in favor of a pay raise. But the intensity of their opposition matters. [11]

To the extent they knew about it, they wanted me to vote against it. . . . It was a sizable issue, but the feeling was that it was the best way to change the system of honoraria. The first attempt to raise pay was abhorred universally. This one attracted support because of the honoraria ban and the substitution of salary for honoraria. [67]

As these comments indicate, in contrast to strong opponent districts, constituents in qualified opponent districts were less certain that the Ethics Act was a bad idea. They agreed that the proposal had costs but also saw a possibility that it would generate benefits, in the form of a more ethical, more responsive Congress.

The third category, supporters, contains districts where the average voter supported or at least tolerated the Ethics Act, either because they felt strongly about the need for ethics reforms or because they agreed with the need for a raise. An example of the former preference is seen in the comments of a Northwestern Democrat: "It didn't get widespread attention in my district. There was some attention to the pay raise, but most constituents were willing to go along with a ban on honoraria and a phased-in raise. Some were opposed, but that's true on any pay raise vote" [15]. In a few other districts, largely those with high costs of living or high average income, constituents reportedly favored the raise outright:

In large part congressional salaries are not unattainable in my district. It's like the member of Congress from Orange County who had an exposé done on him because they found that he'd been out of the country more days than he'd been in it. He said, so what, my constituents are out of the country that much too. Given the salaries where two-thirds of my constituents live, congressional salaries are not seen as outlandish. [42]

Surveys of public opinion arrive at a similar conclusion: in general, well-to-do voters and those facing a high cost of living are sympathetic to pay raises for elected officials (Davidson 1980). The problem, of course, is that in most districts the number of such voters is small.

Summary

These data have a simple implication: if trust was ever needed to enact a piece of legislation, it was needed for the Ethics Act. Assuming the sample is representative of the House, only 15 percent of House members supported the

act and represented constituents who either felt the same way or had no
opinion. An additional 20 percent or so of the House agreed with their constituents that the Ethics Act should be defeated. Thus, the lion's share of a
majority coalition had to come from the remaining 65 percent of the House,
representatives who supported the act and faced constituents who opposed it.

Voting Leeway and the Ethics Act

The high levels of constituent opposition to pay raises in general and to the
Ethics Act in particular suggest that few representatives should have been
trusted to use their judgment on the proposal. That turns out not to be the case.
And trust appears to have made a difference, both in individual vote decisions
and in overall policy outcomes. Consider table 4, which summarizes legislators' votes and their expectations about trust. The table shows that the Ethics
Act is a good case for testing the hypotheses constructed in chapter 4. For one
thing, there is plenty of variance to explain. Overall, 45.5 percent (forty of
eighty-eight) of the representatives interviewed here reported trust on the
Ethics Act. That is, they believed—or said they believed—that their constituents, regardless of how they felt about the proposal, would approve of whatever vote their representative cast. Of these forty representatives, 77.5 percent
(thirty-one) voted yea and 22.5 percent (nine) voted nay. As some of the
representatives in the latter category were supporters of the act, it can be
assumed that their votes reflected a desire to avoid damage to their reputa-

Table 4. Votes and Trust on the Ethics Act

	Vote on the Ethics Act		
Trust	Yea	Nay	Row Totals
Yes	31	9	40
No	16	32	48
Column totals	47	41	

Note: Number in each cell is the cell *n*. Table *N* = 88, with
five cases omitted because of missing data. For information
on variables, see appendix 2.

tions. Table 4 also shows that the absence of trust did not preclude legislators from voting yea: 33.3 percent (sixteen of forty-eight) did so.[2] All of these votes were politically costly, in the sense that these representatives came from districts characterized by opposition or strong opposition. The presumption must be that the members' support for the Ethics Act was strong enough to override political considerations.

Additional analysis (not in table 4) suggests that the Ethics Act was enacted only because of trust. While most legislators in the sample (79.3 percent) supported the act, only sixteen (44.4 percent) of the thirty-six supporters who did not expect trust voted yea. At least in this sample, the remainder of the votes came from supporters who believed that constituents would trust their judgment. Presumably some would have voted yea regardless of their expectations about trust. However, if they voted yea at the same rate as those who did not expect trust, the proposal would not have received enough votes to carry.[3]

The next step is to explain some of this variance. Working from the leeway hypothesis, this section argues that trust on the Ethics Act arose from the perception that a legislator was motivated by a concern with congressional ethics and responsiveness rather than monetary self-interest. This perception should have been generated by attributes or actions that signal that a legislator was either uninterested in a pay raise or would not receive one from the act. With pay discounted as a motive, yea votes are consistent with a concern with ethics or responsiveness. This inference should lead constituents, particularly those in qualified opponent districts, to infer a common interest and grant leeway.

Common Interest and the Ethics Act

Consider what the Ethics Act might do if enacted. Certainly it would increase congressional pay. In addition, the ethics and pay provisions would, in theory, reduce the influence of special interests in the policy process and eliminate potential conflicts of interests, thereby increasing congressional responsiveness to the interests held by the average voter. In the worst case, the act would

---

2. 52.7 percent (49 of 93) of the legislators in the sample and 53.4 percent (47 of 88) of the legislators with valid leeway data voted yea, vs. 59.2 percent (252 of 429) in the entire House.

3. Supporters comprise 79.3 percent of the sample, and only 44.4 percent of supporters without trust voted yea. Assuming these percentages reflect the entire House, if no legislator had leeway, then $(.793) \cdot (.444)$, or 35.2 percent, would have voted yea.

have no effect on responsiveness or ethics and simply give legislators a pay raise.[4]

From these claims, there are three reasons why a member of Congress might favor the Ethics Act: an interest in higher pay, an interest in improving congressional ethics or responsiveness, or a combination of these interests.[5] Each reason defines a set of conditions under which the legislator would vote for the proposal. For example, if she wants higher pay, she would prefer to enact the proposal regardless of whether it will increase responsiveness or improve ethics. In contrast, a legislator who cares about ethics (or who wants pay coupled with ethical improvements) would oppose a simple pay raise bill, favoring the act only if it would generate a better outcome on both dimensions.

Now compare these goals to those held by constituents who are qualified opponents. They oppose the Ethics Act because they think it only raises pay. However, they would prefer to enact the proposal if they knew that it would make sufficient improvements in congressional ethics. Given these interests, qualified opponents do not have a common interest with a legislator who only wants a higher salary. Such a legislator would want to vote for the Ethics Act even if, as constituents suspect, the proposal only raises pay. However, qualified opponents have a common interest with a legislator motivated solely by ethical concerns or one who wants to improve pay and ethics: both types agree with qualified opponents that the proposal should be enacted only if it improves congressional ethics. Put another way, neither of these legislators would ever prefer to deviate from actions that serve the interests of qualified opponents. If they learn that the Ethics Act will improve responsiveness, they would want to vote for it. If they find out that the Ethics Act just raises pay, they would prefer to vote against it. Both actions satisfy the interests of qualified opponents, given the information available to the members.

In sum, the leeway hypothesis suggests that qualified opponent constituents should be more likely to trust their legislator's judgment about the Ethics Act insofar as they can discount the possibility that her vote was driven solely by the desire for higher pay. With pay removed as a motive, constituents are likely to infer that their member's vote was driven by her interest in improving congressional ethics and responsiveness. Thus, in qualified opponent districts, legislators holding attributes or records of past actions that signal they

---

4. Even members who argued that ethics codes are inherently wrong, or who argued for massive reforms to existing ethics codes, did not claim that the Ethics Act would make things worse.

5. This discussion ignores party pressures as a motive for voting yea. While member comments and journalistic accounts agree that there was some internal lobbying, they also indicate that these efforts had a minimal impact. For evidence on other raise votes, see Wilkerson 1991.

had no financial incentive (or at best a minimal one) to vote for the act should be much more likely to report trust compared to legislators who lack these actions and attributes.

Different predictions are made for districts where the predominant sentiment was support or strong opposition to the Ethics Act. In supporter districts, constituents were content with a yea vote, either because they believed that the raise was justified or that the ethics reforms were worthwhile. Given these perceptions, legislators from supporter districts should always be trusted. The reasoning is as follows. Since supporters will approve of a vote for the Ethics Act, a legislator who wants higher pay has no reason to vote nay. The only legislators who will vote nay are those who care about ethics and responsiveness and know that the act will have no effect in these areas. Given this signal, supporters are likely to accept nay as well as yea votes—they will always grant leeway. In contrast, trust is unlikely in strong opposition districts, since constituents there thought it extremely unlikely that the Ethics Act would yield any improvements. Even a high probability of common interest, generated by all the right actions and attributes, might not be enough to persuade them to defer to their representative.

Anecdotal Evidence

Interviews with members of Congress lend support to these predictions. With regard to attributes, a few legislators cited their personal wealth as a source of trust. As two Southern Democrats explained,[6]

> One reason my situation is atypical is that I've given a substantial amount of money to my district each year. My constituents might not think that's a big deal, but they know I'm not dependent on my congressional pay. With my friends I make the argument that for me, a vote for the pay raise is unselfish because I didn't need it. If a thirty thousand dollar raise could become a campaign issue, it's not worth it for me in political terms to vote for it. . . . It's pretty well-known that I have the second-largest net worth in the delegation. Some of my constituents don't like that I was born with a silver spoon in my mouth, but the others just think it's harder to buy me. [67]

> I got criticized during the campaign for spending 450 thousand dollars of my own money. So I told them, "if you're upset about that, you can't say I voted yes only so I could take a twenty-five thousand dollar raise." [11]

---

6. Note that these are the legislators whose comments were used to describe qualified opponent districts.

Each of these legislators expected his constituents to approve of a vote for the Ethics Act—not because they favored the proposal but because they believed that the member would not vote for a bill that just raised pay. Constituents in the two districts behaved as expected. Both legislators reported that their constituents were happy with their votes.

In addition, several actions were cited as a source of trust. One action, voting nay in the case of supporter districts, has already been discussed. In addition, several representatives cited the ethics provisions in the bill—the ban on honoraria and the limits on outside income. Because of these provisions, a substantial fraction of the House, those with substantial honoraria and outside income, received at best a trivial increase in pay as a result of the act's passage.[7] As the following comments indicate, some members expected these circumstances to generate leeway:

> My constituents think I acted in the interests of the country. The raise was overdue; it had to be dealt with. It would be a slam-dunk [to vote nay]. . . . I won't make a nickel more—it's a wash for what goes into my pocket. [24]

> I got hit hard by the bill because I practice law. I'm still a senior partner in a firm with fifty members. Last year I got a check for thirty thousand from that, but I'll have to resign December 31st because of the ethics reforms. So the bill hurt me more than other members. . . . In retrospect, I could have voted for the raise with impunity. [27]

These comments suggest that a legislator's honoraria and outside income had the same effect as personal wealth: they signaled that her vote on the Ethics Act was driven by a concern with ethics and responsiveness, not her desire for higher pay. In addition, many legislators argued that their constituents tend to overestimate the amount of honoraria and outside income that they receive. If so, the restrictions may have generated trust even for members who received a net increase in pay from the act.

Finally, some representatives argued that a refusal to accept the raise would generate leeway.[8] As one said, "If I had believed that the ethics reforms were important, I could have voted for the package and told folks that I didn't agree with the raise and didn't take the money, but that the other reforms were critical because Washington's become corrupted with outside interests. That would couple a yes vote with a refusal to take the money" [53]. This rationale

---

7. In most cases, honoraria were the principal source of lost income. Only eight legislators in the sample lost outside income as a result of the changes mandated by the act.

8. I am grateful to Richard Fenno for alerting me to this possibility.

fits with the earlier discussion. The representative believed that refusing the raise would alter constituent perceptions of his motivations, eliminating monetary self-interest as a possible motive. He anticipated that under these conditions, his constituents would approve a yea vote, thinking it motivated by the goal of improving congressional ethics.

Statistical Evidence

To make a more systematic test of the leeway hypothesis, data were collected for the ninety-three legislators in the sample concerning their personal wealth, honoraria receipts, outside income, and their decision to accept or refuse the pay hike mandated by the Ethics Act. (These variables are defined in appendix 2.) If the hypothesis is correct, holding district sentiments constant, legislators who are wealthy, who received high amounts of honoraria or outside income, or who refused the raise should be more likely to report trust on the Ethics Act compared to legislators who lack these actions and attributes. As discussed previously, this effect should be most evident in qualified opposition districts.

Table 5 contains data on trust as a function of member characteristics and district sentiment.[9] The table provides strong evidence for the leeway hypothesis. Looking at qualified opponent districts (the middle column), legislators holding one or more of the critical actions or attributes were more than three times as likely to have leeway as legislators who had none (15.4 percent versus between 50.0 percent and 66.7 percent). These differences satisfy the usual criteria for statistical significance.[10]

Table 5 also confirms the expectations about trust in supporter and strong opponent districts. All legislators from supporter districts had leeway. In addition, a few legislators from strong opponent districts had leeway, but there is no apparent relationship between leeway and characteristics in these cases.

These results are not perfect. Some legislators—15.4 percent of those

---

9. The reader may wonder why I do not use a multivariate technique, such as logistic regression, to evaluate the effect of member characteristics and district sentiment on the existence or nonexistence of trust. Since the explanatory variables here are ordinal, it is not clear that logit would reveal any information beyond that contained in table 5. In addition, the relatively low sample size would likely confound inferences that might be drawn from a more sophisticated technique. Crosstabs also have the advantage that they are easily described to nonspecialists.

10. The *t*-scores and *p*-values for a difference-of-means test between legislators without any relevant actions or attributes and those falling into one of the other categories in table 5 are as follows:

Refused raise: $t = 1.22$, $p < .1$
Honoraria/outside income: $t = 2.53$, $p < .01$
Personal wealth: $t = 2.06$, $p < .05$
Combination: $t = 2.6$, $p < .01$

from qualified opposition districts and 25.0 percent in strong opposition districts—reported trust even though they did not have any of the actions or attributes listed in table 5. Moreover, of representatives elected from qualified opposition districts who had one or more of these characteristics, almost one-half reported that they were not trusted. While these anomalies are an obvious concern, their existence is no surprise. The obvious possibility is that additional actions or attributes, omitted from table 5, may have functioned as signals of common interest in this case. Their omission would explain why some legislators reported trust without having any of the characteristics that signaled common interest. It is also possible that constituents in some districts were unaware of their representative's actions and attributes. Along the same lines, the stereotypes held by constituents—what does wealth signal?—may also have varied across districts. Both of these possibilities would explain why some legislators were not trusted despite having the "right" actions and attributes. For all of these problems, the only solution is to collect better data on

Table 5. Characteristics and Trust on the Ethics Act

Member Characteristics	District Sentiment		
	Support or No Opinion	Qualified Opposition	Strong Opposition
None	100 (7)	15.4 (26)	25.0 (8)
Didn't accept raise	100 (1)	50.0 (4)	100 (1)
Honoraria or outside income	100 (3)	53.3 (15)	0 (1)
Personal wealth	100 (2)	50.0 (10)	0 (2)
Combination	100 (1)	66.7 (6)	(0) (1)

Note: The top number in each cell is the cell percentage of members who reported trust; the bottom number is the cell *n*. Table $N = 88$, with five cases excluded because of missing data. For details on variables, see appendix 2.

what constituents know about their representative and what kinds of stereo-types they apply to this information.

Another criticism is that table 5 ignores the role of electoral safety. Many analyses of roll call voting incorporate a "marginality hypothesis" (Bartlett 1979): legislators with large election margins are more likely to vote for politically unpopular proposals, such as pay raises, compared to legislators who won by small margins (for applications to pay raise votes, see Bartlett 1979; Hibbing 1983; Wilkerson 1991). In principle, the existence of such a relationship would not falsify the leeway hypothesis. As defined here, trust or voting leeway determines whether a vote is politically costly or not. How a legislator acts in light of political costs is a separate question. It would be no surprise if electoral security, reflected in high election margins, predisposed a legislator to ignore constituent demands in situations in which she did not expect to be trusted. Many legislators made explicit reference to their election margins as a factor in their vote decisions, such as this Northwestern democrat:

> **Were your constituents happy with your vote?** If you asked them in a straight out poll, you'd get eighty percent no. From the guys who brought you the savings and loan mess? Ninety-six thousand looks like a lot of money.
> **They wanted a nay vote?** Oh sure.
> **Then why did you vote yes?** Because if you got seventy-six percent of the vote last time, you have a responsibility to the country, a broader respon-sibility than if you just scraped by with fifty-one percent. [77]

This quote is consistent with the idea that electoral safety represents political capital—capital that can be spent when needed. Safe members simply have more to spend—more votes to lose—than their marginal colleagues. How-ever, voting leeway appears to be distinct from political capital. Many safe legislators did not report leeway on the Ethics Act. Consider what one senior legislator said: "I couldn't even attempt to sell the pay raise. . . . I'm a sitting target at all those town meetings, and I don't need the hassle. I can walk one step on water, but not three or four" [5]. This legislator routinely wins reelec-tion by large margins—sometimes unopposed. Yet he did not have leeway on the Ethics Act. Conversely, some marginal legislators reported trust, like this freshman:

> I don't know why they included me in the article about the pay raise because I haven't heard from my opponent about it. If he includes that in the campaign, he'll lose.
> **Has there been much response?** I haven't heard a whole lot of anything.

There's a talk show back home that bangs away on it, but I haven't heard much at town meetings. I've spoken a couple of hundred times, and it hasn't happened once. As best I can tell, it's not a problem. [52]

Clearly, electoral safety, or political capital, is something different than voting leeway.

However, given the nature of the data used here, one worry is that representatives interpreted questions about trust or leeway as questions about political capital. If they did, their answers to questions about leeway would reflect their feelings of electoral vulnerability and judgments about the damage that a yea vote might cause. The favorable results in table 5 could then be explained by a fortuitous correlation between actions, attributes, and electoral safety.

To examine this possibility, legislators representing qualified opponent districts were split into two categories: marginal (received 60 percent or less of the vote in the 1988 election) or nonmarginal (61 percent or more).[11] The question is: does a control for election margin destroy the relationship between characteristics and leeway? Table 6 shows the percentage of marginal and nonmarginal members with trust as a function of their actions and attributes. Two points are immediately evident. First, having the right actions or attributes did not generate leeway for marginal legislators: the leeway percentages are identical (12.5 percent). Second, actions and attributes have the predicted effect for nonmarginal legislators: a fourfold increase in the leeway percentage (16.7 percent versus 66.6 percent). Moreover, the leeway percentages for legislators without actions and attributes are about the same regardless of whether they are marginal or not (12.5 percent versus 16.7 percent). In other words, without the right characteristics, virtually no one reported trust. But having the right characteristics did not guarantee voting leeway for marginal legislators, although it did for those with somewhat higher margins.

Additional analysis shows that election margins are related to a legislator's willingness to vote against constituent demands. Of the twelve representatives in table 6 who were marginal, represented qualified opponent districts, supported the Ethics Act, and did not have leeway, four (33.3 percent) voted yes, versus eleven (61.1 percent) of the eighteen nonmarginal legislators satisfying the same criteria.

In sum, while electoral safety affects a legislator's vote decisions, con-

---

11. The test focuses on legislators representing qualified opponent districts because, as table 5 shows, this category is the only one where a legislator's chances of leeway vary systematically with her actions and attributes. However, it is interesting to note that the one marginal legislator elected from a supporter district reported trust. Among legislators representing strong opponent districts, the percentage reporting trust is almost identical for marginal and nonmarginal members: 25.0 percent and 22.3 percent, respectively.

trolling for marginality does not falsify the leeway hypothesis. Election margins appear to represent political capital and influence how a legislator votes. However, a separate variable, trust, determines whether deviations from constituent demands are politically costly in the first place. The analysis suggests, however, that electorally vulnerable legislators assess leeway using more stringent criteria than colleagues with higher margins. A legislator who received, say, 65 percent of the vote in the last election might believe she had leeway even though she knew a few constituents would be upset by her vote. Given her high election margin, she could ignore a few malcontents. In contrast, a legislator who won with 51 percent could not afford to be so cavalier. She might well define leeway as the virtual absence of political costs—everyone has to trust her. In the case of the Ethics Act, the fact that all districts, regardless of the prevailing sentiment, contained a few strong opponents may have eliminated the possibility of leeway for marginal legislators.

The Explanation Hypothesis

The structure of the Evaluation game, as well as the empirical analysis presented in this chapter, is built on the assumption that a representative's expla-

Table 6. Marginality and Trust on the Ethics Act

	Action or Attribute	
Member Safety	None	One or More
Marginal	12.5 (8)	12.5 (8)
Nonmarginal	16.7 (18)	66.7 (27)

Note: Nonmarginal seats are defined as districts where the incumbent received 61 percent or more of the two-party vote in the 1988 election; marginal cases received 60 percent or less. The top number in each cell is the percentage of members in the cell who reported trust; the bottom number is the cell n. Table $N = 61$ (all qualified opponent cases with valid data). For details on variables, see appendix 2.

nations have no effect on her constituents' trust decisions. Chapter 3 specified this assumption as a hypothesis—the explanation hypothesis—and described two implications, one strong, one weak. The first implication is that legislators who were trusted and who voted against their constituents' demands should report a low rate of explanation. This observation would provide strong evidence for the hypothesis: explanations cannot be the source of trust if no one who reported (and exploited) trust did any explaining. However, these legislators might report substantial amounts of explaining that were unrelated to trust, such as if constituents asked questions about their vote during town meetings or if they mentioned the vote as part of a discussion of their work in Washington. This possibility suggests a second implication: legislators who voted against their constituents and had trust should explain their vote at roughly the same rate as those legislators who did not have trust and voted as their constituents wanted. This pattern would provide weaker support for the hypothesis, since it does not account for the content of an explanation or its effect on constituents' perceptions.

The interview data allow for a direct test of both implications. During the interviews, members were asked whether they had done any explaining of their vote on the Ethics Act. Their answers were grouped into three categories: major, minor, and none. The first category, major explanations, captures cases where a legislator reported that she had made extensive efforts to explain her vote and reported that constituents showed a high level of interest in her efforts. When congressional scholars talk about explanations generating trust, they are talking about major explanations. Cases falling into the minor explanation category are characterized by trivial expenditures of legislatorial resources, a low frequency of situations where explaining actually occurred, and low constituent interest in what a member said. The no-explanation category includes only those cases in which a legislator reported—literally—that she had not volunteered or been asked for an explanation of her vote on the Ethics Act.

Data on the amount of explaining reported by legislators as a function of their vote on the Ethics Act and their expectations about trust are shown in table 7. To prevent bias, the table excludes districts where constituents supported the Ethics Act or had no opinion. The reason is simple: even if explanations were a mechanism for generating trust, a legislator representing such a district would have no need to explain her vote. Thus, including them in the table would presumably lower the amount of explaining reported by legislators with trust who voted yea, thereby biasing the table's contents in favor of the explanation hypothesis. With this exclusion, legislators who complied with constituent demands voted nay; those who deviated from constituent demands voted yea.

The first surprise in table 7 is the absence of explanations. Slightly less than two-thirds (63.9 percent) of legislators in the sample reported that they did no explaining of their vote on the Ethics Act. *They didn't talk about it at all.* Only a small fraction, 12.5 percent, reported a major explanation. Thus, the picture in our heads, of legislators acting in Washington then going home to explain, does not always hold, even on a high-salience issue like the Ethics Act.

The data also support both implications of the explanation hypothesis. Virtually no legislator (5.6 percent) who voted yea with leeway reported a major explanatory effort. A substantial percentage (44.4 percent) reported making minor explanations. But it seems unreasonable to think that minor explanations—answering an occasional question at a town meeting or sending out a press release—can generate trust across an entire district. Moreover, the percentage of major explanations among members in this category is actually lower than the percentage reported by legislators who voted nay and were not trusted.

Finally, the table confirms one legislator's adage: "when you're explain-

Table 7. Explanations of the Ethics Act

Trust	Vote	Type of Explanation		
		Major	Minor	None
No	Nay	10.0	16.7	73.3
		(3)	(5)	(22)
	Yea	31.3	25.0	43.7
		(5)	(4)	(7)
Yes	Nay	0	0	100.0
		(0)	(0)	(8)
	Yea	5.6	44.4	50.0
		(1)	(8)	(9)
Column average		12.5	23.6	63.9
and *n*		(9)	(17)	(46)

Note: In each cell, the top number is the row percentage; the bottom number is the cell *n*. Table $N = 72$, with ten support districts omitted, four no-opinion districts omitted, and seven additional cases deleted because of missing data. For details on variables, see appendix 2.

ing, you're losing." The only group of legislators who reported a high percentage of major explanations (31.3 percent) are those who deviated without leeway. Rather than generating trust, their explanations appear to have been aimed at acknowledging constituent anger and giving the appearance of accessibility. Several legislators who faced these circumstances reported that they avoided opportunities to explain their vote, believing that communication would only publicize their action and increase the political fallout.

Reputations and Vote Decisions on the Ethics Act

In a world where actions signal motivations, representatives should look beyond the immediate political and policy consequences of different votes and consider how these votes might affect these reputations. As described in chapter 3, these considerations arise when constituents believe that their representative's vote reflects her personal policy concerns. In these situations, votes that match constituent demands have positive effects on a representative's reputation—they increase the chances that constituents will trust their representative when similar proposals are voted on in the future. Conversely, voting against constituent demands has a negative effect, weakening common interest perceptions and making trust less likely.

While the effects of reputational concerns on a legislator's vote decision are quite complex, the discussions in chapters 3 and 4 suggest one concrete prediction, in the form of an exception to the Evaluation game's predictions. Looking at a single vote decision in isolation from other actions, the Evaluation game predicts that a legislator who expects to be trusted will vote as her policy concerns dictate. However, if reputational effects are taken into account, legislators who expect trust may choose to comply with their constituents' demands—not because they favor the resulting policy outcomes or to build their reputations but to preserve whatever reputation they have for use on future proposals.

Interviews bear out this prediction. Of the thirty-six supporters of the Ethics Act who expected trust, only five (13.8 percent) voted nay. However, all but one of these five legislators cited reputational factors as a reason for their decision. Consider, for example, comments made by two of the legislators in this group:

> I could have gotten away with it. But I always vote against them. I made a big stink about it early in my career, when I voted against a raise and gave the money to charity. So now I'm stuck. That was a stupid position to take, but I took it. I come from a difficult district. I've had a few close elections, and I even lost one. Voting for a pay raise alienates my base, which is mostly working-class Democratic. The raise is a smaller prob-

lem among the Republicans in the district. It's also kind of a litmus test of whether you're anti-establishment, whether you're part of the problem in Congress or not. Privately I'm certainly for it, but I'm locked into voting against it. The leadership knows that, they didn't even ask me to vote for it. [91]

I could have voted either way, but I came down that the second phase of the increase was too much given the quarter of a trillion dollars in debt we're laying down this year. . . . I preach so much that Congress has to amend its profligate spending ways. I've talked about a freeze on spending, or spending only new revenues. The raise went against everything I was talking about. . . . [But] they would have accepted [a vote for the Ethics Act]. There was a lot of good in the package. The ethics reforms were a step in the right direction. [10]

Reputational concerns played a critical role in both decisions. The first legislator thought that a yea vote would signal that he was "part of the problem in Congress," presumably that he was more concerned about his own well-being than with the well-being of his constituents. There seems little doubt that reputational concerns were at work. The second legislator's concerns were more concrete: he expects to face votes on freezing federal spending or on cutting programs that are popular with his constituents. Apparently he believes that a vote against the Ethics Act would strengthen—or not weaken— his reputation for being impartial and judicious, thereby increasing—or preserving—the chances that constituents will accept his judgments about the need for fiscal restraint. Voting for the act would reduce the chances of deference, presumably because it would signal that the legislator was willing to make exceptions to the doctrine of fiscal restraint for proposals that have a direct impact on his welfare.

It is also important to note that voting against the Ethics Act generally did not produce reputational benefits. Legislators who voted nay in the absence of trust did not cite the reputational consequences of their vote. As predicted by the analysis in chapter 4, constituents understood that these representatives had cast "political votes," votes driven by a desire to be reelected, not by personal policy concerns. There is no doubt that these legislators believed that a yea vote would damage their reputations. None expected a nay vote to generate reputational benefits.

During the interviews, several legislators cited a second reputational effect: the idea that "voting no and taking the dough"—voting against the Ethics Act but accepting the raise—would be politically damaging. Their expectation was that constituents would infer that a representative who did so was trying to mislead them, combining public compliance with private shirking. As one legislator put it:

[A nay vote] would have been the easier vote. It might be tough if I took the money. You could argue that was hypocritical, that I voted against it but cashed the check. If you take the increase, it's better to vote for it. There are many who voted against it but are taking the money. Ultimately, those people might be in serious political jeopardy. If I'm their opponent, I'd rather have one who voted no and took it rather than yes and took it, just looking at it in a hard, crass way, looking at attack ads. [89]

Or, as another legislator put it, "If the last guy to vote voted no and then took the money, that poor SOB is going to face a 30-second spot that'll blow him away." Both comments suggest that part of a legislator's reputation is composed of beliefs about whether she is consistent or honest. Presumably, voting against the act but accepting the raise would suggest that a legislator's fidelity to constituents existed only as long as she thought they were watching.

Unfortunately, an analysis of legislators' decisions to accept or refuse the raise does not provide much support for this proposition. Table 8 presents data

Table 8. Refusing the Raise

Vote on Ethics	Legislator Preference	Accepted Raise	Deferred Raise	Refused Raise
Yea	Support Ethics	87.0 (40)	4.3 (2)	8.7 (4)
Nay	Support Ethics	70.8 (17)	20.8 (5)	8.3 (2)
	Oppose Ethics	60.0 (9)	13.3 (2)	26.7 (4)
Column average and n		76.7 (66)	10.5 (9)	11.6 (10)

Note: Top number in each cell is the row percentage of legislators who accepted, deferred, or refused the raise; the bottom number is the cell n. The table omits rows for legislators who opposed the Ethics Act and voted yea because there are no such legislators in the dataset. Table $N = 86$, with eight cases omitted because of missing data. For details on variables, see appendix 2.

on these decisions as a function of legislators' votes on the Ethics Act and their personal feelings about the proposal. (The table does not include a row for legislators who opposed the act but voted yea, since there are no legislators in this category.) Overall, 78.2 percent (sixty-eight of eighty-seven) of legislators in the sample accepted the raise outright, 10.3 percent (nine) waited until after the 1990 elections to accept it, and only 11.5 percent (ten) refused it. Dividing legislators into the three groups shown in table 8 reveals two critical points. First, opponents of the act made up a large fraction of the group who refused the raise: 31.6 percent of opponents made some sort of refusal and 40.0 percent rejected the raise outright. (Note also that opponents make up only 17.2 percent of the legislators in table 8.) While their refusal may have had political consequences, for at least some opponents the decision was driven by their antagonism to the proposal. The second critical point is that there is not much difference in the percentage accepting the raise between supporters who voted yea and supporters who voted nay: 87.0 percent versus 70.8 percent. In other words, over two-thirds of legislators who supported the Ethics Act but voted against it ultimately "took the dough." Thus, while the slogan may have been useful as a rallying cry, an argument aimed at fence-sitters who wanted a higher salary, it does not appear to be an accurate statement of reality. (Of course, the vote may have had consequences that legislators did not anticipate at the time they voted, or at the later time when they decided whether to take the raise or refuse it. I am unaware of any evidence that supports this claim.)

Summary

The analysis of trust on the Ethics Act of 1989 confirms the leeway hypothesis. Trust on the Ethics Act was generated by actions and attributes that signaled that legislators did not have a financial incentive to vote yea. This result makes sense given the goals held by constituents and their beliefs about the Ethics Act. The analysis also highlights an important, but unsurprising, possible caveat to the hypothesis: electoral vulnerability may raise the threshold at which a legislator is willing to say that she has leeway.

The data also confirm the explanation hypothesis. The Ethics Act is the classic case of a high-salience proposal that legislators need trust to enact. If explanations generate trust, legislators who reported trust should also report a lot of explaining. But they did not. Major efforts at explanation, when they occurred at all, tended to be attempts to mitigate the political fallout from voting yea in the face of unswerving constituent opposition. Finally, the interviews showed that for some legislators, vote decisions were colored by reputational concerns. This influence is most obvious in the case of legislators who supported the Ethics Act, expected trust, but decided to vote against the proposal. However, it is also apparent that reputational factors gave supporters without trust an additional reason to vote against the act—a nay vote did not enhance their reputation, but a yea vote would certainly have damaged it.

CHAPTER 6

Analyzing the Inexplicable: The Repeal of the Medicare Catastrophic Coverage Act

Catastrophic is inexplicable. Something triggered an emotional response beyond the norm of any legislation. I can't explain why that issue triggered that level of emotion. I'm not going to research that, I'll let you do it. I don't have the time. If you find out, let me know.

—Another senior Democrat

This chapter continues the empirical analysis by examining the repeal of the Medicare Catastrophic Coverage Act. To many pundits, the enactment and subsequent repeal of this program was no surprise: Congress simply responded to demands expressed by an important voting bloc. By this logic, seniors favored Catastrophic Coverage when it was enacted, then changed their minds when they learned more about the program—and Congress did what seniors wanted, both times. But at almost the same time Catastrophic Coverage was repealed, Congress passed the Ethics Act, a proposal that generated similar amounts of opposition. Why were legislators able to enact one controversial proposal but forced to repeal another?

This chapter analyzes the repeal of Catastrophic Coverage to test the leeway and explanation hypotheses. (Because of time limitations during the interviews, a substantial number of legislators could not be asked about the circumstances surrounding the program's enactment. Moreover, over a quarter of the legislators in the sample were not in office when Catastrophic Coverage was enacted.) In one sense, the question raised in the above paragraph has a simple answer. There *were* large shifts in senior opinion between the time Catastrophic Coverage was enacted and the time of its repeal. And many legislators either opposed Catastrophic Coverage or had no strong feelings about the program. Thus, once seniors demanded repeal, a clear majority in Congress had no reason to resist. Moreover, claims about the initial public support for Catastrophic Coverage are well off the mark: in many districts, seniors were indifferent about the program or unaware of its provisions. In voting to enact the program, many members of Congress accepted claims made by interest groups of what seniors would think about the program after they learned something about it.

The analysis also reveals a second interesting fact: the near absence of trust. In contrast to the Ethics Act, where nearly half of the legislators in the sample reported trust, less than a fifth of the same legislators did so on the repeal vote. What made Catastrophic Coverage special, that trust did not arise on an obviously complex policy proposal? As the case of the Ethics Act shows, strong constituent sentiments about a proposal are not enough to deter trust. The answer appears to lie in the way constituents assess common interest. Faced with a proposal like Catastrophic Coverage, seniors will assess a high probability of common interest only if they believe that their representative favors continuation or expansion of programs that favor senior citizens. This perception is difficult to create—regardless of a legislator's true preferences. Because seniors are a sizable, well-organized voting bloc in most districts, actions taken on their behalf tend to signal a legislator's interest in reelection, not her policy concerns. Only if a legislator sends costly signals—mobilizing support for prosenior legislation and overseeing its implementation rather than just voting for it—will her actions signal common interest. That few legislators are willing to incur these costs, as evidenced by their indifference or opposition to Catastrophic Coverage, seems to explain the absence of trust on repeal.

Additional analysis supports the explanation hypothesis. In comparison to the Ethics Act, representatives spent more time talking to constituents about Catastrophic Coverage. However, there is scant evidence that their explanations generated trust. Moreover, of the legislators who voted against repeal and believed they had leeway, almost half reported minimal explaining of any of their votes, enactment or repeal.

The final section of this chapter returns to the question raised in chapter 2 about the level (general or specific) at which trust decisions are made, looking for correlations in legislators' reports about trust across the Ethics Act and Catastrophic Coverage. Analysis shows that trust decisions involving the two proposals were essentially independent: few legislators were trusted on both proposals; most were trusted on one but not the other. Thus, trust decisions appear to be made one-at-a-time, based on the context as constituents see it.

Setting the Stage: Constituent Demands and Legislatorial Preferences

Table 9 begins the analysis by detailing what members of Congress and their constituents thought about Catastrophic Coverage at the time it was enacted. Table 9 contains data only for those legislators who voted on the enactment of Catastrophic Coverage. As in the analysis of the Ethics Act, constituent demands are measured at the aggregate, district level, for simplicity and because legislators described them that way. Throughout the analysis, the term *constituents* is used to refer to senior citizens—virtually no one else

Table 9. Enacting Catastrophic Coverage: Constituent Demands and Legislatorial Preference

| Legislator Preference | Constituent Demands | | | | Row Total and Percentage *n* |
	No Opinion	Support	Oppose	Strong Oppose	
Support	8.3 (6)	19.4 (14)	0 (0)	0 (0)	27.7 (20)
Leaner	12.5 (9)	31.9 (23)	0 (0)	0 (0)	44.4 (32)
Oppose	4.2 (3)	18.1 (13)	0 (0)	5.6 (4)	27.9 (20)
Column total and percentage *n*	25.0 (18)	69.4 (50)	0 (0)	5.6 (4)	

Note: In each cell, the top number is the cell percentage; the bottom number is the cell *n*, with row and column totals along the right-hand side and the bottom, respectively. Total percents do not always match cell percents due to rounding. Table $N = 72$, with remaining cases omitted because of missing data. For details on variables, see appendix 2.

knew or cared about the proposal. Thus, Catastrophic Coverage is an archetypal example of a high-salience proposal that attracted the attention of only a minority of constituents.

Table 9 indicates that at the time Catastrophic Coverage was enacted, opposition was the prevailing sentiment in only 5.6 percent (four of seventy-two) of the districts in the sample. A substantial number of legislators, 25.0 percent (eighteen of seventy-two), reported that seniors in their district had no clear opinion about the proposal. Support for Catastrophic Coverage dominated in the remaining districts—although even in these districts, support was described as extremely thin, with most seniors being uncertain about the proposal's effects.

Table 10 shows that by the time of the repeal vote, a sea change had occurred in senior opinion: virtually *all* districts were characterized by opposition or strong opposition.[1] Districts that opposed Catastrophic Coverage early

---

1. The opposition category includes two districts where there was some support for Catastrophic Coverage. In one, the percentage of supporters was estimated by the legislator to be 50 percent; support in the other district was even lower. (The latter district has missing data on the leeway variable, so it is omitted from much of the analysis.) In all other districts, the overwhelming majority of seniors opposed the program.

on remained steadfast; support and no-opinion districts uniformly moved into the opposition camp.

In contrast to constituents, congressional preferences stayed roughly the same between enactment and repeal. Early on, supporters and opponents of Catastrophic Coverage were evenly divided: each group contained 27.8 percent (twenty of seventy-two) of the representatives in the sample. The remaining legislators, leaners who did not express a strong preference either way, comprised 44.4 percent (thirty-two of seventy-two). Moving to repeal, despite the addition of twenty-one freshmen and two shifts from support to opposition, only minor changes were observed: 26.1 percent (twenty-four of ninety-two) of the sample were supporters, an identical percentage opposed the program, and 47.8 percent (forty-four of ninety-two) were leaners.

Constituent Demands

Based on the interviews, district sentiment about Catastrophic Coverage at the time it was repealed was coded into two categories: *opposition* and *strong*

Table 10. Repealing Catastrophic Coverage: Constituent Demands and Legislatorial Preference

Legislator Preference	Constituent Demands				Row Total and Percentage *n*
	No Opinion	Support	Oppose	Strong Oppose	
Support	0 (0)	0 (0)	17.4 (16)	8.7 (8)	26.1 (24)
Leaner	0 (0)	0 (0)	26.1 (24)	21.7 (20)	47.8 (44)
Oppose	0 (0)	0 (0)	15.2 (14)	10.9 (10)	26.1 (24)
Column total and percentage *n*	0 (0)	0 (0)	58.7 (54)	41.3 (38)	

Note: In each cell, the top number is the cell percentage; the bottom number is the cell *n*, with row and column totals along the right-hand side and the bottom, respectively. Table *N* = 92, with one case omitted because of missing data. For details on variables, see appendix 2.

opposition. In both types of district, seniors appeared to be unanimous or nearly unanimous in demanding repeal. However, there was a critical difference between the two types: seniors in opposition districts were less intense in their calls for repeal. To see the distinction, consider one legislator's description of senior opinion in her strong opposition district:

> They wanted it repealed. They were very strong about it. John Smith, who started up the repeal effort, came from my district. They were very aggressive, and very demanding. . . . They felt it was something they hadn't asked for and didn't want. They wanted to provide it on their own, and they resented that they were not asked about it. They were not interested in having a rational discussion about it. [89]

Contrast these strong words with a second legislator's description of his district, coded as an opposition district:

> I got less of a response than other people, not like Rostenkowski, who was mobbed at his office. I heard from real polite people who said, "this is what I want." It wasn't an adamant response. . . . It wasn't the type of thing where they said, "you're my representative, you've got to do this." It was more like, "I've been told this, is it true?" [13]

In the language of chapter 4, seniors in strong opposition districts were virtually certain that repeal was best; those in opposition districts, while favoring repeal, had some uncertainty.

Why this opposition? One flaw was that Catastrophic Coverage did not address seniors' first priority: coverage for long-term care—extended stays in nursing homes. As one freshman noted:

> Catastrophic provided increased hospital benefits, but people figured that if they had to stay in the hospital that long, they weren't coming out. There is clear interest in what seniors want, long-term care. They are petrified about going into a nursing home and losing every dime they've ever had. They felt disappointed that long-term care was not provided. [83]

Apparently, at least some of the initial support for Catastrophic Coverage arose from the belief that it would pay for long-term care. This support disappeared as seniors learned what the program actually provided.

But what about payment for extended hospital stays, prescription drug coverage, and the other provisions? Two problems made these provisions unattractive. First, for some seniors, Catastrophic Coverage simply was not a good deal.[2] Approximately seven million out of the thirty million retirees eligible for benefits received free or partially subsidized coverage from their former employers. For these seniors, Catastrophic Coverage duplicated their existing coverage—and they had to pay more for it.[3] In addition, while it is impossible to be sure, some legislators argued that future increases in the surtax would make Catastrophic Coverage more expensive than private sector insurance for seniors who faced the maximum or near maximum surtax.

For the vast majority of seniors, however, Catastrophic Coverage was a good deal—good in the sense that coverage would cost them almost nothing and yield attractive benefits. Why were they opposed? Simply put, the average senior held a wild overestimate of what they would have to pay. Time and again, representatives complained that "everyone thought they had to pay eight hundred dollars a year."[4] As one said,

> What I was getting were people who were writing in frightened, scrawled hands, saying "I'm seventy-five, on social security, and I can't afford to pay eight hundred dollars a year." The only people who were paying eight hundred were wealthy. The people who were writing were paying only four dollars a month. There was more misunderstanding on this than on any other issue. [72]

Apparently seniors accepted claims made by the National Committee to Preserve Social Security and Medicare, whose spokespeople, "later conceded that they could have misled members into believing that all beneficiaries would have to pay the $800.00 maximum [premium]" (*CQ Almanac 1989*, 150). In contrast, seniors appeared to ignore the AARP's efforts to build support for the program. As legislators described it, "the AARP had people resigning over this issue, saying they'd never join again", "the AARP took a beating", "AARP was in a furor, they almost had a revolt going on."

---

2. It is possible that strong opposition districts contained a higher proportion of these individuals. Unfortunately, the interview data do not provide enough information to test this conjecture. The same is true for available district-level data.

3. In principle, coverage was optional. However, an individual could opt out only by refusing to participate in Part B of Medicare, a heavily subsidized program that provides many valuable benefits. As a result, the "option" was no choice at all: seniors, even those subject to the full surtax, would find it cheaper to pay the tax than to buy equivalent insurance (Part B plus Catastrophic Coverage) from the private sector.

4. Even some legislators misunderstood the surtax—or so their comments indicate. One described the surtax as follows: "A constituent who had retired and was paying a little bit of taxes snapped a trigger and had to pay an additional tax. In the first year of the program, a couple paying 150 dollars in income tax had to pay an additional 1600 dollar surtax" [29]. In fact, under the program, the couple would pay less than a hundred dollars per year.

These comments illustrate the difficulties inherent in educating constituents about policy proposals. Not only are people hard to reach, they are also hard to convince. As one representative said,

> [Senior citizens] were stupid, and misled endlessly. One-half of those people were yelling, "you've got to repeal it." I asked them whether they made thirty thousand a year, and they said, "of course not." So I told them about the surtax, and how they probably wouldn't pay any tax at their income levels. And then they yelled, "you've got to repeal it." There was no way to talk with them, the misinformation was complete. [77]

The representative was almost certainly right: most seniors would pay almost nothing for coverage. However, even with the benefit of his position, an aggressive staff, and all the handouts and newsletters the taxpayers could provide, he was unable to change their opinions.

These comments also suggest an explanation for the massive shift in uncertainty between enactment and repeal. Apparently, many seniors, particularly those in strong opposition districts, went from being weak, uncertain supporters of Catastrophic Coverage to being dead-sure opponents. Many legislators attributed this change to the National Committee's unilateral opposition to the program. At first glance, this explanation seems plausible: Lupia (1992), for example, shows that rational constituents will alter their beliefs about policy proposals in light of interest group endorsements. But where did the almost complete reduction in uncertainty come from? While the intensity and the certainty of seniors' opposition are consistent with the National Committee's position, it is not obvious why many seniors bought into this position without reservation. The earlier comments about the AARP's lack of credibility with seniors suggest an explanation. Apparently many seniors interpreted the AARP's initial support for Catastrophic Coverage as a sign that the program supplied long-term care coverage, which the AARP has supported for many years. Some members of Congress also asserted that local representatives of the AARP had misled seniors about the program's benefits. As a result, when the true purpose of the program became clear, the AARP and its arguments lost all credibility with seniors, leaving the National Committee as the only group that could make a credible endorsement and deliver it to seniors across the country. A second possibility that yields the same prediction is that seniors attributed the AARP's position to the fact that the organization is a major supplier of prescription drugs and stood to gain a considerable amount of business from the drug provision included in the program.

Representatives

Representatives fell into three groups. The first group, comprising about one-fourth of the sample, were members who were unambiguous supporters of Catastrophic Coverage, such as this Democrat:

> I sensed that the opposition I was hearing was from people who felt they were paying too much, but that in the long run their interests were better served if it was not repealed. . . . I knew that the bill was done correctly. What needed to happen was for people in Congress to say, "we appreciate your views, but in the long run this is something you have to have." [62]

These legislators saw Catastrophic Coverage as a good deal: it did not provide long-term care, but it was unquestionably an advance. Some admitted to problems, such as the duplication of benefits for seniors who had free coverage from former employers, but thought the appropriate remedy was revision, not repeal.

There was an equally large group of opponents. A few voiced deep philosophical objections, citing the dangers of socialized medicine and extolling the virtues of private sector health insurance. By and large, however, opponents described Catastrophic Coverage as a bad deal. The benefits were not questioned, although most agreed that long-term care would be preferable. The problem was the surtax:

> [Catastrophic Coverage] was needed, but it should have been financed differently. The financing mechanism was simply not acceptable. It should have been added to the Medicare tax rate, and the benefits put in as part of the system that individuals pay for as an ongoing tax. Some may object, but that's the way to do it. You pay the tax when you're earning a salary, then you get the benefits when you're on a fixed income. [60]

Many opponents were also worried about the program's long-term viability: "no one could tell me what it was going to cost in five years," was a common complaint.

However, the largest group of representatives consisted of those who did not have a strong preference about Catastrophic Coverage. Some were basically indifferent: "I told [my constituents], 'I didn't think I made a mistake, but you think so. So I'm going to vote to repeal.' . . . I thought it was a good bill, but repeal didn't cost me anything" [33]. Others, such as these legislators, had an opinion, but an extremely weak one:

. . . it was perhaps the first step needed to be taken to answer the problem of the uninsured. But people rebelled. If I'm in the country and someone raises objections to Catastrophic, I tell them, what do we do about someone who's uninsured? What do we do? . . . [It was] a typical idea that ran into trouble. I didn't vote for it, but I have empathy for what we were trying to do. [78]

I thought the funding mechanism was better than not having any program, but it was the worst possible solution. It set a precedent for making people pay a user fee for basic health care. It was the worst thing to do, except for nothing at all. [30]

While each of these representatives had some sort of preference, the truth is that all three were on the fence, leaving them with little reason to vote against their constituents' wishes. If seniors wanted Catastrophic Coverage, they would vote for it; if seniors changed their minds, they would switch their votes as well.

Summary

It is clear that the nearly unanimous vote to enact Catastrophic Coverage vastly overstated both public and congressional support. Few legislators were strong supporters. Most legislators who voted in favor of the program did so only because they were assured that senior citizens wanted it. In truth, a significant number of seniors did not have a clear understanding of what kinds of benefits the proposal would provide. Moreover, a majority of the House either opposed the program on its merits or had no strong feelings. Once seniors decided repeal was preferable and their uncertainty disappeared, repeal was virtually a done deal.

Trust and the Repeal of Catastrophic Coverage

The simplest way to characterize trust on the repeal of Catastrophic Coverage is to say that no one had it. Only 19.5 percent (seventeen of eighty-seven) of the legislators in the sample reported trust on repeal. Moreover, only twelve members of the sample voted against repeal—ten with trust, two without. (The percentage of votes against repeal in the sample, 12.9 percent, is comparable to the percentage for the entire House.) While the absence of trust suggests why the program was repealed by a lopsided margin, it also complicates tests of the leeway hypothesis. Put simply, there is not much variance to explain. (Of course, as noted earlier, this problem was exacerbated by the decision to interview a simple random sample of the House.) The low variance makes it impossible to test the marginality hypothesis like in chapter 5 and complicates tests of the explanation hypothesis. In addition, the fact that so many legislators complied with seniors' demands for repeal means that few saw any reputational consequences—good or bad—from their votes. Of course, one of the reasons that compliance was endemic was that voting against repeal had a reputational cost—it would signal disagreement with seniors' interests. However, these costs cannot be investigated: few legislators voted against repeal, and virtually none did so without trust.

Notwithstanding these problems, this section applies the leeway hypothesis to the question of why some representatives were trusted on repeal while others—most—were not. It shows that the relative absence of trust can be explained by two factors: the intense opposition to the program in many districts and, more importantly, the problems inherent to signaling a common interest with a politically salient group of constituents. The analysis shows, first, that a representative was more likely to be trusted if she represented an opposition district rather than a strong opposition district. In addition, trust was more likely insofar as a representative had a record of past actions that indicated sympathy with seniors' concerns—their desire for additional benefits from the federal government. The best example of an action that had this effect was a representative's membership on the House Select Aging Committee. However, the analysis shows that representatives with records of strong support for proposals favored by senior citizens were no more likely to be trusted than legislators who were moderate or weak supporters. This finding is consistent with the logic advanced in chapter 3: in the main, attempts to assess common interests will exclude actions that are politically beneficial and low cost.

Beliefs about the Proposal

The effect of seniors' beliefs about Catastrophic Coverage on their willingness to grant leeway is easy to describe. The leeway hypothesis states that constituents are more likely to trust their representative insofar as they are unsure what outcome a proposal will produce if it is enacted. Recall that at the time Catastrophic Coverage was repealed, seniors in strong opposition districts were almost sure that repeal was preferable, while those in opposition districts had some doubts—although, as noted earlier, the absolute amount of uncertainty was small in both cases. In addition, beliefs in strong opposition districts may have failed to satisfy the lottery condition or the private information condition.[5] Therefore, holding other factors constant, legislators from opposi-

---

5. For a description of these conditions, see chapter 4.

tion districts should be trusted at a higher rate than those from strong opposition districts.

Beliefs about Common Interest

Defining the conditions for a common interest on Catastrophic Coverage requires, first, a definition of the interests senior citizens hold. Consider a simple definition: when considering these programs, seniors are net benefit maximizers (benefits minus taxes) who want more from government, not less.[6] Thus, their interests are served by enacting proposals that increase their net benefits and defeating (or repealing) proposals that would implement reductions. This conception of seniors as rapacious consumers of government largesse may seem immoral or unrealistic. Certainly some legislators argued that senior citizens have unrealistic expectations about what government can or should do for them. As one said, "Seniors are used to getting something for nothing, they're not used to paying something for something. They think it's their God-given right to get benefits at low or no cost" [89]. This analysis makes no judgment about the morality of seniors' interests. And, while it is possible to come up with exceptions, this assumption seems reasonable as a first-cut, general characterization. Most members of Congress would agree. As one Southern Democrat said, "When the country's running a deficit and someone gives you an entitlement, you should take it" [67].

Given this definition of seniors' interest, when would they infer a common interest with their representative on Catastrophic Coverage? Recall that seniors, regardless of their economic well-being, believed that the program made them worse off. Given this perception, a senior citizen will infer a common interest if he believes that his representative favors increases—or at least opposes reductions—in government transfers to seniors.[7] Leaving political considerations aside, such a representative would favor proposals that increased the senior's net benefits and oppose measures that reduced them. That is, if the representative knew that enacting Catastrophic Coverage made the senior better off, she would favor keeping it in place, and if she knew that the senior was worse off, she would favor repeal.

This answer suggests a simple prediction: a legislator was more likely to

---

6. The reader may object, citing chapter 2's criticisms of this motivational assumption. However, the discussion there centered on the use of this assumption to operationalize a legislator's interest in reelection. To say that seniors are fundamentally net benefit maximizers—within the limits of available information, of course—seems much less objectionable.

7. Given that the benefits and costs of Catastrophic Coverage were relatively modest, it seems unlikely that the program overshot a representative's preferences for increases or cuts.

be trusted on Catastrophic Coverage only insofar as she was thought to favor increases, or at least oppose cuts, in government transfers to senior citizens. Trust would not exist for a legislator who was thought to favor reductions in seniors' benefits. Similarly, trust would not exist for representatives who were thought to prefer that some seniors be made better off at the expense of others. For example, suppose a representative favored taxing Social Security benefits for high-income seniors but opposed taxing low-income seniors. In this case, seniors who saw themselves on the losing end of the representative's preferences would refuse to defer, regardless of what seniors on the winning end decided to do. Such a representative cannot be said to have voting leeway, since a substantial number of seniors would protest votes that ran against their demands.

These predictions suggest a partial explanation of why Catastrophic Coverage was repealed by such a wide margin and why trust was so rare at the time of repeal. For one thing, the condition for common interest is quite stringent: a representative has to favor increased benefits for virtually all seniors in her district. Any hint that a representative favors redistribution across senior citizens will lead some seniors to decide against trust. Even if a majority of seniors were willing to defer, the cost of voting against the demands of the remainder would remain substantial.

In addition, representatives also face fundamental limits on their ability to signal their beliefs about programs that benefit seniors. At first glance, there are many ways for a representative to signal her agreement with seniors' concerns: by going home and meeting with seniors, by voting in favor of programs that benefit seniors, or by making aggressive efforts to take care of seniors' casework. The problem is that a representative has reason to take these actions regardless of her policy concerns. Representatives invariably describe senior citizens as one of the most powerful voting blocs in their district, the one they would least like to anger. One truism on Capitol Hill labels Social Security as "the third rail of American politics: touch it and die." All of this is to say that members of Congress, regardless of their policy concerns, have reason to take actions of which seniors will approve. Insofar as seniors recognize this fact, actions that ostensibly signal a legislator's sympathy toward senior citizens may not have any reputation-building effect. Seniors are likely to see them as efforts to build support and win reelection, not as an expression of a legislator's policy concerns.

This problem is extremely acute for members of Congress whose principal activity on seniors' behalf was to vote in favor of programs that benefited seniors. Using voting scores compiled by the National Committee to Preserve Social Security and Medicare, the average voting score for members of the 100th Congress was 60.1 on a scale of 0 to 100, with high scores implying a higher proportion of "correct" votes. (For details on this index, see appendix

2.) Moreover, the average is somewhat depressed, since it includes "wrong" votes to enact Catastrophic Coverage. (Only two legislators received a perfect score of 100 for their votes in the 100th Congress, while in the 99th Congress fully 41.4 percent did so.) However, the logic described in chapter 3 suggests that even a perfect voting record, by itself, will not generate the perception of shared interests: the votes will be discounted as political gestures.

Does this mean that seniors will disregard all their legislator's actions? No. For one thing, actions that benefit seniors but that go far beyond what would be needed to attract their support indicate that a representative's apparent agreement with seniors' interests is in fact sincere. In contrast, the decision to act against seniors' demands will send the politically damaging signal that she does not share their interests. Examples would include votes in favor of taxing Social Security benefits or votes against increasing benefits for the "notch babies," seniors who lost benefits as a result of the 1982 Social Security reforms. The reasoning is simple. Given that political considerations would motivate a legislator to vote with seniors, not against them, the only type of legislator who would cast these votes is one who does not share seniors' interests—who believes that seniors should get less from government, not more. Thus, while a prosenior voting record by itself will not serve as a signal of common interest on Catastrophic Coverage, weak support or opposition should signal the absence of common interest.

Anecdotal Evidence

Representative's comments about trust on the repeal vote are consistent with the leeway hypothesis. For one thing, almost all of the legislators who reported trust came from districts characterized by opposition rather than strong opposition. Moreover, in opposition districts, trust came from actions that signaled a legislator's sympathy to seniors' interests. However, this signal was sent only by actions that went well beyond the minimum needed to attract seniors' support in the next election. The canonical description was offered by a Southern Democrat:

> I have a pretty good reputation on senior issues. I have one of the few offices with a senior coordinator, a retired person who keeps in contact with seniors. I'm on the Aging Committee. I fight for issues that concern them. For example, when repeal was finalized the Social Security Administration didn't plan to stop deducting the catastrophic premiums from Social Security checks for six months because it would be too much trouble to reprogram their computers. I was outraged. We've given them money to reprogram their computers, and while four dollars per month isn't a lot of money, it's vital if people were paying increased premiums

for medigap coverage. So [we] got them to issue the refund checks every two months. [72]

In political terms, all this representative had to do to generate favorable retrospective evaluations was vote for repeal, perhaps combined with a speech favoring prompt refund of the surtax. But he did more: he was part of a group that went to considerable length to force the Social Security Administration to begin the refund process. This action has the ring of a costly signal: only someone who sincerely cared about seniors' interests would invest so much time and energy getting the surtax refunded. A representative who was indifferent, or who thought seniors received too much from government already, would be content to vote for repeal, which would make seniors happy at no cost to her.

The contrast between members who had sent such costly signals and those who had not can be seen by comparing the above quote with one from a senior Democrat:

I spoke at some town meetings where [Catastrophic Coverage] was the issue, and heard those who came to talk about it. We decided there was an information gap. We had already put an item in our newsletter which explained the bill. When we started getting complaints, we figured they didn't have the facts. So we put out a special mailing just on Catastrophic that spelled out who would pay and the extent of the benefits. We found it made no difference. . . . I've spent 12 years in Congress, and 9 years on the City Council before that, but for the first time I found in social situations that I was fighting with my constituents over an issue. They were not persuadable, so I didn't see any gain in insisting I knew better. So I supported repeal. [30]

Both of these representatives voted for Catastrophic Coverage when it was enacted. Both came from districts that were coded into the opponent category. Both received high ratings from the National Committee to Preserve Social Security and Medicare—in fact the second legislator's rating is slightly higher.[8] Moreover, the second legislator is a strong supporter of liberal causes. One article even described his name as a synonym for "liberal." Liberal he may be, but nothing written about him, nor his comments during the interview, sug-

---

8. The first legislator received a rating of 88 based on his votes in the 100th Congress (1987–1988). The second legislator was not given a rating for the 100th Congress, since he missed too many votes. His score based on votes during the 98th and 99th Congresses was a perfect 100.

gests that he is an advocate for senior citizens. Thus, it is no surprise that the first legislator reported trust on Catastrophic Coverage while the second did not.

The point is simple. The interviews suggest that a variety of actions served as costly signals of common interest on Catastrophic Coverage— assigning staff to focus on legislation of interest to seniors, membership on committees such as the House Select Committee on Aging, and a variety of activities associated with markup, floor proceedings, and oversight. The common factor appears to be intensity. Decisions about staff allocation, committee assignments, or policy leadership are costly signals: they shape the range of legislation that a representative can knowledgeably involve herself in.

In contrast, the interviews confirm that actions such as voting in accordance with seniors' demands or holding frequent town meetings with senior citizens were not viewed as signals of a legislator's policy concerns. A large percentage of the Congress has such a voting record; virtually all members try to meet with seniors whenever possible. Yet there is no evidence that these actions helped to generate trust on the repeal vote. By the logic discussed in chapter 3, this negative effect is not surprising. Such actions can reasonably be seen as political gestures designed to win support rather than expressions of genuine concern. Certainly the actions are politically beneficial: seniors would rather have a representative who votes their way and meets with them rather than one who does not. However, precisely because the actions are politically valuable, they say nothing about a representative's policy concerns.

The interviews also produced a surprise: several legislators believed that membership on the Ways and Means Committee helped to generate trust. For example, when asked why seniors deferred to his judgments about Catastrophic Coverage, one Northern Democrat simply said, "I'm on the [Ways and Means] committee where it originated. We deal with numbers and ratios every day. Four hundred other members don't" [47]. Since Ways and Means has jurisdiction over Social Security and Medicare, in principle it seems reasonable that membership on the committee could function as a signal of common interest. The problem is that members of Ways and Means are thought to act as prudent managers of Social Security and Medicare, not as agents of benefit-hungry seniors (Strahan 1990, especially chaps. 2 and 6). However, because seniors believed that enacting Catastrophic Coverage made them worse off, perhaps the perception that a legislator was a "prudent manager" and favored the status quo with regard to senior citizens would be enough to generate the perception of shared interests. An alternate explanation is that membership on Ways and Means signals a member's expertise on complicated entitlement programs such as Catastrophic Coverage. If so, among legislators who, for whatever reason, were thought to have a common interest with seniors, those on Ways and Means may evidence higher rates of trust because they were more likely to be seen as having private information about Catastrophic Coverage.

The idea that committee membership signals a member's sympathy to senior concerns may seem inconsistent with chapter 2's description of constituents as uncertain and ill informed. However, representatives who noted the reputational effects of committee membership believed that constituents knew about their assignments. As noted in chapter 3, explanations might serve to disseminate such verifiable information, particularly over time. It is also possible that constituents are unaware of their representative's assignments but that membership on committees such as Select Aging is a proxy for a pro-senior reputation—a reputation that constituents are well aware of. Either way, dividing legislators on the basis of their assignments to Select Aging and Ways and Means should separate them on the basis of common interest assessments. However, if in fact committee membership proxies reputation, rather than serving as a signal of it, a committee-based analysis is likely to produce a substantial number of anomalies—cases in which trust exists when it ostensibly should not, or the reverse. Such anomalies would arise if, for example, legislators not on Select Aging have strong prosenior reputations because of their efforts to legislate new benefits for seniors. Alternately, legislators who are on the committee might have no reputation at all among seniors, or a reputation that indicates hostility to seniors' concerns.

Statistical Evidence

The anecdotal evidence suggests that a legislator whose record signals that she favors maintaining or increasing transfers to seniors should be trusted at a higher rate than a legislator who lacks such a record or who is seen as favoring reductions. As noted earlier, membership on the House Select Committee on Aging and membership on Ways and Means stand out as possible signals of this motivation. In addition, a record of consistent opposition to seniors' demands, expressed in terms of past votes, should signal the absence of common interest and be associated with lower rates of trust. In this analysis, voting scores issued by the National Committee are used as an estimate of a legislator's voting record on issues of interest to senior citizens. Both effects should be strongest among representatives elected from opposition districts: as noted earlier, the intensity of anti-Catastrophic feeling from strong opposition districts makes leeway unlikely there in any case. (All of the variables are defined and discussed in appendix 2.)

Table 11 examines legislators' reports about trust on the repeal of Catastrophic Coverage as a function of their committee assignments and voting records. The columns of table 11 divide legislators according to whether they represented a district that was opposed or strongly opposed to Catastrophic Coverage. The rows further divide legislators into four groups. Legislators who were not members of Select Aging or Ways and Means are divided into three groups: those with moderate or prosenior voting records, those with antisenior voting records, and freshman, who did not receive a rating from the National Committee. The final group contains legislators who were members of Select Aging or Ways and Means, all of whom had prosenior voting records.

Overall, the table provides modest support for the leeway hypothesis. The most obvious pattern is no surprise: virtually none of the legislators from strong opposition districts reported trust. Moreover, the table supports the hypothesis about voting records: looking at opposition districts, *no* legislator with an antisenior voting record reported trust, compared to approximately a third of legislators with a moderate or prosenior record. Freshmen lie somewhere in the middle, which seems sensible given that their constituents probably did not know much about their policy preferences. In addition, the table suggests that membership on Select Aging or Ways and Means signaled

Table 11. Trust on Catastrophic Coverage

		District Sentiment	
Committee Member?	Voting Record	Opposition	Strong Opposition
No	Freshman	22.2 (9)	0 (6)
	Antisenior	0 (6)	0 (4)
	Moderate, prosenior	31.6 (19)	0 (20)
Select Aging or Ways and Means	Prosenior	46.2 (13)	12.5 (8)

Note: In each cell, the top number is the cell percentage of legislators who reported trust on repeal; the bottom number is the cell *n*. Table *N* = 85, with eight cases omitted because of missing data. For details on variables, see appendix 2.

common interest. For one thing, the only legislator elected from a strong opposition district who reported trust was a member of Select Aging. Overall, 46.2 percent of legislators who belonged to one of the two committees reported trust. Taken by themselves, 50.0 percent (four of eight) of the members of Select Aging in this cell reported trust. Since all of these legislators were strong supporters of senior demands, this percentage can be compared to the 31.6 percent rate reported by legislators with similar records who were not on these committees. Clearly, there is a difference. And it is precisely the difference that would occur if committee assignments (or a reputation proxied by assignment) signaled common interest. However, it falls short of the usual grounds for statistical significance.[9] Still, the difference is in the right direction, as well as consistent with anecdotal data.

Testing the Explanation Hypothesis

The final step in the analysis is to test the explanation hypothesis—the assertion that explanations do not generate trust. Chapter 3 outlined two implications of this hypothesis. The first, strong implication is that legislators who deviate from constituent demands (here, vote against repeal) and report trust should also report a low rate of explanation. The second, weaker implication is that legislators who deviate and who report trust should do similar amounts of explaining compared to those legislators who complied with constituent demands (here, voted for repeal) and did not have leeway.

Tests of these implications are complicated by the nature of the data. First, only twelve legislators in the sample voted against repeal. Of these, ten believed they had leeway on repeal, while two did not. The small sample works in favor of the explanation hypothesis, making it harder to discern a statistically significant difference in the amount of explaining performed by legislators in different categories. The second problem arises from the circumstances of the repeal vote. During the time between enactment and repeal, various interest groups, such as the AARP and the National Committee, conducted extensive outreach efforts. These efforts undoubtedly increased the chances that all legislators would be asked for an explanation, regardless of how they had voted initially or on repeal. In addition, when asked about their explanatory efforts, many legislators did not distinguish between explanations of their vote on enactment and explanations of their later vote on repeal. Taken together, these complications inflate reports of explaining of

---

9. The percentage for legislators not on the committees is 31.6 percent. A difference-of-proportion test between this percentage and that reported by legislators on the two committees yields a t-score of 1.09, with $t = 1.3$ needed for rejection of the null hypothesis of no difference at the .10 level, one-tail.

Catastrophic Coverage—and reduce differences in the rates of explanation across categories.

With these problems in mind, the hypothesis is tested as follows. First, in order to eliminate a potential bias, legislators (mostly freshmen) who did not vote on enactment are excluded. These legislators might be expected to report lower amounts of explaining simply because they had nothing to explain. Second, the variable that codes a legislator's reports about explanation (major, minor, or none) combines her answers to two questions, one concerning explanations of the enactment vote, the other dealing with explanations of repeal. (Details are in appendix 2.) With these qualifications, the analysis proceeds as in chapter 5: legislators are divided into four groups depending on their vote on repeal and their expectations about trust. Data on explanations for legislators in each of these four groups are presented in table 12.

The data in table 12 do not provide strong support for the explanation

Table 12. Explanations and Catastrophic Coverage

Trust	Vote	Type of Explanation		
		Major	Minor	None
No	For repeal	40.4 (21)	26.9 (14)	32.7 (17)
	Against repeal	0 (0)	100.0 (1)	0 (0)
Yes	For repeal	25.0 (1)	50.0 (2)	25.0 (1)
	Against repeal	55.5 (5)	33.3 (3)	11.1 (1)
Column average and *n*		40.9 (27)	30.3 (20)	28.8 (19)

Note: For each category, the table reports the number and percentage of legislators who reported major, minor, or no explaining. Table $N = 66$, with remaining cases omitted because of missing data or because they did not vote on enactment. For details on variables, see appendix 2.

hypothesis. For one thing, it shows higher rates of explanation on Catastrophic Coverage compared to the Ethics Act. Recall that in the case of the Ethics Act, except for legislators who ignored constituent disapproval to vote yea, virtually no legislator reported a major explanation. However, in the case of Catastrophic Coverage, 40.9 percent (twenty-seven of sixty-six) of legislators reported a major explanation. Moreover, of the nine legislators who deviated with leeway, 55.5 percent (five of nine) reported a major explanation. But the glass is half full: even on Catastrophic Coverage, which legislators agreed was one of the most salient issues of the 100th Congress, nearly half of the legislators interviewed did not report a major explanation. Some did no explaining at all. Thus, even in the case of Catastrophic Coverage, the picture of legislators going home en masse to report on their actions vastly overstates the amount of explaining that actually took place.

However, the data do provide weak support for the explanation hypothesis. As shown in table 12, the difference in explanation rates between legislators who deviated with leeway and those who complied without leeway (40.9 percent versus 55.5 percent), while certainly in the right direction, is nowhere near statistical significance.[10] In other words, while we can say that a substantial number of legislators explained their votes on Catastrophic Coverage, there is no evidence that their efforts built trust. Skeptics might counter by saying that the table shows that many legislators tried to explain their way to trust, but only a few were successful. While this claim is difficult to test, it is not supported by legislators' comments about their explanations. The best example is from a freshman Democrat:

> I explained [my vote] by telling the ones who were on SSI that they'd only pay 4 dollars a month and get expanded services. Plus, I felt that people with the ability to pay should be taxed, not those without the ability to pay. The majority of my constituents are low-income, and they reacted positively. [25]
> *Why did the explanation work?* People know me, I've been around a while and my record is consistent. I grew up poor, I live in a poor district, I've never had the support of the big people in the party. I ran for ten years against the organization to become Ward Chairman. So I have the confidence of the people. They felt that if I did it, it must be the right thing. [25]

True, the legislator explained his actions. And constituents deferred to his judgment. But the explanation did not generate trust or defuse the contro-

---

10. Formally, the t-score is .848 with df = 59, with t = 1.3 required for rejection of the null hypothesis of no effect at the .10 level, one-tail.

versy. The critical factor was that constituents interpreted the representative's action in light of what they knew about him—their belief that he shares their interests. On learning that he had voted to save Catastrophic Coverage, their response was to think that he had private information about the program, not that he had acted against their interests.

Summary

This chapter's analysis of the repeal of the Medicare Catastrophic Coverage Act has provided evidence that is consistent with both the leeway hypothesis and the explanation hypothesis. Trust on the repeal vote arose from perceptions of common interest—the belief, engendered by actions such as joining the Select Aging Committee, that a member of Congress favored increased (or sustained) government transfers to senior citizens. Simply voting in favor of senior-preferred proposals was not enough to generate this reputation: a legislator had to have a well-established, long-term record of tending to seniors' concerns. A consistent record of votes against seniors did, however, signal that a legislator disagreed with the interests held by this group. Moreover, while a substantial number of legislators explained their votes on Catastrophic Coverage, there is little evidence that their efforts built trust. A majority of legislators who were trusted did little or no explaining. And many legislators who did a great deal of explaining found that their efforts had no effect.

Comparing Trust on the Ethics Act and Catastrophic Coverage

The leeway hypothesis is built on the assumption that trust decisions are made one proposal at a time. As noted earlier, this assumption would cause great distress to many legislative scholars, who argue that trust is largely an all-or-nothing phenomenon. In their view, a representative is either trusted on matters great and small, or she is not.[11] Both empirical chapters provide circumstantial evidence for the contextual view. For one thing, when members of Congress think about trust, they appear to ask, "will my constituents trust me in this particular situation," not, "in general, do my constituents trust me?" In addition, assessments of common interest, which play a critical role in trust decisions, are made in context—they depend on what constituents know about the proposal being voted on and whether their representative has taken

---

11. By itself, the assertion is not inconsistent with the rational actor assumption or the Evaluation game. For example, some action or attribute (probably the latter) might be seen as proof that a representative shares all of her constituents' policy concerns. If so, some representatives, those who hold the action or attribute, will be trusted across a range of proposals.

certain actions or holds certain attributes. It is also important to note that none of the actions or attributes that signaled a common interest on the Ethics Act did so on Catastrophic Coverage, or vice versa.

With two case studies in hand, additional evidence can be presented in favor of the contextual view. This evidence involves a comparison of legislators' reports about trust on the two proposals, the Ethics Act and Catastrophic Coverage. The question is, of those legislators who reported trust on one proposal, how many were trusted on both? The idea that trust is a blanket decision implies that out of the set of legislators reporting trust on at least one proposal, the proportion reporting trust on both proposals should be high. A low proportion would support the contextual view, although a high proportion could be explained by establishing that a large number of legislators happened to have the right mix of actions and attributes that generated trust in both situations.

The comparison of trust on the two proposals is shown in table 13. The table divides legislators on the basis of their reports about trust on the Ethics Act and Catastrophic Coverage. For example, the top-right cell shows the number of legislators who said they were trusted on Catastrophic Coverage but not on the Ethics Act; the top-left cell shows the number who were not trusted at all. In general, the table supports the assumption that trust decisions are made at the level of individual proposals. A near majority, forty (47.1 percent), of legislators reported that they were not trusted on either proposal. And, of the forty-five legislators who were trusted on at least one proposal, only nine (20.0 percent) were trusted on both. The rest, thirty-six (80.0

Table 13. Comparing Trust on the Ethics Act and Catastrophic Coverage

	Trust on Catastrophic	
Trust on Ethics	No	Yes
No	47.1 (40)	8.2 (7)
Yes	34.1 (29)	10.6 (9)

Note: Numbers in each cell are the cell percentages and cell *n*, respectively. Table $N = 85$, with 8 cases deleted due to missing data.

percent), were trusted on one proposal, usually the Ethics Act, but not on the other. Moreover, while trust on one proposal is associated with higher levels of trust on the other, the relationship is modest at best. For example, of the legislators who reported trust on Catastrophic Coverage, 56.3 percent were trusted on the Ethics Act, versus 42.0 percent of those who reported no trust on Catastrophic Coverage. And 23.7 percent of the legislators who reported trust on the Ethics Act also reported trust on Catastrophic Coverage, compared to 14.9 percent of those who reported no trust on the Ethics Act. Thus, if there is some underlying factor that generates trust regardless of context, few legislators in the sample had it.

While a firm conclusion will require the analysis of additional proposals, the overwhelming message from table 13 is that constituent trust is a contextual phenomenon. Constituents do not appear to make overarching decisions about trust. Rather, they make independent decisions on individual proposals, based on what they know about the proposal and about their representative. The reader might argue that the Ethics Act and Catastrophic Coverage were completely different proposals and that there is no reason to expect trust on one to imply trust on the other. That is exactly the point. Trust depends on context. Perhaps some representatives hold reputations for being altruistic or for agreeing with all of their constituents' policy concerns. It would be no surprise to see representatives trying to engender one or both of these perceptions. However, it appears that few legislators are successful in these efforts to the point that they are trusted regardless of what they vote on.

CHAPTER 7

Conclusions

My dad, who was the mayor when I was growing up, said to me once, "you can't succeed in this business if you don't know things other people can't see, feel, or touch."[1]

—A Midwestern Democrat

This book began with a series of questions. Why do constituents trust elected officials? What factors make trust likely—or unlikely? And how do a representative's expectations about trust influence her behavior? I am now in a position to offer some answers. The first section of this chapter reiterates and extends the findings of the analysis. The remaining two sections address the issues raised in chapter 1. How should the electoral connection be modeled? Is representative democracy viable in the modern era? What do its failures signify? Can it be improved?

These answers rely heavily on information supplied by members of Congress. The analysis has specified the world as representatives see it: the idea that constituents are rational actors, the assumption that constituents view explanations as cheap talk, and the belief that motives are assessed using stereotypes. In addition, most of the data used to test the leeway and explanation hypotheses came from interviews with legislators. While this approach is certainly reasonable, and perhaps inevitable, skeptics might argue it fails to capture trust decisions as constituents see them. Perhaps constituents take explanations seriously. Perhaps they overlook stereotypes in favor of another technique. Perhaps they are boundedly rational. It is impossible to say. Of course, the assumptions held by legislators are consistent with the logic of game theory. And since legislators face a considerable incentive to develop accurate expectations about trust, it would be surprising if their perceptions were far off the mark.

In addition, the results are limited in their focus on vote decisions, rather than considering the processes that bring proposals to the floor and determine how they are voted on. I cannot say that trust or expectations about trust have a direct impact on these decisions. However, insofar as expectations

---

1. Caro (1982, 319) attributes a similar quote to the late Sam Rayburn.

about trust influence members' vote decisions, they should also have an indirect impact on choices made in anticipation of these decisions, including the formulation of legislative proposals and the selection of procedures that govern floor consideration. Now that we have a better idea of where trust comes from, and a better idea of how legislators act in light of expectations about trust, we are in a better position to understand the processes that generate vote decisions and trust decisions.

Results

This section is organized around four general statements: two deal with trust and trust decisions, one discusses explanations, and one focuses on reputations. The emphasis is on setting out general principles about legislatures, representation, and the findings of this analysis.

Trust Is Rational

The analysis shows that once some necessary conditions are satisfied, trust hinges on two factors: how much constituents know about the options before their representative and their beliefs about common interest. Of these perceptions, the latter is more important by far. As long as constituents assess a high enough probability of common interest, they will trust their representative regardless of how much they know about policy options. Conversely, if constituents think that a common interest is unlikely, they will never trust their representative, even if they know very little. The analysis also shows that assessments of common interest are made in context, in light of information about a proposal's possible effects. As a result, rational constituents can opt for trust even if they are sure that their representative disagrees with their preferences across policy outcomes. Trust decisions do not involve a general assessment of motive; rather, the critical question for constituents is whether their policy concerns are compatible with those held by their representative in light of the options before her: enacting or defeating a specific policy proposal.

These findings concern behavior on high-salience proposals. While the Evaluation game does not address the question directly, it appears that trust is ubiquitous on low-salience proposals, in the sense that few constituents are interested enough to monitor the legislator's behavior or to form evaluations after votes are cast. In these cases, trust arises from indifference or perceived unimportance. Even in these cases, however, a representative's vote decisions are politically significant—they signal information about her policy concerns.

The analysis also reveals that constituents use stereotypes to form beliefs about their representative, including beliefs about common interest. This finding explains why a representative's visible attributes are often imbued with political significance: these characteristics signal policy concerns. Thus, to say that voters want a representative who shares their religious views, their ethnicity, or their race, or a representative who is a war hero, a businessman, or a famous athlete does not imply that they are motivated by cultural forces or extrapolicy goals. Instead, appearance and actions outside politics matter because these characteristics signal motivation, talent, and character. Moreover, voters appear to be sensible in their use of stereotypes. Voters appear to discount actions that they see as the product of calculation—particularly verbal assertions—as well as actions or attributes that do not signal anything about a representative's policy concerns. Voters do not blindly assume that a representative who looks like them will share their policy concerns. Instead, voters assess their representative's motives by forming conjectures about the kinds of goals and motives that are signaled by different actions and attributes.

As stated in chapter 2, these findings assume that voters consciously monitor their incumbent's behavior with an eye toward evaluating her performance in office. However, the alternate assumption, that monitoring is largely an elite-level phenomenon, would not change any of the conclusions developed here. In both cases, we could say that incumbents make vote decisions based on expectations about how their constituents would react to different votes—expectations that reflect the substance and certainty of constituents' beliefs about a proposal and their assessments of common interest. The only difference is that in the case of elite-level monitoring, constituents would do much less evaluating, as potential challengers would have no incentive to transmit information about an incumbent's fidelity to constituent demands or deviations that could be explained in terms of trust.

These findings about trust have been confirmed by empirical analysis—again, with the caveat that the data reflect a representative's perspective on trust and trust decisions. On the Ethics Act vote, trust arose from actions and attributes that signaled a legislator's agreement with constituent interests: no pay raise without ethics reform. In particular, wealthy legislators and those who had substantial honoraria and outside income were more likely to report trust than middle-class legislators who lived off their congressional salaries. The irony of the Ethics Act was that on a proposal intended to help middle-class people stay in Congress, reduce the influence of special interests, and eliminate conflicts of interest, deference was most likely to arise for wealthy members and those most vulnerable to charges of capture and conflict. Similarly, in the case of Catastrophic Coverage, only those legislators who had taken costly, policy-relevant actions on seniors' behalf—allocating staff, joining committees, building legislative coalitions and monitoring implementation—had leeway on the repeal vote. Simply voting in favor of senior-preferred proposals, or taking other actions consistent with the pursuit of reelection, did not build trust.

These results confirm the premise stated in chapter 1: constituent trust is a rational response to asymmetric information. It does not arise because constituents abdicate their power to control elected officials. It does not arise because representatives hoodwink the electorate with rhetorical tricks. Rather, trust occurs because constituents want to tap their representative's private information and expertise. And trust occurs only when constituents believe that it improves the chances of achieving favorable policy outcomes. Much of the apparently "irrational" character of real-world trust decisions can be explained as the product of rational behavior under asymmetric information. Rational, sensible constituents may refuse to trust their representative even when they know very little and are sure that she knows all. On the other hand, deference can be a sensible choice even when constituents are sure that their representative's preferences differ from their own. Thus, if constituents are observed to make bizarre decisions about trust, the presumption should be that the explanation lies in their beliefs, not in their inability to make good decisions.

Of course, to say that trust is rational does not mean that constituents always make the right decision. The results presented here support the view expressed a generation ago by V. O. Key: ". . . the electorate behaves about as rationally and responsibly as we should expect, given the clarity of the alternatives presented to it and the character of the information available to it" (1966, 7). Uncertain, misinformed constituents are vulnerable to mistakes. They may refuse to defer in situations where deference would lead to superior policy outcomes. They may defer in situations where refusing trust would yield a preferable result. However, these mistakes should be understood as an inevitable product of behavior under asymmetric information. They do not represent a departure from a rational calculus. Of course, we cannot say that all constituents meet this standard. Within the central tendency of rational, goal-directed behavior, there may be citizens who are seemingly irrational, whose decisions follow a different logic, or no logic at all.[2] This finding should be no surprise: even Key believed that some voters behaved "in odd ways indeed" (1966, 7). It appears that these voters are few in number, few enough that a model that presumes rational calculation can make accurate predictions about trust. Even as legislators disparage attempts to model their behavior or the behavior of constituents, they seem to make decisions based on the assumption that most of their constituents are rational actors, who behave much as the Evaluation game says they do.

---

2. Of course, this label must be used with care, since apparently irrational behavior may well be a sensible response to extremely peculiar beliefs.

Trust Varies with Context

The analysis has replaced the idea that constituents make blanket, overarching decisions about trust with the idea that trust is conditional and contextual. Trust depends on who a representative is—or is thought to be—and what she votes on. Therefore, it should be no surprise to find that the average representative is trusted in some situations but not in others. Moreover, looking at a single policy proposal, we should expect to find that some representatives are trusted while others are not. And, looking across a range of proposals, we should expect to find that some representatives are trusted more often than others.

Many factors generate this variation. Constituents may know a lot about some proposals and little about others. Beliefs about a proposal may vary across districts. Representatives may have different attributes or different records of past actions. Moreover, beliefs about common interest are fundamentally driven by context. Even if two representatives have the same actions and attributes, their constituents may arrive at different judgments about common interest, owing to variation in their beliefs about a proposal or in the content of their stereotypes. Finally, if constituents believe that their representative disagrees with their notions of good policy, they may assess a high probability of common interest on one proposal and a low probability on another, even if the two proposals deal with similar policy questions.

These factors were observed in the empirical analysis. While a substantial number of legislators reported trust on the Ethics Act and a smaller number did so on Catastrophic Coverage, very few reported trust on both proposals. Moreover, none of the factors that generated common interest on the Ethics Act did so on Catastrophic Coverage, or vice versa. The overwhelming picture is of constituents making independent decisions in different contexts.

These findings may seem incompatible with the conventional wisdom. In works such as Fenno 1978, Jewell 1982, or Kingdon 1981, legislators talk in general terms, as though trust did not vary with context. It appears that these quotes capture a legislator's overall assessment of trust, looking across the entire range of actions she takes. In that limited sense, the assessments are trivially accurate: most of a legislator's actions are of such low salience that she has trust by default—no one cares. Asking legislators about trust in the context of specific, high-salience actions reveals a different answer. Here legislators do not rely on abstract assessments. Rather, they ask, "what do my constituents know about this proposal?" and "what do they think my motives are?" A legislator's general statements about trust may provide insight into kinds of proposals she expects to vote on or confirm the idea that few proposals arouse much interest among voters. However, these statements do not bear much relation to the legislator's expectations about trust in the context of specific high-salience proposals.

Of course, to say that trust will vary with context does not guarantee that this variation will always be observed. Almost any congressional scholar could name representatives who apparently have leeway in all contexts—or never have leeway, regardless of what they are voting on. These anecdotes can easily be explained in terms of the theory developed here. For cases of universal trust, some legislators may hold a mix of actions or attributes that signals common interest across a wide range of policy areas. Alternately, certain actions or attributes might signal a legislator's overall agreement with constituent concerns, or signal that she is an altruist whose only goal is to serve their interests. Such "principled agents" would be trusted regardless of context. (One problem for future research is to identify the actions or attributes that might have these effects.) On the other side, it would be no surprise to find some number of luckless representatives who lack the characteristics needed to signal common interest in any context, and who therefore will be trusted rarely, if at all. These exceptions do not invalidate the general principle developed here: decisions about trust and expectations about trust are formed in context and can be understood only in context. The fact that a legislator almost always has leeway—or never does—is the product of decisions made by constituents one vote at a time, based on the information available to them at the time of their decision.

The Content of Reputations

Congressional scholars agree that reputations—beliefs about a representative's abilities and motivations—are politically salient. Our theories fall short on the specifics. What kinds of beliefs are contained in a reputation? Where do reputations come from? The analysis of trust, augmented by legislators' broader comments, does not provide complete answers to these questions, but it supplies a number of useful insights.

At a minimum, it appears that a legislator's reputation includes beliefs about her policy concerns. As we have seen, these beliefs provide constituents with a basis for assessing common interest and thus for making decisions about trust. Certainly that is what members of Congress expect, both when forming expectations about trust and when assessing the reputational consequences of their behavior. Presumably reputations incorporate other beliefs that are relevant to trust decisions, such as assessments of a legislator's expertise—the set of policy areas in which she can be expected to have private information.

It appears that reputations are fairly complex. When making judgments about common interest, constituents do not simply ask, "is our representative a good person?" Nor do they see her as a member of Congress, undistinguishable from her colleagues. Rather, their judgments are fairly specific and couched in terms of the proposals at hand. Does the representative care about pay and ethics, or just pay? Does she believe that government should do more for seniors, or less? These findings imply that we cannot explain trust, or election outcomes, by talking about Congress's reputation among the voters; we must speak of the reputations held by this representative or that representative. Moreover, the content of a legislator's reputation can be explained only by considering the situations—the trust decisions—that led constituents to form certain judgments about their representative.

The analysis also sheds some light on where reputations come from: at least in part, they are the product of stereotypes. In general, constituents ignore their legislator's statements about her motives or talents—perhaps because they do not hear them, perhaps because they discount them as cheap talk. As a substitute, constituents look to actions and attributes, signals that speak louder than words, or at least with more meaning. The analysis has shown that stereotyping can be explained by the logic of rational choice. In other words, constituents appear to be rational actors when they form beliefs, as well as when they act on them. The only caveat is that we do not know where stereotypes come from. The possibility that they are formed by a nonrational process cannot be dismissed. However, given the results presented here, and the literature reviewed in chapter 3, it would be extremely surprising if people were any less systematic and careful about forming stereotypes as they are when using them.

Finally, the analysis highlights a number of difficulties that legislators face when trying to shape their reputations. One problem is contact: constituents are hard to find. In addition, representatives are prisoners of the stereotypes held by their constituents. Representatives can publicize their actions or attributes, or take some actions over others, but they cannot shape the inferences that voters draw from these factors. In addition, politically beneficial reputations are hard to build. It is easy for a representative to signal a disagreement with her constituents—all she has to do is act against their demands. However, actions that nominally indicate agreement will often be interpreted as signals of a legislator's interest in reelection or her desire to build a reputation for trustworthiness. As a result, these actions will not affect beliefs about the legislator's policy concerns, even if they have real policy consequences. The only exception is if a politically beneficial action is so extreme or so costly that an interest in reelection or a concern with reputation would not provoke a legislator to take it. Only then will the action be viewed as a signal of policy concerns.

The Significance of Explanations

Congressional scholars describe explanations as a means for persuasion—a way for representatives to shape constituent opinion, influence retrospective evaluations, and build trust. Their descriptions suggest the image of a representative casting the proverbial tough vote, then returning home to educate constituents. This view does not jibe with reality or with the expectations of members of Congress. It is clear that legislators expect to explain their votes and worry about how different votes can be explained. However, legislators do not think about explanations in terms of persuasion. Legislators certainly offer explanations when asked and sometimes volunteer explanations without being asked, but they are under no illusions that their efforts will build trust.[3] These suspicions were confirmed by empirical analysis. In the case of the Ethics Act, the only group of legislators who reported significant amounts of explaining were those who angered their constituents by voting for the proposal. These efforts appeared to be aimed more at appearing accountable than at altering evaluations of the vote. Almost no explaining occurred in districts where legislators exploited trust to vote for the proposal. Data from Catastrophic Coverage are less clear-cut but provide no support for the conventional wisdom.

These findings, together with comments made during the interviews, suggest that when a legislator describes a vote as explainable, what she means is that she expects constituents to evaluate the vote favorably, because it is consistent with their demands or because they are inclined to trust her judgment. It does not imply that the legislator expects to be called on to explain, plans to volunteer an explanation, or believes that an explanation, *by itself,* will alter constituents' beliefs or generate trust. Rather, explainability is defined in terms of how constituents will react to a vote, as they assess what their representative has done in light of what they know about her motives and the options before her.

These findings leave plenty of room for legislators to be strategic about explaining. Explanations may be informative when they reveal information that constituents can verify independently. Moreover, decisions about venue —the identity of the audience or of other speakers—may speak volumes about a legislator's motivations, even as her comments are discounted. Explanations may help legislators signal accessibility and accountability. Alternatively, explanations themselves may not send this signal, but a failure to

---

3. There is no reason to think that legislators underestimated their powers of persuasion. If anything, their comments might be expected to be biased toward the conventional wisdom, since this view is consistent with normative concepts of good representation such as Pitkin's (1967) definition, offered in chapter 2.

explain may be a politically damaging signal of inaccessibility, particularly in situations when a legislator deviates from constituent demands.

Of course, while the interviews suggest that persuasive explanations are few and far between, they do not imply that such explanations never occur. The possibility of persuasive explanations is also suggested by analyses of signaling such as those discussed in chapter 3, which suggest that talk is not inevitably cheap, even among eminently rational actors. But even in these analyses, the decision to listen to another player's statements is driven by assessments of motive—assessments that are similar to the concept of common interest developed in this study. Thus, in highlighting the importance of common interest perceptions, the analysis presented here provides insight into the vast majority of trust decisions, where explanations apparently have no effect on the beliefs held by constituents, but also into the comparatively rare case where explanations have a direct and immediate effect.

Modeling the Electoral Connection

For congressional scholars, this book has a simple implication: if we want to predict behavior in the modern Congress, we need to account for expectations about trust. We cannot assume that legislators, even those who put reelection first, will blindly implement constituent demands or opinions. We cannot assume legislators always have the freedom to act on the basis of their private information. And finally, we cannot make simplistic assumptions about trust. Trust is not a random variable, nor is it a constant across representatives and across contexts. Rather, it is the product of a rational, systematic, and predictable calculus.

This finding has three wider implications for models of congressional behavior. First, scholars should accept, once and for all, that legislators pursue reelection by implementing constituent demands, not constituent interests—by taking actions, not securing outcomes. Second, scholars must realize that the votes that are typically used to estimate a representative's policy concerns—votes on high-salience policy proposals—contain this information only under fairly restrictive circumstances. Finally, scholars should focus on explaining legislatorial behavior at the level of individual votes or other actions rather than analyzing behavior in terms of summary indices.

Demands, Interests, and Induced Ideal Points

The analysis presented in chapter 4 improves on the work of Mayhew (1974) and others by explaining why, in a world where constituents care about policy outcomes, legislators earn political credits as a function of their actions rather than for the consequences of their actions. This regularity does not exist because constituents are stupid or because they care about actions independent of policy consequences. Rather, constituents focus on actions because, in general, legislators cannot be rewarded and punished on the basis of outcomes. As a result, legislators pursue reelection by doing what their constituents want—by implementing constituent demands, not by serving constituent interests. A representative has no reason to implement constituent interests, except insofar as actions along these lines are politically expedient or conform to her own ideas of what is best. Scholars may wish to evaluate legislatorial behavior in terms of constituent interests, but they cannot assume that these interests directly influence behavior.

This admonishment may seem obvious and well accepted, but it is not. As noted in chapter 2, statistical analyses of legislatorial behavior often specify the reelection goal in terms of constituent interests. A similar assumption underlies the use of induced ideal points. These analyses begin with a false premise. This is not to say that representatives never implement constituent interests: it is easy to imagine situations in which they do. This is not to say that constituents do not care about outcomes: they do. The point is that fidelity to constituent interests is at best a consequence of a legislator's decisions or a criterion for evaluating policy outcomes, not a direct influence on behavior.

One implication of this finding is quite simple: scholars who use demographic or socioeconomic variables as proxies for the constituency in analyses of roll-call behavior need to find variables that tap demands rather than interests. This distinction is not a matter of semantics. Insofar as constituents are ill informed about the policy process, variables that are good proxies for interests may be bad proxies of demands. For example, suppose constituent interests reflect a desire to maximize net benefits from government. Intuitively, one could determine whether the enactment of a distributive proposal served these interests by comparing the benefits that constituents would receive from the proposal with the cost they would pay in the form of additional taxes. This measure could be proxied by variables that capture a district's demographics or its industrial base. However, if benefits are concentrated and costs dispersed, as they usually are in the case of distributive proposals, it would be easy for constituents to overestimate benefits and underestimate costs. Moreover, across a number of districts with the same interests, beliefs about a proposal's financial impact may vary because of idiosyncratic local events or factors such as education and political awareness. Either way a proxy variable might be an adequate measure of interests but fail to account for demands.

In addition, scholars must abandon attempts to model legislatorial behavior using induced ideal points. The intuition behind this construction is simply wrong. In general, legislators do not pursue reelection by serving constituent interests. Even on high-salience proposals, a legislator's actions are a function of her policy goals, the demands made by constituents, and the legislator's expectations about trust. Moreover, behavior is not the product of a trade-off between reelection and policy goals; rather, different goals are relevant in different contexts. These suspicions were confirmed in chapter 4. While representatives motivated by policy and reelection will sometimes behave as though they held induced ideal points, this assertion does not hold in general. In some cases, it is impossible to locate an induced ideal point that accounts for a representative's behavior. In other cases, such points exist but lie far outside the range where they intuitively should be located. These difficulties arise even in relatively simple situations where policy outcomes and policy goals can be specified in a one-dimensional space. Therefore, models that use the induced ideal point assumption are flawed. Regardless of their elegance or their simplicity, they begin with an incorrect specification of the forces that generate legislatorial behavior.

Votes as Ideological Measures

As noted in chapter 2, many scholars use a legislator's voting behavior, typically votes on high-salience proposals, to measure her ideology or policy concerns. This tactic is dangerous. In a legislature such as the modern Congress, where the reelection goal is ubiquitous, high-salience votes are often driven by political considerations—the desire to avoid unfavorable evaluations or reputational damage. While these votes may be useful predictors of a representative's future behavior, they say nothing about her policy goals. Moreover, the votes signal ideology only in a limited range of situations: first, when a proposal taps an intense policy concern—intense enough to override the reelection imperative; second, when the representative expects trust and ignores the reputational consequences of her vote—or when the vote has positive consequences for her reputation; and third, when a proposal is of sufficiently low salience that a representative's vote decision has no political consequences.

These findings imply that the standard type of data used to construct ideological scales for members of Congress, votes on high-salience proposals, are precisely the wrong ones to use. These votes have the advantage that they address issues that capture the public's attention and, owing to their salience, are likely to be the product of considered, calculated decisions. However, in some unknown proportion of the time, a legislator's votes on these issues will reflect political considerations rather than ideological concerns. While the proportion of such political votes is likely to vary across legislators, the impression from the interviews is that most legislators cast a substantial number. Under these conditions, ideological estimates derived from high-salience votes are likely to reflect constituent demands, not a legislator's policy concerns. High-salience votes can be used to measure ideology only if it can be established that they are uncontaminated by political concerns. This is a difficult requirement to meet. As a result, measures that use votes cast on low-salience proposals are likely to produce better measures of ideology, even if the proposals arouse little interest among legislators or their constituents. Of course, even these votes might be contaminated by reputational considerations. However, this danger is offset by the fact that votes on low-salience proposals are unlikely to be the focus of retrospective evaluations.

The problem, of course, is to devise a better measure of ideology. One possibility, currently under study by Patrick Sellers and me, is a measure derived from legislators' affiliations with congressional caucuses (e.g., the Democratic Study Group and the Conservative Opportunity Society). However, the availability of such data, as well as the internal and external validity of an ideological index derived from it, remain open questions at this time.

One Action at a Time

Finally, the analysis suggests that studies of the legislative process should aim at explaining individual decisions, such as a legislator's votes, rather than focusing on aggregates of individual-level decisions, such as ADA scores. Intuitively, aggregate-level analyses yield general principles about legislatorial behavior rather than findings that are contingent on the specifics of a particular vote or decision. This intuition is wrong, at least when applied to voting on high-salience policy proposals. There, representatives appear to make vote decisions one at a time, based on the particulars of the situation before them. At most, vote decisions are linked by reputational concerns. Thus, aggregate-level analyses run the risk of modeling behavior at a level that representatives do not consider when making their decisions.

Additional questions can be raised about measurement and model specification in aggregate-level analyses. Looking at individual votes, it makes sense to talk about a legislator choosing between personal policy concerns and constituent demands, contingent on her expectations about trust and her appreciation of reputational costs and benefits. Can these factors be specified at the aggregate level? It would be difficult. One problem would be to develop a summary measure of a legislator's policy concerns across a range of policy areas. A similar problem would arise when trying to measure constituent demands. Even if such measures could be developed, an aggregate-level model would also have to account for members' expectations about trust—expectations that vary across members and across proposals. Thus, even if the intuition about aggregate-level analysis were true, it might be impossible to specify a reasonable aggregate-level model.

A similar argument applies to elite interviews: if we want to know how legislators make decisions, we need to ask them specific questions about actual decisions.[4] For example, when asked about vote decisions in the abstract, most legislators will identify themselves as a delegate or as a trustee—usually the latter. However, such statements do not reveal much about the forces that determine legislators' behavior, particularly their votes on high-salience proposals. Many times during my interviews, a legislator would begin by saying that she was a trustee, or a delegate, and then explain her votes on the Ethics Act and Catastrophic Coverage as exceptions to the general rule. At best, the frequent references to trustee behavior might reflect the fact that in most situations legislators use their judgment, but only because the political consequences of different actions are nil.

Of course, the interviews reveal that when legislators discuss actual decisions, they use the delegate-trustee distinction as a summary description of the forces driving their vote decision. In other words, a legislator who complied with constituent demands in order to attract favorable evaluations would say she acted as a delegate, while a legislator who used her judgment would say she acted as a trustee.[5] But there is no evidence that legislators hold role orientations that determine their actions across a range of proposals. Having said she acted as a trustee on one proposal, a member was just as likely to say that she was a delegate on the other. The overriding impression is that most legislators are politicos; the forces driving their actions, and thus whether they behave as delegates or as trustees, vary across contexts.

In sum, since legislatorial behavior depends so heavily on context, we cannot hope to study it in the abstract or at the aggregate level. And we cannot ask legislators to do the abstracting for us. It appears that general propositions about vote decisions—or any other kind of legislatorial behavior—must be derived from the study of actual decisions, however difficult this task might be.

Evaluating Congress, Reforming Congress

Democratic theory posits that legislators will act in accordance with constituent interests. Yet even a cursory glance through the scholarly literature or the op-ed pages suggests that real-world politics does not match our expectations. Many of these arguments center on the claim that constituents are unable to make good decisions about trust—either they trust too little, or they trust too much. These charges are troubling. Much of our faith in democratic institutions rests on the assumption that democratic theory is a descriptive as well as a normative theory. Continued faith in representative government requires, at a minimum, a response to the charge that constituents cannot take the actions

---

4. I am indebted to David Price for this insight.
5. This finding is similar to a point made by Fenno (1978, 161–62).

needed to give elected officials the right incentives—the incentives needed to produce fiduciary behavior.

Are these charges true? While we cannot say they are completely false, we can say at least that they are overdrawn. Much of the behavior cited as evidence against democratic theory admits to a different explanation. Even if constituents know very little about policy options, they may do better—better in terms of policy outcomes—by deciding against trust. Similarly, trust may be the preferred option for policy-minded constituents who are well-informed about the policy process. Moreover, trust can be preferable even if constituents are unsure about their representative's policy goals—even if they know that her goals differ from their own. Of course, the ability to identify these alternate explanations does not mean that the critics are wrong. It suggests, however, that the real world is more complex than they appreciate.

More importantly, the case studies of the Ethics Act and Catastrophic Coverage, as well as discussions with members of Congress, suggest that constituents in contemporary America make good decisions about trust. They do not defer randomly. They do not make once-and-for-all decisions. Rather, trust decisions are made in context. Constituents take into account what their representative is voting on. What outcomes might be produced? To what extent can they say different outcomes are likely or unlikely? In addition, constituents take account of their representative's possible motives and her expertise. What is the likelihood of a common interest? What are the chances that she knows something that they do not? Thus, to the extent that we see constituents making good decisions about trust—or bad ones—our analyses should begin with the assumption that these decisions are the product of calculation, not good fortune or bad luck.

Will rational decisions about trust restore the fiduciary ideal? No. For one thing, constituents can decide, correctly, that trust is unwarranted, even if they are sure that their representative knows much more about policy options than they do. In these situations, the best that constituents can do is force their representative to implement their demands or follow their opinions, even though this strategy may yield inferior policy outcomes. In addition, constituents will sometimes make the wrong decision about trust. Their beliefs about a proposal may be incorrect. Stereotypes may lead them to the wrong conclusion about their representative's goals. As a result, constituents may decide against trust in situations where a common interest exists or decide in favor of trust when it does not. Finally, even if constituents allow their representative to act as a free agent, there is no assurance that she will take advantage of her discretion. Constituents can only create the opportunity for trustee behavior; they cannot mandate it or be sure that it has occurred.

Moreover, even rational constituents will sometimes find themselves at the mercy of politicians who are willing to gain office and political power by playing into the electorate's ill-conceived notions about the policy process. Again, this possibility does not imply that voters are unable or unwilling to make good decisions about trust. It is yet another consequence of the fact that constituents do not have—and cannot be expected to have—full information about policy options and motivations. Under these conditions, it is no surprise to observe political demagogues being rewarded for choices that have unfavorable consequences. Voters are simply doing the best they can given what they know. The problem is that they do not know everything.

What is to be done? Here the answers are less certain. The analysis does not reveal a magic bullet, a change in constituent behavior or political institutions that would bring legislators closer to the fiduciary ideal. If anything, it suggests that this effect will be extremely difficult to produce. Insofar as voters appear to be rational actors, it is difficult to imagine how their behavior might be improved; any advice is vulnerable to the charge that if it had merit, voters would be using it already. Real reform will require modifications in the game that representatives play with their constituents, such as changes in available information, in the types of people who are elected to office, or in the content of proposals they are made to vote on. Yet it is difficult to identify a beneficial change. The remainder of this chapter critiques three reforms that have received much attention in recent years: enhanced deliberation of policy options, the centralization of congressional power, and the imposition of term limits. I close with some remarks about the viability of democratic theory in light of contemporary criticisms.

Deliberation

For some scholars, meeting the expectations of democratic theory requires changes that would eliminate, or at least mitigate, the informational gap between voters and elected officials. Dodd, for example, offers the following diagnosis of contemporary politics:

> More so than at any other time in the nation's history, Congress is elected and organized to serve the disparate elements of a self-interested public rather than to identify and foster the shared concerns of a public-spirited citizenry. Congress increasingly lacks the ability to recognize the mutual concerns and shared interests of the public, and the ability to discover new governing principles that could resolve our policy dilemmas and renew public faith in government. (1993, 418)

Dodd's comments mirror the views advanced by Elizabeth Drew (1992) in chapter 2: citizens fail to see that their interests are best served by measures that require short-run sacrifice. Because of this misperception, citizen demands are based on a narrow conception of interests—one that excludes mutual concerns and shared interests, one that relies on existing policy solutions rather than searching for better ones.

Based on his diagnosis, Dodd (1993) calls for the formation of an emergency joint committee of Congress.[6] This committee would hold televised national hearings that would ". . . shift the public debate away from a focus on the nature and extent of bureaucratic service delivery, and the role of legislators in facilitating that process, and toward an emphasis on government restructuring. . . . In shifting the logic of politics, Congress and its leaders would shift the electoral calculus of voters, and thus the political strategies of politicians" (Dodd 1993, 433). In other words, Dodd expects that the committee's proceedings would inform the electorate and change the nature of their demands. As a result, members of Congress would face new incentives and would be able—or forced—to enact better policies.

A similar solution is proposed by Smith, who argues in favor of measures that would increase the amount of congressional deliberation: " . . . discussion among legislators is the means by which common interests are distilled from narrow interests, innovative public policy is identified and nurtured, and members of the public become educated about the substantive and political implications of the policy options they face" (1989, 238). Again, the expectation is that additional deliberation would inform citizens about the true effects of policy options, thereby creating support for painful but necessary policy choices. In addition, the process would presumably help citizens to recognize situations in which they know very little about policy options, allowing them to consider whether trust might be preferable.

The results developed here suggest that Dodd and Smith are putting too much faith in deliberation. Their expectation is that citizens would actually listen to arguments made in committee hearings or on the floor, as though they were all attending a town meeting on the state of the nation. But as noted in chapters 2 and 3, the average citizen shows a sensible lack of interest in the political process. Whether the changes proposed by these authors would increase citizen interest in politics is very much an open question.

Even if the problem of contact can be overcome, proponents of deliberation face a second problem: credibility. Will the electorate believe statements made by their representatives, who may have a stake in the outcome? Deliberation sounds a lot like cheap talk. Constituents might see deliberation as an attempt to build support for proposals that benefit elected officials or organized interests rather than offering unbiased information.[7] Some proponents

---

6. Both in intent and method, Dodd's emergency joint committee is much the same as Ross Perot's "electronic town meeting."

7. An example of this response is seen in the debate over the pay recommendations made by the Quadrennial Commission in late 1988. For more details, see Wilkerson 1991.

of deliberation recognize this problem. Dodd, for example, suggests that his emergency joint committee include "a diversity of members, across ethnic, gender, and ideological lines" (1993, 432). Even then, voters may not be sure enough about common interest to defer to the committee's collective judgment—or even to the judgment of some individuals on the committee. Moreover, even if the membership of the committee mirrors the demographic makeup of the electorate, the mere fact that they are representatives may be enough to skew perceptions of their goals and motives.[8]

The authors' response to these criticisms might be that increased deliberation is intended to help members of Congress develop new policy solutions, not just sell new solutions to the public. However, as Krehbiel (1991) notes, mechanisms already exist in Congress for developing new proposals and informing members about their details. Recall Elizabeth Drew's comment in chapter 2: "It's not the processes that are the main problem now but the public's aversion to giving anything up, and our leaders' reluctance to lead" (1992, 88). Deliberation, to have any effect at all, must be aimed at educating the public, not members of Congress. In sum, measures designed to increase congressional debate and deliberation on issues of the day will certainly produce more talk. But there is considerable doubt that anyone will listen, or having listened, be swayed.

Empowering the Leadership

Recent studies of the House of Representatives emphasize the policy-making powers of the congressional leadership. Rohde (1991) describes how Speaker Jim Wright used agenda-setting powers to facilitate the enactment of controversial proposals. Bach and Smith (1988) show how Special Rules are used to implement outcomes preferred by majorities in the Democratic Caucus. Kiewiet and McCubbins (1991) show that the caucus stacks the membership of the Appropriations Committee to similar ends. And Arnold (1990) highlights the role of the leadership in enacting tax reform.

With these examples in mind, reform might involve giving the leadership additional control over committee membership and proceedings, as well as new powers to shape floor debate and voting. The hope would be that the leadership will use these powers to oversee the writing of controversial proposals and to expedite their consideration by the full House. The leadership would also choose policy instruments and procedures that minimized political

---

8. Again, consider the Ethics Act. Intuitively, constituents would be likely to defer to someone who faces the same financial pressures they do or who voluntarily decides to follow good-conduct codes. However, legislators fitting this description were unlikely to have leeway. Middle-class legislators could not escape the charge that they wanted a raise under any circumstances. A previous decision to refuse honoraria and curtail outside income ensured that a legislator faced a financial incentive to vote for the proposal.

costs. In the language of the Evaluation game, the aim would be to maximize policy uncertainty and engender perceptions of common interest.

The successful enactment of the Ethics Act suggests that the leadership can, on occasion, act to smooth the passage of controversial proposals. Combining a pay raise with ethics reforms helped generate trust, since it altered voters' beliefs about their representative's incentives to vote for the package. Policy uncertainty was increased by bringing the proposal to a vote on short notice and with little debate. In addition, the Ethics Act was voted on under a closed rule, which prevented amendments designed to strike the raise provisions. Finally, the leadership concealed an additional piece of information: the order in which members voted on the Ethics Act.[9] Secrecy was of enormous benefit to legislators who supported the act but who ultimately voted against the proposal. Many waited to vote until the measure received a majority. An assistant whip cited the potential danger of this strategy:

> A pollster told me that I only had two options: vote yea and take the money, or vote no and refuse it. If I were running against someone who voted nay, I'd look at when they voted. Some of the opponents voted nay only after there were 218 yea votes and the motion was sure to pass. I'd rather run against someone who voted no late than someone who voted yea early. [11]

By making it impossible to find out when a legislator voted, the leadership shielded late-voting members from the politically damaging charge that they had gone on the record only after the result was certain.

However, focusing on the leadership's success in the case of the Ethics Act ignores fundamental limits on their ability to shape policy outcomes. As noted in chapter 4, tactics that increase voter uncertainty may not be enough to generate trust. If voters think that a common interest is unlikely, they will refuse to trust their representative regardless of their uncertainties about policy options. Markup specialists must also find policy instruments that engender perceptions of common interest. Such instruments will not always be available. Consider the next attempt to raise congressional pay. For the moment, congressional salaries are revised annually to control for inflation. History suggests that these yearly raises are likely to be postponed or repealed entirely.[10] The problem is, now that honoraria and outside income have been banned, what new provisions can be included in the next raise proposal to

---

9. Several legislators indicated that the electronic voting system in the House records this information as a matter of course. However, no one in the Office of the Majority Whip, who controls the voting system, would admit that such data exist.

10. A similar mechanism was in effect during the 1980s, but attempts to appropriate funds to cover yearly adjustments were always defeated when brought to a vote.

reinforce perceptions of common interest? Having raised pay once, the leadership may find it hard to repeat their success.

Finally, perceptions of common interest may be negatively correlated with attempts to manipulate constituent beliefs. In early 1989, Congress attempted to enact a pay raise without a roll call vote. Voters may have been opposed to a pay increase, but they were even more opposed to the idea that legislators could get a raise without voting on it. Rather than shielding members from political fallout, the procedure created a political problem for anyone who did not vote against it—including legislators who would have been trusted on a straight up-or-down raise vote. Wilkerson (1991) makes a similar point in his historical survey of raise proposals. He argues that tactics designed to enact these proposals have a limited lifetime: after repeated use, voters come to see them as political camouflage and penalize members who agree to their use.

In sum, empowering the congressional leadership will not eliminate, and perhaps not even mitigate, the problems caused by asymmetric information. Certainly the leadership can help to solve the coordination problem among competing coalitions or speed the consideration of majority-preferred proposals. And perhaps the leadership can, on occasion, enact laws by manipulating constituent uncertainties. But it appears difficult for the leadership to engender perceptions of common interest for backbench legislators. Moreover, the history of raise votes suggests that attempts at political engineering may destroy the very perceptions they are designed to create. Thus, we cannot rely on the congressional leadership to solve our problems.

Term Limits

As of January 1993, voters in twenty-four states have approved term limits for their state legislature and, in most cases, for their congressional delegations.[11] Arguments for term limits center on two conjectures. The first is that term limits will change the mix of people elected to office. The expectation is that representatives elected under term limits would be more likely to know of and share their constituents' interests on major issues of the day. Fund argues that with term limits, ". . . no longer would those political offices be held by longtime incumbents. They would be held by citizen legislators, who would be more disposed to represent the will of the people and rein in the out-of-control bureaucracy that now substitutes for a general government" (1992, 237).

The second conjecture is that, holding congressional composition constant, term limits will increase the probability that elected officials will act in

---

11. For details, see Galvin 1992.

accordance with their constituents' interests. This change would be produced in two ways. For one thing, legislators who know their tenure is limited would have little reason to favor special interests as a way of attracting campaign funds and other electoral resources. Term limits would also reduce a legislator's incentive to take actions that are politically attractive but ultimately harmful to constituents. Voting against constituent demands might cost a member her seat, but this penalty would have little bite if the member knew that she would have to retire soon in any case. This conjecture looms large in arguments for term limits, as a change in legislatorial incentives is the only sure consequence of putting limits in place.[12] Moreover, the argument receives support even from opponents of term limits. Fiorina, for example, argues against term limits, but notes, " . . . if our legislators were less vulnerable and less responsive, they might be willing to make tough, but nationally beneficial decisions, and we would probably rate our legislatures more highly" (1992, 55).

The Evaluation game allows an analysis of this conjecture. This evaluation, contained in appendix 3, shows that term limits never increase the probability of fiduciary behavior. If anything, the probability is lower under term limits. The intuition is simple: term limits reduce the options available to constituents. A representative who puts reelection first is a valuable asset, in that constituents can affect, if not determine, whether she implements their demands or uses her judgment. If constituents are rational actors, their decision between control and discretion takes into account the likelihood of fiduciary behavior in each case. This choice is lost under term limits. With limits, a representative acts as a free agent regardless of whether constituents want her to. Thus, in situations where constituents are inclined to trust their representative in any case, term limits will not increase the probability of fiduciary behavior.[13] However, in situations where constituents believe that trust is unwarranted, term limits will reduce the probability of fiduciary behavior.

The test in appendix 3 does not resolve the debate over term limits. However, it shows that the first-order effect of limiting tenure does not produce beneficial effects. Term limits may stiffen the backbones of elected officials, enabling them to make hard choices. The problem is that constitu-

---

12. Because of limitations in our current understanding of candidacy decisions, it would be difficult to evaluate the argument that term limits will bring new blood into the political process. The seminal works in this area are Black 1972 and Rohde 1979. Canon 1990 is a notable recent effort.

13. The only caveat is that term limits might eliminate a legislator's incentive to consider the reputational consequences of her actions. If so, imposing limits might increase the probability of fiduciary behavior in situations in which a representative expects trust but conforms to constituent demands out of reputational concerns. However, these concerns would probably remain under a system of term limits insofar as legislators anticipated running for other offices after their forced retirement from Congress.

ents often do better with a representative whose backbone is subject to their recall. While term limits may elect a better class of legislator or reduce the power of organized interests, these benefits must be balanced against the costs identified here. Firmer conclusions must await results from an experiment now underway. In more than twenty states, politicians and would-be politicians are beginning to make career decisions with term limits in mind. By the beginning of the next century, we will be in a position to assess whether legislatures elected under term limits are qualitatively different from those elected under unlimited tenure and to evaluate the policy implications of this change. At that point we will be able to determine, empirically, whether term limits help to elect a different breed of legislator. For now, term limits are an experiment—one with sure costs and uncertain benefits.

What Next?

These reform proposals share a common expectation: if we make the right changes to the legislator-constituent game, representatives will have the right incentives and behave as democratic theory says they should. Yet even in a world where deliberation occurs, terms are limited, and the congressional leadership is empowered, it is easy to think of situations in which constituents will not know enough to make good decisions about public policy and cannot rely on elected officials to make the decision for them. Moreover, unless a reform somehow eliminates constituent uncertainty about policy options or leads to the election of representatives who share their constituents' interests—effects that seem impossible to achieve—congressional behavior will always fall short of the fiduciary ideal.

The problem is our expectations. Democratic theory tells us how representatives should act, but we cannot expect such behavior under real-world conditions. The situation may be unfortunate, but it appears inevitable. Representatives will always have private information about policy proposals. Their motives will always be difficult to assess. Under these conditions, our inability to give representatives the right incentives is no surprise: perfect control is impossible in all other situations characterized by asymmetric information. To put it another way, the problem is not with representative government; rather, representative government is an example of a generic and intractable problem. The solution is not to abandon this form of government or to explain its failures by saying that voters or elected officials fall short of some normative ideal. The solution is to accept the nature of the representational game.

Appendixes

APPENDIX 1

The Evaluation Game

This appendix describes the Evaluation game using formal game-theoretic language. It also states, and proves, Proposition 1, which characterizes equilibrium behavior in the Evaluation game.

The Evaluation Game

In the Evaluation game, a representative (R) votes on a policy proposal (β). Following the terminology in chapter 4, β is a policy proposal which, if enacted, will produce a new policy outcome. (Recall that policies are means, outcomes are ends, and players have policy preferences across policy outcomes.) After the vote, constituents, modeled as a unitary actor (C), make retrospective evaluations. R has two kinds of private information. First, she knows what her policy goals are. Second, she knows what will happen if β is enacted. C has some information about these factors, but R always knows more. Both players are fully informed about other features of the game.

Asymmetric information. Before R and C choose their strategies, a nonstrategic player, Nature, selects the values of two random variables, E and D. E determines the outcome produced by enacting β; D determines R's preferences across policy outcomes. All other features of the game are fixed and known to both players.

Variable E takes on two values, 0 (with probability $1 - e$) and 1 (with probability e), where $0 < e < 1$. If $E = 1$, the enactment of β yields outcome b_3; while if $E = 0$, the enactment yields outcome b_1. Given Nature's move, b_y is defined as the outcome (b_1 or b_3) that will be produced if β is enacted. The status quo outcome, which prevails if β is defeated, is labeled b_2.

Variable D takes on values 0 (with probability $1 - d$) and 1 (with probability d), with $0 < d < 1$. If $D = 0$, R holds the same policy goal and policy preferences as C: $b_1 \, p \, b_2 \, p \, b_3$.[1] If $D = 1$, R holds one of five orderings, all of which differ from C's:

---

1. The $D = 0$ case can be seen as capturing two scenarios: R shares C's policy goal, or R is motivated by an altruistic concern over C's welfare.

Case 1: b_3 p b_2 p b_1
Case 2: b_2 p b_1 p b_3
Case 3: b_2 p b_3 p b_1
Case 4: b_3 p b_1 p b_2
Case 5: b_1 p b_3 p b_2.

The proof of Proposition 1 is organized in terms of the five cases. However, Proposition 1 itself describes equilibria in terms of certain assessments held by C. (These will be defined later.) These assessments provide a common metric for describing equilibrium behavior in all five cases.

A situation of asymmetric information exists in the Evaluation game because when R votes, she knows the values of E and D. In contrast, when C makes his evaluation, he knows the values of e and of d but not E and D. These asymmetries reflect the ideas discussed in chapter 1: constituents are uncertain about the policy effects of legislative proposals and about their representative's policy goals. C knows what R's policy preferences *might* be and the likelihood that R has each possible ordering but does not know what R's preferences actually are. C also knows the likelihood that enacting β will produce either b_1 or b_3 and knows how desirable each outcome is given his goals but does not know what the actual result will be if β is enacted.[2]

Finally, C's beliefs about the probability of Nature making different choices are labeled as follows:

$p_1 = p$ (E = 1 and D = 1)

$p_2 = p$ (E = 0 and D = 1)

$p_3 = p$ (E = 1 and D = 0)

$p_4 = p$ (E = 0 and D = 0).

For example, at the beginning of the game, before observing R's vote, C's beliefs are $p_1 = $ (e)(d), $p_2 = (1 - e)(d)$, $p_3 = (e)(1 - d)$, and $p_4 = (1 - e)(1 - d)$.

Strategies and trust. A strategy for R specifies her vote, yea or nay, as a function of her policy goals and information about β. Formally, R's strategy, denoted r(####), tells whether she votes yea or nay given E and D. The first

---

2. For example, suppose e = .4. In this case, C knows there is a 60 percent chance that β will produce b_1, and only a 40 percent chance that it will produce b_3. Thus, b_1 is C's best guess about what outcome will follow from enacting β. But there is a good chance—40 percent—that the guess is wrong.

number gives R's vote (1 = yea, 0 = nay) when D = E = 1, the second if D = 1 and E = 0, the third if D = 0 and E = 1, and the fourth if D = E = 0. If, for example, R uses the strategy r(0101), she votes yea if E = 0, and nay otherwise.[3] R is pivotal in the Evaluation game, meaning that if she votes yea, β is enacted, yielding outcome b_y (b_1 or b_3, depending on E). Similarly, if R votes nay, β is defeated, preserving the status quo outcome b_2. Finally, given R's preferences, r(m) is defined as her policy-max strategy, the strategy that yields her preferred policy outcome given values for E and D and R's preferences when D = 1. The definition of r(m) varies across cases 1 through 5 as follows:

Case 1:   r(1001)

Cases 2–3: r(0001)

Cases 4–5: r(1101)

C's strategy gives his evaluation, favorable or unfavorable, of a yea vote and a nay vote. Formally, C's strategy is denoted c(##), where the first number tells how C will evaluate a yea vote (1 = favorable, 0 = unfavorable) and the second gives his evaluation of a nay vote. For example, by using the strategy c(10), C evaluates a yea vote favorably and a nay vote unfavorably. Trust exists only when C uses c(11)—he evaluates both yea and nay votes favorably.

Payoffs. The payoffs of R, $E(u_R)$, and C, $E(u_C)$, are composed of two elements: one a function of the realized outcome, denoted u (.), the other a function of C's evaluation (k for R, t for C).

C's policy goals are defined by an ordering across b_1, b_2, and b_3: b_1 p b_2 p b_3. Thus, if C knew that E = 0 and b_y = b_1, he would prefer to enact β, since he prefers b_1 to the status quo b_2. If, however, C knew that E = 1 and b_y = b_3, he would want to defeat β, since he prefers b_2 over b_3. C's outcome payoff is labeled $u_C(.)$; the three possible payoffs he can receive are ordered $u_C(b_1) > u_C(b_2) > u_C(b_3)$. This ordering follows C's preferences across b_1, b_2, and b_3. The payoffs are abbreviated as follows:

$$u_C(b_1) = u_1$$

$$u_C(b_2) = u_2$$

$$u_C(b_3) = u_3.$$

---

3. The analysis is limited to pure strategies.

In addition, C incurs a cost $t = 1$ whenever he makes an inaccurate evaluation of R's vote.[4] This can happen two ways. The first possibility is when C issues an unfavorable evaluation in a situation where R's vote maximizes $u_C(.)$ given E. For example, suppose $E = 0$, R votes yea, and C uses $c(01)$: here R's vote is consistent with C's interests (it yields b_1, which C prefers to the product of a nay vote, b_2), yet C issues an unfavorable evaluation. The second situation is when C issues a favorable evaluation given R's vote does not maximize $u_C(.)$ given E. An example is if $E = 0$, R votes nay, and C uses $c(01)$: now R is rewarded for deviating from C's interests.

R's outcome payoffs when $D = 0$ are labeled $u_{R0}(.)$, and take on the same relative magnitudes as those held by C. R's outcome payoff when $D = 1$ is denoted $u_{R1}(.)$. The relative magnitudes of $u_{R1}(b_1)$, $u_{R1}(b_2)$, and $u_{R1}(b_3)$ vary across cases 1 through 5 and conform to the definition of R's policy preferences when $D = 1$:

Case 1: $u_{R1}(b_3) > u_{R1}(b_2) > u_{R1}(b_1)$
Case 2: $u_{R1}(b_2) > u_{R1}(b_1) > u_{R1}(b_3)$
Case 3: $u_{R1}(b_2) > u_{R1}(b_3) > u_{R1}(b_1)$
Case 4: $u_{R1}(b_3) > u_{R1}(b_1) > u_{R1}(b_2)$
Case 5: $u_{R1}(b_1) > u_{R1}(b_3) > u_{R1}(b_2)$

R also incurs a cost k if she receives an unfavorable evaluation from C. This portion of R's payoff reflects the electoral value of favorable retrospective evaluations.[5] Formally,

$$k > | u_R(b_y) - u_R(b_2) | \quad \text{for } b_y = \{b_1, b_3\}.$$

The magnitude of k is sized such that R always prefers to cast a vote that will be evaluated favorably over one that will be evaluated unfavorably, regardless of the policy consequences—that is, R values reelection over policy. If R valued policy over reelection, the sign would be reversed.

C's Assessments. The conditions for equilibria in Proposition 1 are expressed as a function of two transformations of e and d.[6] The first is **c**:

---

4. As long as t is positive, equilibria are not sensitive to its value. Assuming that t takes on different values given C makes different kinds of mistakes (rewarding a deviation versus punishing fidelity) changes the conditions under which strategy pairs are equilibria but does not eliminate them entirely.

5. These costs could also be specified by assuming that R benefited from favorable evaluations but did not incur costs from unfavorable evaluations or if she incurred both benefits and costs. None of these changes would alter the characterization of behavior in Proposition 1.

6. These transformations, particularly the formula for **c**, may seem arbitrary. To some degree, they are. (In particular, the fact that **c** varies from 0 to 1 is purely a matter of convenience.) The principal value of the transformations is that they capture equilibrium behavior in cases 1 through 5 within a common metric. In addition, they facilitate an easily explained, empirically relevant interpretation of Proposition 1.

$$\mathbf{c} = 2(.5 - e) \qquad e < .5$$

$$0 \qquad e = .5$$

$$2(e - .5) \qquad e > .5.$$

Informally, this variable measures how much C knows about β. It equals 0 when e = .5, increasing linearly to 1 as e goes to 0 or to 1. A higher value for c indicates that C is better-informed. For example, when e = .4, C knows that enacting β will produce b_3 with probability .4 and b_1 with probability .6. Thus, if C were forced to guess what the product of enacting β will be, he would say b_1. However, there is a 40 percent chance that his guess is incorrect. In contrast, suppose e = .1. Now C knows that enacting β yields b_3 with probability .1, and b_1 with probability .9. His best guess about the policy outcome associated with β is still b_1, but now there is only a 10 percent chance that he is wrong. All of this is to say that C has a better idea of what β will do when e = .1 than when e = .4. This difference is reflected in the value of c: it equals .2 when e = .4, and .8 when e = .1.

The second transformation of e and d, $\mathbf{z}$, is defined as a function of R's preferences when D = 1. (Recall that these preferences vary across cases 1 through 5. These are given in parentheses below):

$$\mathbf{z} = 1 - d \qquad \qquad \text{Case 1 } (b_3 \text{ p } b_2 \text{ p } b_1)$$
$$1 - d(1 - e) \qquad \text{Case 2 } (b_2 \text{ p } b_1 \text{ p } b_3), \text{ Case 3 } (b_2 \text{ p } b_3 \text{ p } b_1)$$
$$1 - ed \qquad \qquad \text{Case 4 } (b_3 \text{ p } b_1 \text{ p } b_2), \text{ Case 5 } (b_1 \text{ p } b_3 \text{ p } b_2)$$

Informally, $\mathbf{z}$ is C's estimate, given e and d, of the likelihood that he and R have a common interest on β. A common interest is defined as a situation in which, given R's policy preferences and the outcome b_y that β will produce if enacted, R and C have identical induced preferences with regard to β—that is, they agree that it should be enacted, or agree that it should be defeated. Because C does not know the values of E and D, he cannot determine for sure whether a common interest exists. However, he can use what he knows—e and d—to calculate the probability of a common interest.

To see how this calculation works, suppose that e = .4, d = .7, and R's preferences given D = 1 are b_2 p b_3 p b_1 (Case 3). (This situation corresponds to fig. 2 in chap. 4.) Table 14 summarizes the factors driving common interest in this example. Reading across table 14, the first column gives possible combinations of moves—values of E and D—that Nature can make; the second gives the probability that these values are realized given e and d. (In substantive terms, this is C's estimate of the joint probability that Nature has made the set of moves.) The third column identifies b_y, or the outcome that will result if R votes yea given Nature's move—b_1 when $E = 0$ and b_3 when $E = 1$. The fourth and fifth columns show whether C and R would each prefer to enact β or to defeat it in light of their policy preferences. Under the conditions defined by each row, a common interest exists if both players agree—that is, they have the same induced preferences regarding β given their preferences across outcomes and the value for b_y.

For example, suppose $E = 0$ and $D = 1$ (the third row in table 14). The probability of Nature making these choices equals $(1 - e)(d) = (.6)(.7) = .42$. Given $E = 0$ and $D = 1$, a yea vote by R enacts β, yielding outcome b_1 (recall that b_2 is always the product of a nay vote), and R holds policy preferences b_2 p b_3 p b_1. Thus, in substantive terms, .42 is C's estimate, given what he knows at the start of the Evaluation game, of the probability that he is in a game where enacting β will produce outcome b_1 and R's policy preferences are b_2 p b_3 p b_1. By assumption, C's preferences are b_1 p b_2 p b_3. R prefers to defeat β, as she has b_2 p b_1. C, on the other hand, prefers to enact β, as he has b_1 p b_2. Under these conditions, a common interest does not exist. In contrast, a common interest exists when $E = 0$ and $D = 0$ (the first row in table 14): enacting β yields b_1, which both players prefer to the status quo, b_2, which prevails if β is defeated. Note the probability of Nature making these choices equals $(1 - e)(1 - d) = (.6)(.3) = .18$.

Finally, from C's perspective, the likelihood of a common interest is the probability that Nature's choices of E and D yield a common interest—in table 14, $.18 + .12 + .28 = .58$, which is identical to the definition of **z** given above for case 3: $\mathbf{z} = 1 - d(1 - e) = 1 - (.7)(.6) = .58$.

Sequence of moves and extensive form. The sequence of moves in the Evaluation game is as follows:

Table 14. Common Interest in the Evaluation Game

Values of E and D	Probability of Occurence	Outcome from Enacting β (b_y)	C Prefers	R Prefers	Common Interest?
$E = 0$ $D = 0$	$(.6)(.3) = .18$	b_1	Enact $(b_1$ p $b_2)$	Enact $(b_1$ p $b_2)$	Yes
$E = 1$ $D = 0$	$(.4)(.3) = .12$	b_3	Defeat $(b_2$ p $b_3)$	Defeat $(b_2$ p $b_3)$	Yes
$E = 0$ $D = 1$	$(.6)(.7) = .42$	b_1	Enact $(b_1$ p $b_2)$	Defeat $(b_2$ p $b_1)$	No
$E = 1$ $D = 1$	$(.4)(.7) = .28$	b_3	Defeat $(b_2$ p $b_3)$	Defeat $(b_2$ p $b_3)$	Yes

1. Nature chooses E and D and informs R about the choices.
2. R chooses r(.).
3. After viewing R's vote, which depends on r(.), E, and D, C selects c(.).
4. C learns the values of E and D, and both players receive their payoffs.

In light of this sequence, figure 7 gives the extensive form of the Evaluation game. This extensive form is assumed to be common knowledge. Note R's information sets are all singletons, while C's information sets contain several nodes, reflecting the information asymmetry between the players.

Equilibrium Behavior in the Evaluation Game

This section presents Proposition 1, a characterization of sequential equilibria (Kreps and Wilson 1982a, 1982b) for the Evaluation game.

The combination of sequential moves and asymmetric information in the Evaluation game makes sequential equilibrium the obvious solution concept. In a sequential equilibrium for the Evaluation game, R's strategy maximizes $E(u_R)$ given C's strategy and Nature's choices (E and D); C's strategy maximizes $E(u_C)$ given R's strategy, her observed vote, and C's beliefs about E and D, and C's beliefs are calculated using Bayes' rule whenever possible. In addition, in the proof of Proposition 1, C's off-equilibrium beliefs satisfy two criteria. The first is the "intuitive" criterion (Banks and Sobel 1987; Cho and Kreps 1987) that C assigns zero probability to types of R who certainly lose by deviating from whatever equilibrium strategy R is supposed to be playing. The second criterion is that C's beliefs about all remaining types (who could conceivably have an incentive to deviate) are proportionate to his priors.

To begin with, Lemma 1 identifies the r(.) that is a best response to a given c(.).

Lemma 1: In the Evaluation game,

1. r(m) is R's best response to c(11), or c(00);
2. r(0000) is R's best response to c(10); and
3. r(1111) is R's best response to c(01).

Proof: If C uses c(11) or c(00), R's vote has no effect on whether she incurs the cost k, so his best response is the strategy that maximizes $u_{R0}(.)$ and $u_{R1}(.)$, r(m). If C uses c(01), R incurs k iff she votes yea, so her best response is r(0000). Similarly, if C uses c(10), R's best response is r(1111).

Next, Proposition 1 characterizes equilibrium behavior in the Evaluation game:

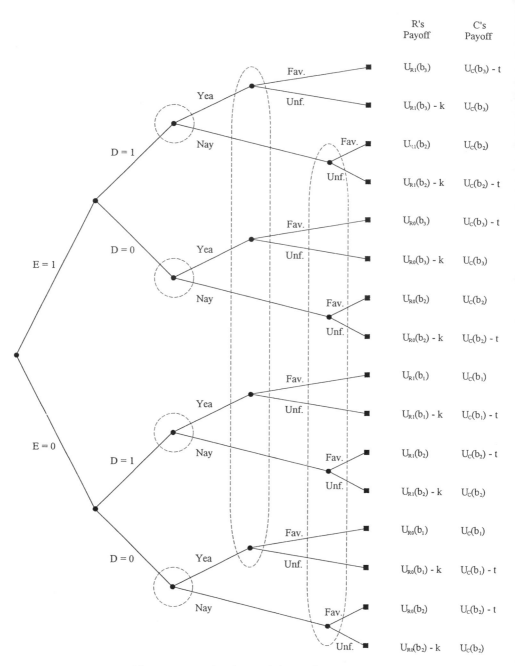

Fig. 7. Extensive form of the Evaluation game

Proposition 1: When the Evaluation game is played, R and C will use the following strategies:

$r(m)$, $c(11)$ if $c \leq 2(z) - 1$

$r(1111)$, $c(10)$ if $c \geq 2(z) - 1$ and $e \leq .5$

$r(0000)$, $c(01)$ if $c \geq 2(z) - 1$ and $e \geq .5$

$r(m)$, $c(00)$ if $c \leq 1 - 2(z)$.

Proof: The proof of Proposition 1 is organized in terms of cases 1 through 5. For each case and strategy pair, table 15 expresses the c, z conditions given in Proposition 1 as a function of e and d. Consider the $r(m)$, $c(11)$ pair, which Proposition 1 identifies as an equilibrium to the Evaluation game if $c \leq 2(z) - 1$. In case 1, where $r(m) = r(1001)$ and $z = (1 - d)$, $c \leq 2(z) - 1$ implies $d \leq (1 - e)$ when $e \leq .5$ (note $c = 1 - 2e$), $d \leq .5$ when $e = .5$ (and $c = 0$) and $d \leq e$ when $e \geq .5$ (and $c = 2e - 1$). In other words, Proposition 1 implies that if R's policy preferences correspond to Case 1 and $e < .5$, the $r(1001)$, $c(11)$ strategy pair is a sequential equilibrium given $d \leq e$. Similarly, when $e = .5$, the requirement is that $d \leq .5$. And finally, if $e \geq .5$, the condition is $d \leq (1 - e)$. Accordingly, these conditions are given in the top cell of the case 1 column in table 15.

As a second example, consider cases 2 and 3, where $r(m) = r(0001)$ and $z = 1 - d(1 - e)$. Under these conditions, $c \leq 2(z) - 1$ is always true given $e \geq .5$. When $e < .5$, the condition holds if $d \leq e/(1 - e)$. Thus, under case 2 or case 3 conditions, Proposition 1 implies that the $r(0001)$, $c(11)$ pair is always a sequential equilibrium given $e \geq .5$. When $e < .5$, the requirement is that $d \leq (1 - e)/e$. Again, these conditions are displayed in the top cell of the case 2–3 column in table 15.

Table 15 also indicates that some strategy pairs are never sequential equilibria given certain configurations of R's preferences. Consider the $r(m)$, $c(00)$ pair. In cases 4 and 5, where R's preferences are b_3 p b_1 p b_2 (Case 4) or b_1 p b_3 p b_2 (Case 5), $r(m) = r(1101)$ and $z = 1 - (ed)$. When $e \leq .5$, c is less than or equal to $1 - 2(z)$ only if $(1 - c)/c \leq d$, which is impossible given $e \leq .5$. When $e > .5$, the identity holds only if $d \geq 1$, which is also impossible. Therefore, when R's policy preferences are of the case 4 or case 5 variety, Proposition 1 says that the $r(m)$, $c(00)$ pair is never a sequential equilibrium, as indicated in the corresponding cell of table 15. It is similarly easy to show that the $r(1111)$, $c(10)$ pair is never a sequential equilibrium under case 4–5 conditions, or that the $r(0000)$, $c(01)$ pair is never an equilibrium under the conditions of cases 2–3. Space considerations preclude a detailed treatment of these assertions.

The next step is to show that the strategy pairs identified in Proposition 1 are indeed sequential equilibria under the conditions specified in table 15. For all of the pairs discussed below, R's strategy is a best response by Lemma 1. In addition, all of the off-equilibrium beliefs given below satisfy the criteria described earlier.

Case 1

$r(1111)$, $c(10)$: On equilibrium, where C's beliefs are $p_1 = (ed)$, $p_2 = (1 - e)(d)$, $p_3 = (e)(1 - d)$, and $p_4 = (1 - e)(1 - d)$, $c(10)$ is a best response iff

Table 15. Translation of Proposition 1 Conditions

Strategy Pair	Value of e	Conditions for Equilibria in Case		
		1	2–3	4–5
$r(m)$, $c(11)$	$e < .5$	$d \le e$	$d \le e/(1 - e)$	Always
	$e = .5$	$d \le .5$	Always	Always
	$e > .5$	$d \le (1 - e)$	Always	$d \le (1 - e)/e$
$r(1111)$, $c(10)$	$e < .5$	$d \ge e$	$d \ge e/(1 - e)$	—
	$e = .5$	$d \ge e$	$d \ge e/(1 - e)$	—
	$e > .5$	—	—	—
$r(0000)$, $c(01)$	$e < .5$	—	—	—
	$e = .5$	$d \ge (1 - e)$	—	$d \ge (1 - e)/e$
	$e > .5$	$d \ge (1 - e)$	—	$d \ge (1 - e)/e$
$r(m)$, $c(00)$	$e < .5$	$d \ge (1 - e)$	—	—
	$e = .5$	$d \ge .5$	—	—
	$e > .5$	$d \ge e$	—	—

$$p_1[u_3 - 1] + p_2[u_1] + p_3[u_3 - 1] + p_4[u_1] \geq$$

$$p_1[u_3] + p_2[u_1 - 1] + p_3[u_3] + p_4[u_1 - 1],$$

or $e \leq .5$. C's off-equilibrium beliefs are $p_1 = p_4 = 0$, $p_2 = d(1 - e)/$ $[d(1 - e) + e(1 - d)]$, $p_3 = (1 - d)e/[d(1 - e) + e(1 - d)]$. Therefore, $c(10)$ is a best response off equilibrium iff

$$p_2[u_2] + p_3[u_2 - 1] \geq p_2[u_2 - 1] + p_3[u_2],$$

or $d \geq e$. Thus, under case 1 conditions, the pair is a sequential equilibrium given $e \leq .5$ and $d \geq e$, as Proposition 1 states; it is never a sequential equilibrium when $e > .5$.

$r(0000)$, $c(01)$: On equilibrium, where C's beliefs are $p_1 = (ed)$, $p_2 = (1 - e)(d)$, $p_3 = (e)(1 - d)$, and $p_4 = (1 - e)(1 - d)$, $c(01)$ is a best response iff

$$p_1[u_2] + p_2[u_2 - 1] + p_3[u_2] + p_4[u_2 - 1] \geq$$

$$p_1[u_2 - 1] + p_2[u_2] + p_3[u_2 - 1] + p_4[u_2],$$

or $e \geq .5$. C's off-equilibrium beliefs are $p_1 = (ed)/[ed + (1 - e)(1 - d)]$, $p_2 = p_3 = 0$, and $p_4 = (1 - c)(1 - d)/[cd + (1 - c)(1 - d)]$. Therefore, $c(01)$ is a best response off equilibrium iff

$$p_1[u_3] + p_4[u_1 - 1] \geq p_1[u_3 - 1] + p_4[u_1],$$

or $d \geq (1 - e)$. Thus, under case 1 conditions, the pair is a sequential equilibrium given $e \geq .5$ and $d \geq (1 - e)$, as Proposition 1 states; it is never a sequential equilibrium when $e < .5$.

$r(m) = r(1001)$, $c(11)$: If R votes yea, C forms beliefs $p_1 = (ed)/[ed + (1 - e)(1 - d)]$, $p_2 = p_3 = 0$, and $p_4 = (1 - e)(1 - d)/[ed + (1 - e)(1 - d)]$. Given these beliefs, $c(11)$ is a best-response following a yea vote iff

$$p_1[u_3 - 1] + p_4[u_1] \geq p_1[u_3] + p_4[u_1 - 1],$$

or $d \leq (1 - e)$. If R votes nay, C forms beliefs $p_1 = p_4 = 0$, $p_2 = d(1 - e)/$ $[d(1 - e) + e(1 - d)]$, and $p_3 = e(1 - d)/[d(1 - e) + e(1 - d)]$. Now $c(11)$ is a best response iff

$$p_2[u_2 - 1] + p_3[u_2] \geq p_2[u_2] + p_2[u_2 - 1],$$

or $d \leq e$. When $e < .5$, $d \leq e$ implies $d \leq (1 - e)$; when $e \geq .5$, the reverse is true. Thus, under case 1 conditions, the pair is a sequential equilibrium when

$e < .5$ iff $d \le e$; when $e = .5$, it is a sequential equilibrium iff $d \le e = (1 - e) = .5$; finally, when $e > .5$, the pair is a sequential equilibrium iff $d \le (1 - e)$.

$r(m) = r(1001)$, $c(00)$: If R votes yea, C forms beliefs $p_1 = (ed)/[ed + (1 - e)(1 - d)]$, $p_2 = p_3 = 0$, and $p_4 = (1 - e)(1 - d)/[ed + (1 - e)(1 - d)]$. Given these beliefs, $c(11)$ is a best response following a yea vote iff

$$p_1[u_3] + p_4[u_1 - 1] \ge p_1[u_3 - 1] + p_4[u_1],$$

or $d \ge (1 - e)$. If R votes nay, C forms beliefs $p_1 = p_4 = 0$, $p_2 = d(1 - e)/[d(1 - e) + e(1 - d)]$, and $p_3 = e(1 - d)/[d(1 - e) + e(1 - d)]$. Now $c(11)$ is a best response iff

$$p_2[u_2] + p_3[u_2 - 1] \ge p_2[u_2 - 1] + p_2[u_2],$$

or $d \ge e$. When $e < .5$, $d \ge (1 - e)$ implies $d \ge e$; when $e \ge .5$, the reverse is true. Thus, under case 1 conditions, the pair is a sequential equilibrium given $e < .5$ iff $d \ge (1 - e)$; given $e = .5$, the pair is a sequential equilibrium iff $d \ge e = (1 - e) = .5$; given $e \ge .5$, the pair is a sequential equilibrium iff $d \ge e$.

Cases 2 and 3

$r(1111)$, $c(10)$: On equilibrium, $c(10)$ is a best response as in Case 1. C's off-equilibrium beliefs are $p_1 = ed/[d + e(1 - d)]$, $p_2 = d(1 - e)/[d + e(1 - d)]$, $p_3 = e/(1 - d)/[d + e(1 - d)]$, and $p_4 = 0$. Therefore, $c(10)$ is a best response off equilibrium iff

$$p_1[u_2 - 1] + p_2[u_2] + p_3[u_2 - 1] \ge p_1[u_2] + p_2[u_2 - 1] + p_3[u_2],$$

or $d \ge e/(1 - e)$. Thus, under case 2–3 conditions, the pair is a sequential equilibrium iff $e \le .5$ and $d \ge e/(1 - e)$; it is never a sequential equilibrium when $e > .5$.

$r(m) = r(0001)$, $c(11)$: If R votes yea, C can infer that $p_4 = 1$; if so, $c(11)$ is a best response iff $p_4[u_1] \ge p_4[u_1 - 1]$. If R votes nay, C's beliefs are $p_1 = ed/[d + e(1 - d)]$, $p_2 = d(1 - e)/[d + e(1 - d)]$, $p_3 = e/(1 - d)/[d + e(1 - d)]$, and $p_4 = 0$, and his strategy is a best response iff

$$p_1[u_2] + p_2[u_2 - 1] + p_3[u_2] \ge p_1[u_2 - 1] + p_2[u_2] + p_3[u_2 - 1],$$

or $d \le e/(1 - e)$. This requirement is always satisfied when $e \ge .5$; it may hold when $e < .5$.

Cases 4 and 5

r(0000), c(01): On equilibrium, c(01) is a best response as in case 1. Off equilibrium, C's beliefs are $p_1 = ed/[(1 - e) + ed]$, $p_2 = d(1 - e)/[(1 - e) + ed]$, $p_3 = 0$, and $p_4 = (1 - e)(1 - d)/[(1 - e) + ed]$, and his strategy is a best response iff

$$p_1[u_3] + p_2[u_1 - 1] + p_4[u_1 - 1] \geq p_1[u_3 - 1] + p_2[u_1] + p_4[u_1],$$

or $d \geq (1 - e)/e$. Therefore, the pair is a sequential equilibrium under case 4–5 conditions iff $e \geq .5$ and $d \geq (1 - e)/e$; it is never a sequential equilibrium when $e < .5$.

r(m) = r(1101), c(11): If R votes nay, C can infer that $p_3 = 1$; if so, his strategy is a best response iff $p_3[u_2] \geq p_3[u_2 - 1]$, which is trivially true. If R votes yea, C's beliefs are $p_1 = ed/[(1 - c) + ed]$, $p_2 - d(1 - e)/[(1 - e) + ed]$, $p_3 = 0$, and $p_4 = (1 - e)(1 - d)/[(1 - e) + ed]$, and his strategy is a best response iff

$$p_1[u_3 - 1] + p_2[u_1] + p_4[u_1] \geq p_1[u_3] + p_2[u_1 - 1] + p_4[u_1 - 1],$$

or $d \leq (1 - e)/e$. This requirement always holds if $e \leq .5$; it may hold if $e > .5$.

Interpreting Proposition 1

Figure 8 plots equilibria for the Evaluation game as a function of **c** and **z**. It is identical to figure 5, except that Region 2 is broken into two parts: 2a and 2b. (This complication will be explained in a moment.) The strategies vary across these regions as follows:[7]

Region 1: r(m), c(11)
Region 2a: r(1111), c(10) $(e \leq .5)$
           r(0000), c(01) $(e \geq .5)$
Region 2b: r(m), c(00)
           or
           r(1111), c(10) $(e \leq .5)$
           r(0000), c(01) $(e \geq .5)$.

The only difference between this depiction and the one in chapter 4 is that it reveals an additional equilibrium that can arise under Region 2b conditions. In

---

7. Multiple equilibria exist along the lines separating different regions. These are ignored to simplify the discussion.

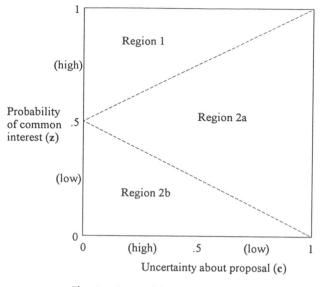

Fig. 8. Proposition 1 equilibria

this equilibrium, R uses her policy-max strategy, while C resorts to unilateral punishment, making an unfavorable evaluation regardless of how R votes. However, the pooling equilibrium that is the unique equilibrium under Region 2a conditions is also an equilibrium in Region 2b.[8]

The discussion in chapter 4 presumes that the pooling equilibrium will result under Region 2b conditions. For one thing, both players have reason to prefer this equilibrium over the one where unilateral punishment occurs. R always receives a higher payoff in the pooling equilibrium. In addition, the probability that R behaves as a fiduciary in the pooling equilibrium is almost always greater—and never less—than the probability in the unilateral punishment equilibrium. Thus, C, who wants R to behave as a fiduciary, has reason to prefer the pooling equilibrium as well. In any case, given the central question in this analysis—when do constituents trust their representative—details on what happens when trust does not exist are of secondary interest.

---

8. The conditions under which unilateral punishment is an equilibrium confirm the intuition given in chapter 4: the only time that C might use this strategy is if the probability of common interest is extremely low. Furthermore, Region 2b conditions can arise only if R's policy preferences given $D = 1$ are $b_3 \; p \; b_2 \; p \; b_1$ (case 1).

The Data

Interviews with ninety-three members of Congress are the principal data source for the analyses in chapters 5 and 6. This appendix provides details on the sample, questionnaire, and variables; assesses the reliability of these data; and gives the source of the additional contextual data used in the analysis.

The Sample

The interviews were conducted during January–June, 1990, in Washington, D.C. Members were promised anonymity. The sample was constructed by taking successive one-fourth subsamples of the 101st House, excluding the Speaker, the majority leader, the minority leader, the minority whip, and the members representing the Second and Fourth Districts of North Carolina.[1] Members in the first wave were contacted during January–February, 1990; those in the second wave, during March–April, 1990; and those in the third, during May 1990. In all, 249 legislators were contacted (everyone in the first and second waves, but only the first 36 in the third). Data on the response rate are in table 16. The sample contains 21.4 percent of the House (93 legislators). The overall response rate (interviews divided by requests) is 37.3 percent. This rate underestimates legislators' willingness to be interviewed, as some requests were unresolved at the end of June 1990.[2]

Next, table 17 compares the sample of ninety-three legislators to the entire 101st Congress. With one notable exception (the oversampling of legislators with low seniority, which is actually an oversampling of freshmen), the sample appears to be representative. In particular, it contains reasonable numbers of party leaders and members with positions of power on committees.

During the interviews, legislators were asked about their votes on two

---

1. The last two legislators were excluded because the author has had numerous contacts with them.

2. Unresolved requests are cases in which a legislator's office staff never gave a definite answer about their principal's willingness to be interviewed. Readers with a cynical mind can simply combine these cases with the "Refused Request" category.

proposals: the Ethics Act of 1989 and the repeal of the 1988 Medicare Cata-strophic Coverage Act. Five questions were asked about each proposal:

1. When [proposal] first came up, what did your constituents want you to do?
2. What were your personal feelings about [proposal]?
3. Did you have to do any explaining of your vote on [proposal]?
4. Do your constituents think you acted in their interest on [proposal]?
5. How would your constituents have reacted if you had voted the other way on [proposal]?

The exact wording of the questions, as well as the use of follow-ups and probes, varied across interviews. Questions about Catastrophic Coverage were usually asked first. If time allowed, legislators were also asked about their votes on the 1989 Quadrennial Commission raise proposal and the enactment of Catastrophic Coverage. In the main, legislators' remarks were written down verbatim (or as close as possible) during the interview.

In addition to interviews with members of Congress, a total of five other interviews were conducted. The subjects included an administrative assistant to a legislator in the sample, three lobbyists who were involved in the debate over the Ethics Act or Catastrophic Coverage, and a senior member of the House Office of Advice and Education. The last individual was asked about the format of legislators' financial disclosure forms.

In general, the quotes used in the book are taken directly from the interview transcripts. The only exception is if a legislator said something that would indicate her identity—e.g., the number of her district or her margin in the last election. In these cases, small changes were made to preserve anonymity.

Table 16. Interview Response Rates

Wave	Contacted	Refused	Unresolved	Interviewed	Response Rate
1	108	62	1	45	41.7
2	105	47	18	40	38.1
3	36	10	18	8	22.2
Total	249	119	37	93	37.3

Table 17. Sample Characteristics

Characteristic	Sample (N = 93) percentage	Population (N = 435) percentage
Party affiliation		
Northern Democrats	37.6 (35)	42.1 (183)
Southern Democrats	26.9 (25)	17.7 (77)
Republicans	35.5 (33)	40.2 (175)
Seniority (terms)		
1–3	38.7 (36)	28.0 (122)
4–9	53.8 (50)	57.9 (252)
10 or more	7.5 (7)	14.0 (61)
Leadership		
Democratic Party	9.7 (9)	8.7 (38)
Republican Party	6.5 (6)	7.1 (31)
Committee chair or RMM	7.5 (7)	12.4 (54)
Subcommittee chair or RMM	36.6 (34)	37.9 (165)

Sources: Seniority: Ornstein, Mann, and Malbin 1990, Table 1.6. Leadership data: Duncan 1991, 1698–1700. Democratic leadership is defined as caucus chair, caucus vice-chair, chief deputy whip, deputy whips, steering and policy committee. Republican leadership includes conference chair, conference vice-chair, chief deputy whips, deputy whips, and policy committee. Party data. Duncan 1991. Southern Democrats are defined as members from Alabama, Arkansas, Florida, Georgia, Louisiana, Mississippi, North Carolina, South Carolina, Tennessee, Texas, and Virginia. Committee data: Duncan 1991, 1666–98. Subcommittee percentages exclude members who are committee chairs or ranking minority members.

Variables Used in Chapter 5

Constituent preference. This variable was coded from answers to question 1.

Representative preference. This variable was coded from answers to question 2.

Explanations. This variable was coded from answers to question 3.

Leeway/trust. This variable was coded from answers to questions 4 and 5. Legislators who are coded as having leeway, or reporting trust, answered that their constituents were happy with the vote they cast and would have approved of the opposite vote as well. Stretching the definition to include legislators who qualified their response would switch four legislators from no leeway to leeway.

Honoraria and outside income. A legislator's honoraria income was calculated from 1989 disclosure forms by subtracting total honoraria from honoraria donated to charity. The outside income listed on the forms was sorted into income that fell under the new prohibitions and income that was still allowed. Deferred compensation from a freshman's employment prior to being elected to Congress (or income received before being elected in a special election) was also excluded. A legislator was coded as having high honoraria and outside income if the total of net honoraria plus lost outside income listed on the 1989 form exceeded $22,000 (approximately 90 percent of the pay increase mandated by the Ethics Act).

Personal wealth. Legislators' listings of assets and liabilities on their 1989 disclosure forms were used to calculate net worth. As assets and liabilities are listed in categories, category midpoints were used to estimate dollar figures. The value of assets and liabilities in the open-ended category was assumed to be twice the midpoint of the previous category. Using these measures, a legislator was defined as wealthy if her estimated net worth (assets minus liabilities) put her in the top 20 percent of the sample. In practice, legislators satisfying this definition (nineteen in all) had an estimated net worth exceeding $925,000.

After some initial analysis, it became clear that these disclosure forms can significantly underestimate a legislator's net worth. Such problems are well known: a senior staffer in the Office of Advice and Education (an arm of the House Committee on Standards of Official Conduct) pointed out to the author that the financial disclosure forms are designed to reveal conflicts of interests, not net worth. Part of the bias results from the nature of the forms: assets and liabilities are reported in categories, with a final open-ended category grouping assets or liabilities over $250,000. Furthermore, while assets must be listed at fair market value, there is no way to check that a legislator's valuation satisfies this definition. In addition, the open-ended category allows legislators to undervalue extremely large assets or to mask a large number of small assets by aggregating them.

In sum, if a disclosure form indicates that a legislator is wealthy, she almost certainly is. However, some legislators whose disclosure forms indicate moderate wealth are actually much better off. (Again, conversations with the aforementioned staffer in the Office of Advice and Education confirmed this suspicion.) These problems must be set against the fact that disclosure forms provide the only systematic data on members' net worth. As a partial solution, legislators who listed two or more assets in the open-ended category on their 1988 or 1989 forms were counted as wealthy, regardless of whether their net assets met the criteria discussed above. This assumption added five legislators to the wealthy category, making twenty-three in all.

Accept/reject raise. This information was obtained from interview transcripts, a survey done by *Roll Call* (Krewatch 1991), or by a call to members' press secretaries. Data could not be obtained for four legislators who were defeated or retired after the 1990 elections. To maximize sample size, these legislators were kept in the analysis and classified based on their remaining attributes. In all, eleven legislators were coded as having refused the raise.

Vote on the Ethics Act. This information was obtained from *Congressional Quarterly Weekly Report,* 120-H.

1988 Election margin. Data are taken from *Congressional Quarterly Almanac 1988,* 28-A.

Variables Used in Chapter 6

Constituent preference. This variable was coded from answers to question 1.

Representative preference. This variable was coded from answers to question 2.

Explanations. This variable was coded from a legislator's answers to two questions, one about her explanations of the initial vote to enact Catastrophic Coverage, the other about her explanations of the repeal vote.

Leeway/trust. This variable was coded from answers to questions 4 and 5, as described previously.

Votes on repeal of Catastrophic Coverage. These variables were obtained from *Congressional Quarterly Almanac 1989.* Since there were several votes to repeal the program and no obvious criteria for deciding which one was most visible or definitive, a legislator was coded as voting against repeal if she voted nay—against repeal—on any occasion. Only a few legislators deviated from a pure pro- or anti-repeal voting record.

Committee assignments. This information was taken from *Politics in America 1990.*

Voting scores. This information is from the September 1989 issue of *Saving Social Security,* a publication of the National Committee to Preserve Social Security and Medicare. Scores ranged from 0 to 100, with higher scores indicating a prosenior voting record as defined by the committee. A legislator was defined as having an antisenior record if her score was 15 or less. All other legislators were defined as prosenior.

Reliability

This book's heavy reliance on interviews raises an important question: do the variables coded from the interviews capture the information they are alleged to capture? There are many reasons to worry that they do not. Legislators may have misrepresented what they knew. They may have misunderstood the questions. They may not have known enough to answer the questions accurately. Finally, errors may have been introduced during the process of coding variables from the interview transcripts.

In some cases, different variables are the most likely candidates for each of these problems. Intuitively, the potential for misrepresentation exists when truthful revelation might be costly—for example, when a legislator disagrees with her constituents' feelings about a matter and is asked to discuss her personal preferences. The possibility of misunderstanding seems highest when legislators are asked about trust; as noted in chapter 5, one worry is that they might interpret these questions in terms of their political safety rather than answering in terms of how they expected constituents to respond to different votes. (This possibility was analyzed, and refuted, in chapter 5's analysis of the Ethics Act.) Mistakes might occur when legislators are asked about a factor that they themselves are not sure of—their constituents' beliefs about a proposal, for example. Finally, all of the variables are vulnerable to coding errors.

It is impossible to prove that these errors did not occur. Alternate measures simply do not exist. That is precisely the reason for conducting interviews. Take, for example, measures of a representative's personal preference about a proposal. It is hard to imagine how this information could be obtained except by asking the representative directly. The same can be said for measures of trust or explanation. Measures derived from interviews may not be perfect, but it is hard to think of something better.

The reader might argue that the problem of availability does not arise for variables that describe constituent demands. In principle, alternate measures could be developed from individual-level survey data or from models that predicted district sentiment as a function of demographic characteristics. (These possibilities were raised by reviewers of an early version of this manuscript.) Both were explored and discarded. One problem is simple: there are no surveys that measure district opinion on the Ethics Act or Catastrophic Coverage with adequate sample sizes. Demographics-based measures run into two problems. First, it is unclear how to specify an equation that predicts district opinion on either proposal. Even assuming a reasonable model of individual-level opinion can be developed, it is not clear that the same specification is valid at the aggregate level. In the absence of clear answers to these questions, interview data, with all their possible drawbacks, seem more attractive.

Still, all this discussion has done is to criticize alternate measures, not to establish the accuracy of the variables coded from interviews. The next three sections attempt to argue this point. The first section compares measures of legislators' preferences on the Ethics Act and Catastrophic Coverage to their votes on procedural questions that came up during consideration of the two proposals. The expectation is that, in contrast to votes on proposals and amendments, procedural votes are more likely to reflect a legislator's personal preferences, since it is much less likely that a procedural vote will become the subject of retrospective evaluations. The second section compares measures of constituent demands to district demographic data. The final section supplies information on intercoder reliability.

Measures of Legislatorial Preference

Whether legislators told the truth about their personal preferences was my biggest worry. Put simply: would they tell an academic, whom they had never met before, that they disagreed with their constituents?[3] My expectation was that if they were comfortable revealing a disagreement on a high-salience proposal like the Ethics Act or Catastrophic Coverage, they would answer any other questions I might ask to the best of their knowledge.

Thankfully, it appears that legislators did not misrepresent their preferences. Consider the Ethics Act: nearly 80 percent of legislators overall and fully 75 percent of those from opposition or strong opposition districts reported that they supported the proposal. Even if one takes the cynical position that all legislators prefer more money to less, the amount of misrepresentation cannot be more than 20 percent. Moreover, even if legislators were purely interested in salary, some might legitimately oppose the Ethics Act because of the restrictions on outside income and honoraria.

Additional confidence can be gained by comparing legislators' reported preference with two indirect indicators. The first is a survey conducted in early 1989 by then-Speaker Jim Wright (Hook 1989a). In this survey, legislators were asked about the Quadrennial Commission's proposal to raise congressional salaries by 50 percent and an alternate proposal to limit the increase to 30 percent. In both cases, the survey proposed that the raise be accompanied by a ban on honoraria and outside income. In all, 326 legislators

---

3. Several offices went to some lengths to verify that I was in fact an academic. One office sent an intern to the Library of Congress to examine a copy of my dissertation. Others ran searches for articles I had published.

responded to the survey. The percentage of legislators supporting each option, and the percentage in the sample reporting support of the Ethics Act, are in table 18. Assuming that a legislator who favored a 50 percent raise would prefer a 30 percent raise over nothing, Wright's survey suggests that 83 percent of the House would support a proposal such as the Ethics Act. This percentage is quite close to the percentage reported in my sample, 79.4 percent.

Voting on the Quadrennial proposal supplies an additional indicator of a legislator's preference on the Ethics Act. At one point during debate on the proposal, supporters attempted to adjourn the House. The aim was to prevent a vote on disapproving the recommendations, which would go into effect unless disapproved. (The expectation was that the recommendations would be disapproved if voted on.) Presumably, no legislator who expressed opposition to the Ethics Act should have voted to adjourn—anyone who opposed a 30 percent raise would oppose one for 50 percent. Supporters, however, should be split: some might think a 50 percent raise was too high, others might worry that their constituents would find out about the vote. The actual comparison is seen in table 19. As predicted, supporters range across the nay, no-vote, and yea categories. However, of the fifteen opponents of the Ethics Act who also voted on the adjournment motion, only one failed to vote against adjournment —and he did not vote at all. Thus, if there are some hidden supporters in the sample—supporters who said they were opponents—their number appears to be small.

A similar test can be made of legislators' reports of personal preference

Table 18. Reported Preference on the Ethics Act Compared to Wright Survey

Survey Response	Percentage
"50% about right"	42
"Roll-back to 30%"	41
Total	83
Support for Ethics in sample	79.4

Source: Hook 1989a.

on Catastrophic Coverage. It is somewhat more complicated, as so many legislators had no strong feelings about the proposal. Nevertheless, the analysis yields roughly the same result: while the possibility of misrepresentation cannot be eliminated, the number of cases where it might have occurred appears to be small. These results are omitted for space reasons.

Measures of Constituent Demands

With regard to constituent demands, the problem is not so much misrepresentation as mistakes. Legislators have no reason to lie about their constituents' demands. Even if legislators wanted to profess a false agreement with their constituents, presumably they would accomplish this goal by biasing reports of their personal preferences. However, there is the possibility that legislators have no idea—or an imprecise one—of their constituents' demands. As noted in chapter 4, many scholars would argue otherwise. Still, the possibility of mistakes cannot be ignored. In the absence of survey data, however, it is impossible to be sure that legislators knew what they were talking about. However, two tests provide a measure of confidence in the data.

The first test focuses on constituent opinion regarding the Ethics Act. Recall in chapter 5 that many legislators explained their constituents' feelings about the proposal in terms of their district's economic conditions. Well-to-do districts were usually described as supporters of the Ethics Act; rural or poor districts as strong opponents. If this assertion is true and legislators' assessments of district opinion are indeed accurate, measures of district economic conditions should vary across the categories used to describe constituent opinion—supporter, opponent, and strong opponent—with supporter districts best off and strong opponent districts worst off. Two obvious measures of economic conditions in a district are mean home prices and mean rents. Both

Table 19. Reported Preference on the Ethics Act Compared with Procedural Votes

Reported Preference	Vote on Motion to Adjourn		
	Nay	Did Not Vote	Yea
Support	36	20	15
Oppose	14	1	0

are available from census data. (These tests use 1980 census data, as 1990 data is unavailable for 1980s-era districts.) Mean values for the categories of constituent opinion are shown in table 20. The economic variables vary as predicted. Supporter districts have the highest home prices and rents; strong opposition districts have the lowest. While this comparison does not prove that legislators' assessments of district opinion were accurate—for one thing, these assessments may be derived from a legislator's sense of economic conditions in her district—it suggests that the constituent demand variable is not complete nonsense.

The second test turns to Catastrophic Coverage. Here the task is somewhat complicated: it is difficult to find a separate indicator of seniors' demands. However, a negative test is possible. One criticism of the variables used here is that legislators' comments about the intensity of senior demands, used to code districts into the opposition and strong opposition categories, simply reflect the number of seniors in their districts. If this misunderstanding occurred, opposition districts should have fewer seniors than districts coded as strong opponents of Catastrophic Coverage. Table 21 compares the two types of districts using data from the 1990 census to measure the percentage of seniors in a district. As the table shows, the mean percentages of seniors in the two types of districts are virtually identical. Thus, in assessing their constituents' demands on Catastrophic Coverage, legislators apparently did not substitute raw numbers for opinion.

Table 20. Constituent Demands on the Ethics Act and
District Economic Conditions

Constituent Demands	Mean House Value	Mean Rent
Support ($n = 10$)	$60,340	$236.60
Qualified opposition ($n = 65$)	$46,167	$187.12
Opposition ($n = 13$)	$34,715	$144.70

Intercoder Reliability

A final worry about the data is that statements made by respondents have been misinterpreted, introducing either random measurement error or systematic bias into the analysis. To guard against this possibility, each variable derived from the interview transcripts was coded by myself and one of two research assistants. My codes are used in the analysis. The second set of codes are used here to check on reliability.

Some disagreements were inevitable: I did not ask follow-up questions during the interview if I believed that the member had said enough to code the case, and I coded variables with the interview fresh in my mind. The coders only had the printed transcripts to work with. Even with this caveat, table 22 shows that the data score well on measures of intercoder reliability. The table compares the two sets of codes for the constituent preference, representative preference, explanation, and trust variables. (The Catastrophic Coverage variables measure demands, etc., on repeal.) The first column (Codes) gives the percentage of cases where the two coders agreed that a case could be coded as nonmissing and agreed on which code it should receive. The second column (No Information) gives the percentage of cases where the coders agreed that a variable could not be coded. The third and fourth columns (Disagree–Codes and Disagree–Information) give the percentage of cases where the coders disagreed, either on how a variable should be coded or whether there was sufficient information to assign a code. The final column (Percentage Agreement) is the percentage of times the coders agreed about how to code a particular variable.

Table 22 shows a relatively high level of intercoder reliability. While

Table 21. Constituent Demands on Catastrophic Coverage and the Size of the Senior Bloc

Constituent Demands (Repeal)	Mean Percent Seniors
Opposition	13.1 (52)
Strong opposition	12.4 (38)

Table 22. Intercoder Reliability

Case	Variable	Agree		Disagree		Percentage of Agreement
		Codes	No Information	Codes	Information	
Ethics Act	Constituent demands	75.3 (70)	1.1 (1)	23.7 (22)	0 (0)	76.3
	Representative preferences	84.9 (79)	0 (0)	15.1 (14)	0 (0)	84.9
	Trust	82.8 (77)	5.4 (5)	6.5 (6)	5.4 (5)	88.2
	Explanation	78.5 (73)	0 (0)	16.1 (15)	5.4 (5)	78.5
Catastrophic Coverage	Constituent demands	61.3 (57)	1.1 (1)	32.3 (30)	5.4 (5)	62.4
	Representative preferences	87.1 (81)	1.1 (1)	10.7 (10)	1.1 (1)	88.2
	Trust	82.8 (77)	6.4 (6)	10.7 (10)	0 (0)	89.2
	Explanation	79.6 (74)	2.2 (2)	16.1 (15)	2.2 (2)	81.8

coder agreement does not reach the levels typically seen in mass surveys (90 percent or so), the percentages are respectable. Moreover, only one variable, the one that codes constituent demands for Catastrophic Coverage, has a percentage of agreement below 75 percent. Agreement for other variables, typically those coding trust or representative preference, is close to the mass survey benchmark.

Fiduciary Behavior under Term Limits

This appendix shows that the probability of fiduciary behavior in the Evaluation game is at least as high, and often higher, under unlimited tenure as under term limits.

As constructed in appendix 1, the Evaluation game models the behavior of a career-oriented representative elected under a system of unlimited tenure who values reelection over policy concerns. Such a representative will conform to constituent demands if she does not expect trust and vote according to her personal policy goals if she does. Formally, the interpretation of Proposition 1 shows that her behavior varies as a function of c, z, and e as follows:

$r(m)$ if $c < 2(z) - 1$

$r(1111)$ if $c \geq 2(z) - 1$ and $e < .5$

$r(0000)$ if $c \geq 2(z) - 1$ and $e \geq .5$

From chapter 4 and appendix 1, recall that

$z = 1 - d$ Case 1

$\quad\quad 1 - d(1 - e)$ Cases 2 and 3

$\quad\quad 1 - ed$ Cases 4 and 5,

where cases 1 through 5 describe possible configurations of R's policy goals, and

$c = 2(.5 - e)$ $e < .5$

$\quad\quad 0$ $e = .5$

$\quad\quad 2(e - .5)$ $e > .5$.

Given this characterization, the probability of fiduciary behavior under each of these conditions is as follows:

z if $c < 2(z) - 1$

$(1 - e)$ if $c \geq 2(z) - 1$ and $e < .5$

(e) if $c \geq 2(z) - 1$ and $e \geq .5$.

For example, when $c < 2(z) - 1$, R uses her policy-max strategy. If so, the probability that her vote yields the best policy outcome for C equals z, the probability of a common interest. Conversely, when $c \geq 2(z) - 1$ and $e < .5$, R will vote yea, expecting that C will evaluate yea votes favorably and nay votes unfavorably. Therefore, the probability of fiduciary behavior equals $(1 - e)$, or the probability that enacting β yields outcome b_1.

Now suppose R is elected under term limits, rendering her interest in reelection moot. With this change, presumably she will always use her policy-max strategy, or vote as her policy goals dictate, regardless of how she expects C to react. Therefore, the probability of fiduciary behavior under term limits equals z, regardless of the values of c, z, and e.

Comparing the probability of fiduciary behavior in these scenarios yields two findings:

1. When $c < 2(z) - 1$, unlimited tenure and term limits yield the same probability of fiduciary behavior: z.
2. When $c \geq 2(z) - 1$, the probability of fiduciary behavior in the two scenarios is different. However, for each case, simple algebra shows that the probability is higher under unlimited tenure.

As an example of (2), consider case 1, where $z = (1 - d)$. When $e < .5$, $c = 2(.5 - e)$. Therefore, unlimited tenure yields a higher probability of fiduciary behavior when $e < .5$ iff

$(1 - e) > (1 - d)$ or $d > e$.

Given the values of c and z, $c \geq 2(z) - 1$ implies

$2(.5 - e) > 2(1 - d) - 1$ or $d > e$.

So, the required condition is met. Similarly, when $e > .5$, $\mathbf{c} = 2(e - .5)$, unlimited tenure yields the higher probability iff

$$e > (1 - d).$$

Now, the values of $\mathbf{c}$ and $\mathbf{z}$ imply

$$2(e - .5) > 2(1 - d) - 1 \quad \text{or} \quad e > (1 - d).$$

Again, the identity holds.

References

Aldrich, John H., and William T. Bianco. 1992. "A Game-Theoretic Model of Party Affiliation of Candidates and Office-holders." *Mathematical and Computer Modeling* 16:103–16.

Almond, Gabriel A. 1988. "Separate Tables: Schools and Sects in Political Science." *PS* 21:828–42.

Alston, Chuck. 1990. "Warning Shots Fired By Voters More Mood Than Mandate." *Congressional Quarterly Weekly Report,* November 10, 1990, 3796–97.

Arnold, R. Douglas. 1990. *The Logic of Congressional Action.* New Haven: Yale University Press.

Austen-Smith, David. 1990. "Information Transmission in Debate." *American Journal of Political Science* 34:124–52.

———. 1992. "Explaining the Vote: Constituency Constraints on Legislative Strategy." *American Journal of Political Science* 36:68–95.

Bach, Stanley, and Steven S. Smith. 1988. *Managing Uncertainty in the House of Representatives: Adaptation and Innovation in Special Rules.* Washington, D.C.: Brookings.

Banks, Jeffrey. 1991. *Signaling Games in Political Science.* London: Harwood Academic Publishers.

Banks, Jeffrey, and Joel Sobel. 1987. "Equilibrium Selection in Signaling Games." *Econometrica* 55:647–61.

Barber, James David. 1985. *The Presidential Character.* 3d ed. Englewood Cliffs, N.J.: Prentice-Hall.

Baron, David. 1990. "Majoritarian Incentives, Pork Barrel Programs, and Procedural Control." *American Journal of Political Science* 35:57–90.

Bartels, Larry M. 1991. "Constituency Opinion and Congressional Policymaking." *American Political Science Review* 85:457–74.

Bartlett, Robert V. 1979. "The Marginality Hypothesis: Electoral Insecurity, Self-Interest, and Voting Behavior." *American Politics Quarterly* 7:498–508.

Berelson, Bernard R., Paul F. Lazarsfeld, and William N. McPhee. 1954. *Voting.* Chicago: University of Chicago Press.

Bernstein, Robert A. 1989. *Elections, Representation, and Congressional Voting Behavior: The Myth of Constituency Control.* Englewood Cliffs, N.J.: Prentice-Hall.

———. 1991. "Strategic Shifts: Safeguarding the Public Interest? U.S. Senators, 1971–1986." *Legislative Studies Quarterly* 16:263–79.

Bianco, William T. 1989. "Doing the Politically Right Thing: Results, Behavior and Vote Trading." *Journal of Politics* 51:886–99.

Black, Duncan. 1958. *The Theory of Committees and Elections*. Cambridge: Cambridge University Press.

Black, Gordon. 1972. "A Theory of Political Ambition: Career Choices and the Role of Structural Incentives." *American Political Science Review* 66:144–59.

Blondel, Jean. 1973. *Comparative Legislatures*. New York: Prentice-Hall.

Calvert, Randall L. 1993. "Lowi's Critique of Political Science: A Response." *PS* 26: 196–98.

Canon, David T. 1990. *Actors, Athletes, and Astronauts: Political Amateurs in the United States Congress*. Chicago: University of Chicago Press.

Caro, Robert A. 1982. *The Years of Lyndon Johnson: The Path to Power*. New York: Alfred A. Knopf.

Carson, Richard T., and Joseph A. Oppenheimer. 1984. "A Technique for Estimating the Personal Ideology of Political Representatives." *American Political Science Review* 78:163–78.

Cho, In-Koo, and David Kreps. 1987. "Signaling Games and Stable Equilibria." *Quarterly Journal of Economics* 12:179–221.

Congressional Quarterly Almanac 1989. Washington, D.C.: Congressional Quarterly Press.

Conover, Pamela Johnston, and Stanley Feldman. 1986. "The Role of Inference in the Perception of Political Candidates." In *Political Cognition,* Richard R. Lau and David O. Sears, eds. Hillsdale, N.J.: Erlbaum Press.

———. 1989. "Candidate Perceptions in an Ambiguous World: Campaigns, Cues, and Inference Processes." *American Journal of Political Science* 33:912–40.

Converse, Phillip E., and Roy Pierce. 1986. *Political Representation in France*. Cambridge, Mass.: Harvard University Press.

Cook, Karen Schweers, and Margaret Levi, eds. 1990. *The Limits of Rationality*. Chicago: University of Chicago Press.

Dahl, Robert A. 1956. *A Preface to Democratic Theory*. Chicago: University of Chicago Press.

Davidson, Roger H. 1980. "The Politics of Executive, Legislative, and Judicial Compensation." In *The Rewards of Public Service*, Robert W. Hartman and Arnold R. Weber, eds. Washington, D.C.: Brookings Institution.

Denzau, Arthur, William H. Riker, and Kenneth A. Shepsle. 1985. "Farquharson and Fenno: Sophisticated Voting and Home Style." *American Political Science Review* 79:1117–34.

Dodd, Lawrence C. 1993. "Congress and the Politics of Renewal: Readdressing the Crisis of Legitimation." In *Congress Reconsidered*, 5th ed. Lawrence C. Dodd and Bruce Oppenheimer, eds. Washington, D.C.: Congressional Quarterly Press.

Downs, Anthony. 1957. *An Economic Theory of Democracy*. New York: Harper and Row.

Drew, Elizabeth. 1992. "Letter From Washington." *The New Yorker,* May 18, 1992, 86–94.

Duncan, Phil. 1990a. 'Budget May Shift Advantage in Congress' Close Races." *Congressional Quarterly Weekly Report,* October 13, 1991, 3279–83.

———. 1990b. "Large Turnover Seems Unlikely, But Campaign Won't Be Dull." *Congressional Quarterly Weekly Report*, February 17, 1990, 433–39.

———. ed. 1989. *Politics in America: 1990*. Washington, D.C.: Congressional Quarterly Press.

———. 1991. *Politics in America: 1992*. Washington, D.C.: Congressional Quarterly Press.

Enelow, James M., and Melvin J. Hinich. 1984. *The Spatial Theory of Voting*. Cambridge: Cambridge University Press.

Erikson, Robert S. 1978. "Constituency Opinion and Congressional Behavior: A Reexamination of the Miller-Stokes Representation Data." *American Journal of Political Science* 22:511–35.

Eulau, Heinz. 1987. "The Congruence Model Revisited." *Legislative Studies Quarterly* 12:171–214.

Eulau, Heinz, and Paul D. Karps. 1977. "The Puzzle of Representation: Specifying Components of Responsiveness." *Legislative Studies Quarterly* 2:233–54.

Fenno, Richard F. 1973. *Congressmen in Committees*. Boston: Little, Brown.

———. 1978. *Home Style*. Boston: Little, Brown.

Ferejohn, John A. 1984. "Logrolling in an Institutional Context: A Case Study of Food Stamps Legislation." Unpublished paper, Stanford University.

———. 1986. "Incumbent Performance and Electoral Control." *Public Choice* 50:5–25.

———. 1990. "Information and Elections." In *Information and Democratic Processes*, John A. Ferejohn and James H. Kuklinski, eds. Urbana: University of Illinois Press.

Fiorina, Morris P. 1981. *Retrospective Voting in American National Elections*. New Haven, Conn.: Yale University Press.

———. 1992. *Divided Government*. New York: Macmillan.

Fisher, Louis. 1980. "History of Pay Adjustments for Members of Congress." In *The Rewards of Public Service*, Robert W. Hartman and Arnold R. Weber, eds. Washington, D.C.: Brookings Institution.

Fiske, Susan T. 1990. "The Motivated Tactician: Cognition and Motivation in Research on the Presidency." Typescript, University of Massachusetts.

Fowler, Linda L., and Ronald G. Shaiko. 1987. "The Grass Roots Connection: Environmental Activists and Senate Roll Calls." *American Journal of Political Science* 31:484–510.

Fund, John H. 1992. "Term Limitation: An Idea Whose Time Has Come." In *Limiting Legislative Terms*, Gerald Benjamin and Michael J. Malbin, eds. Washington, D.C.: Congressional Quarterly Press.

Galvin, Thomas. 1992. "Term Limits Score a Perfect 14-for-14, But Court Challenges Loom." *Congressional Quarterly Weekly Report*, November 7, 1992, 3593.

Gigerenzer, Gerd. N.d. "How to Make Cognitive Illusions Disappear: Beyond 'Heurestics and Biases.'" Typescript, Universität Konstanz, Germany.

Gilligan, Thomas, and Keith Krehbiel. 1990. "Organization of Informative Committees by a Rational Legislature." *American Journal of Political Science* 34:531–65.

Goffman, Erving. 1959. *The Presentation of Self in Everyday Life*. New York: Doubleday.

Grafstein, Robert. 1992. "Rational Choice Inside and Out." *Journal of Politics* 54:259–68.

Harrington, Joseph E. 1988. "The Revelation of Information through the Electoral Process: An Exploratory Analysis." Typescript, The Johns Hopkins University.

Harsanyi, John. 1967. "Games of Incomplete Information Played by Bayesian Players." *Management Science* 14:159–82, 320–34, 486–502.

Hershey, Marjorie Randon. 1984. *Running for Office: The Political Education of Campaigners*. Chatam, N.J.: Chatam House Publishers.

Herstein, John A. 1981. "Keeping the Voter's Limits in Mind: A Cognitive Process Analysis of Decision Making in Voting." *Journal of Personality and Social Psychology* 40:843–61.

Hibbing, John B. 1983. "Washington on 75 Dollars a Day: Members of Congress Voting on Their Own Tax Break." *Legislative Studies Quarterly* 8:219–30.

Hoffman, Ross, and Paul Levack, eds. 1949. *Burke's Politics*. New York: Alfred Knopf.

Hogarth, Robin M., and Melvin W. Reder. 1986. "Introduction: Perspectives from Economics and Psychology." In *Rational Choice: The Contrast Between Economics and Psychology*, Robin M. Hogarth and Melvin W. Reder, eds. Chicago: University of Chicago Press.

Hook, Janet. 1989a. "Congress Wavering on 51 Percent Salary Hike." *Congressional Quarterly Weekly Report*, February 4, 1989, 203.

———. 1989b. "How the Pay Raise Strategy Came Unraveled." *Congressional Quarterly Weekly Report*, February 11, 1989, 264–67.

Jackson, John E., and David C. King. 1989. "Public Goods, Private Interests, and Representation." *American Political Science Review* 83:1143–65.

Jackson, John E., and John W. Kingdon. 1990. "Ideology, Interest Group Scores, and Legislative Votes." Unpublished paper, University of Michigan.

Jacobson, Gary. 1991. "Divided Government, Strategic Politicians, and the 1990 Congressional Elections." Paper presented at the 1991 Annual Meeting of the Midwest Political Science Association, Chicago, Ill.

———. 1992. *The Politics of Congressional Elections*. 3d ed. New York: Harper Collins.

Jewell, Malcolm E. 1970. "Attitudinal Determinants of Legislative Behavior: The Utility of Role Analysis." In *Legislatures in Developmental Perspective*, Allan Kornberg and Lloyd Musolf, eds. Durham, N.C.: Duke University Press.

———. 1982. *Representation in State Legislatures*. Lexington: University of Kentucky Press.

Kalt, Joseph P., and Mark A. Zupan. 1984. "Capture and Ideology in the Economic Theory of Politics." *American Economic Review* 74:279–300.

———. 1990. "The Apparent Ideological Behavior of Legislators: Testing the Principal-Agent Slack in Political Institutions." *Journal of Political Economy* 33:103–31.

Kaplan, Dave. 1990. "The Tally: Democrats, Up Nine; Republicans, Down Eight." *Congressional Quarterly Weekly Report*, November 10, 1990, 3801–5.

Kau, James B., and Paul H. Rubin. 1979. "Self-Interest, Ideology, and Logrolling in Congressional Voting." *Journal of Law and Economics* 22:365–84.

Key, V. O., with Milton C. Cummings. 1966. *The Responsible Electorate*. New York: Vintage Press.

Kieweit, D. Roderick, and Mathew D. McCubbins. 1991. *The Logic of Delegation: Congressional Parties and the Appropriations Process*. Chicago: University of Chicago Press.

Kinder, Donald R. 1993. "Rational and Not-So-Rational Processes of Judgement and Decision." In *Experimental Foundations of Political Science*, Donald R. Kinder and Thomas R. Palfrey, eds. Ann Arbor: University of Michigan Press.

Kinder, Donald R., and Thomas R. Palfrey, eds. 1993. *Experimental Foundations of Political Science*. Ann Arbor: University of Michigan Press.

King, Gary, and Andrew Gelman. 1992. "Why Do Presidential Election Campaign Polls Vary So Much When The Vote Is So Predictable?" Center For Political Studies, Harvard University Occasional Paper.

Kingdon, John W. 1980. *Congressmen's Voting Decisions*. 2d ed. New York: Harper and Row.

Krehbiel, Keith. 1986. "A Technique for Estimating Congressmen's Ideal Points." *Journal of Politics* 48:97–115.

———. 1988. "Spatial Models of Legislative Choice." *Legislative Studies Quarterly* 8:259–319.

———. 1990. "Are Congressional Committees Composed of Preference Outliers?" *American Political Science Review* 84:149–63.

———. 1991. *Information and Legislative Organization*. Ann Arbor. University of Michigan Press.

Krehbiel, Keith, and Douglas Rivers. 1988. "The Analysis of Committee Power: An Application to Senate Voting on the Minimum Wage." *American Journal of Political Science* 32:1151–74.

Kreps, David. 1983. "Signaling Games and Stable Equilibria." Typescript, Stanford University.

Kreps, David, and Robert Wilson. 1982a. "Reputation and Imperfect Information." *Journal of Economic Theory* 27:253–79.

———. 1982b. "Sequential Equilibria." *Econometrica* 50:863–90.

Krewatch, Mark. 1991. "Another 33 Members Say They'll Keep Hike." *Roll Call*, January 28, 1991, 14.

Lazear, Edward, and Sherwin Rosen. 1980. "The Economics of Compensation of Government Officials." In *The Rewards of Public Service*, Robert W. Hartman and Arnold R. Weber, eds. Washington, D.C.: Brookings Institution.

Lippman, Walter. 1922. *Public Opinion*. New York: Macmillan.

Lowi, Theodore J. 1992. "The State in Political Science: How We Became What We Study." *American Political Science Review* 86:1–7.

Lupia, Arthur. 1992. "Busy Voters, Agenda Control, and the Power of Information." *American Political Science Review* 86:390–403.

Maas, Arthur. 1983. *Congress and the Common Good*. New York: Basic Books.

March, James G., and Johan P. Olsen. 1984. "The New Institutionalism: Organizational Factors in Political Life." *American Political Science Review* 78:734–48.

Mayhew, David R. 1974. *Congress: The Electoral Connection*. New Haven: Yale University Press.

McKelvey, Richard D., and Richard G. Niemi. 1978. "A Multistage Game Representation of Sophisticated Voting for Binary Procedures." *Journal of Economic Theory* 18:1–22.

Miller, Warren E., and Donald E. Stokes. 1963. "Constituency Influence in Congress." *American Political Science Review* 57:45–56.

Moe, Terry M. 1990. "Political Institutions: The Neglected Side of the Story." Unpublished paper, Stanford University.

Niou, Emerson, and Peter C. Ordeshook. 1985. "Universalism in Congress." *American Journal of Political Science* 29:246–59.

Oleszek, Walter J. 1989. *Congressional Procedures and the Policy Process*. 3d ed. Washington, D.C.: Congressional Quarterly Press.

Olson, Mancur. 1967. *The Logic of Collective Action*. Cambridge, Mass.: Harvard University Press.

Ornstein, Norman J., Thomas E. Mann, and Michael J. Malbin. 1990. *Vital Statistics on Congress 1989–1990*, Washington, D.C.: Congressional Quarterly Press.

Page, Benjamin I., and Robert Y. Shapiro. 1992. *The Rational Public*. Chicago: University of Chicago Press.

Parker, Glenn. 1989. *Characteristics of Congress: Patterns in Congressional Behavior*. Englewood Cliffs, N.J.: Prentice-Hall.

Parker, Suzanne L., and Glenn R. Parker. 1993. "Why Do We Trust Our Congressman?" *Journal of Politics* 55:442–53.

Pitkin, Hanna F. 1967. *The Concept of Representation*. Berkeley: University of California Press.

Plott, Charles R. 1986. "Rational Choice in Experimental Markets." In *Rational Choice: The Contrast between Economics and Psychology*, Robin M. Hogarth and Melvin W. Reder, eds. Chicago: University of Chicago Press.

Poole, Keith T., and Howard Rosenthal. 1991. "Patterns of Congressional Voting." *American Journal of Political Science* 35:228–78.

Popkin, Samuel L. 1991. *The Reasoning Voter*. Chicago: University of Chicago Press.

Quattrone, George A., and Amos Tversky. 1988. "Contrasting Rational and Psychological Analyses of Political Choice." *American Political Science Review* 82:720–36.

Rahn, Wendy M. 1993. "The Role of Partisan Stereotypes in Information Processing about Political Candidates." *American Journal of Political Science* 37:472–96.

Rahn, Wendy M., John H. Aldrich, Eugene Borgida, and John L. Sullivan. 1990. "A Socio-Cognitive Model of Candidate Appraisal." In *Information and Democratic Processes*, John A. Ferejohn and James H. Kuklinski, eds. Urbana: University of Illinois Press.

Rasmussen, Eric. 1989. *Games and Information*. New York: Basil Blackwell.

Rohde, David. 1979. "Risk-Bearing and Progressive Ambition: The Case of the United States House of Representatives." *American Journal of Political Science* 23:1–26.

———. 1991. *Parties and Leaders in the Post-Reform House*. Chicago: University of Chicago Press.

Ruder, Catherine E. 1990. "Review of *Budget Reform Politics: The Design of the Appropriations Process in the House of Representatives, 1865–1921.*" *Congress and the Presidency* 16:185–87.

Salisbury, Robert H., and Kenneth A. Shepsle. 1981. "U.S. Congressman as Enterprise." *Legislative Studies Quarterly* 4:559–76.

Schlozman, Kay Lehman, and John T. Tierney. 1986. *Organized Interests and American Democracy*. New York: Harper and Row.

Schumpeter, Joseph A. [1942] 1975. *Capitalism, Socialism, and Democracy*, 3d. ed. New York: Harper and Row.

Shepsle, Kenneth. 1979. "Institutional Arrangements and Equilibria in Multidimensional Voting Models." *American Journal of Political Science* 23:27–59.

Shepsle, Kenneth A., and Barry R. Weingast. 1981. "Political Preferences for the Pork Barrel: A Generalization." *American Journal of Political Science* 25:96–111.

———. 1987. "The Institutional Foundations of Committee Power." *American Political Science Review* 81:85–104.

Sherman, Steven J., Charles M. Judd, and Bernadette Park. 1989. "Social Cognition." *American Review of Psychology* 40:281–326.

Simon, Herbert A. 1947. *Administrative Behavior*. New York: Free Press.

———. 1985. "Human Nature in Politics: The Dialogue of Psychology with Political Science." *American Political Science Review* 79:293–304.

Sinclair, Barbara. 1992. "Framing, Interpreting, and Explaining Senate Behavior: The Importance of Looking Up-Close-and-Personal." *Extension of Remarks*, November 1992.

Smith, Steven S. 1989. *Call to Order: Floor Politics in the House and the Senate*. Washington, D.C.: Brookings.

Stewart, Charles, III. 1989. *Budget Reform Politics: The Design of the Appropriations Process in the House of Representatives, 1865–1921*. Cambridge: Cambridge University Press.

Storing, Henry J. 1981a. *The Anti-Federalist*. Chicago: University of Chicago Press.

———. 1981b. *What the Antifederalists Were For*. Chicago: University of Chicago Press.

Strahan, Randall. 1990. *New Ways and Means: Reform and Change in a Congressional Committee*. Chapel Hill: University of North Carolina Press.

Taylor, Shelley E., Susan T. Fiske, Nancy L. Etcoff, and Audrey J. Ruderman. 1978. "Categorical and Contextual Bases of Person Memory and Stereotyping." *Journal of Personality and Social Psychology* 36:778–93.

Tversky, Amos, and Daniel Kahneman. 1986. "Rational Choice and the Framing of Decisions." In *Rational Choice: The Contrast between Economics and Psychology*, Robin M. Hogarth and Melvin W. Reder, eds. Chicago: University of Chicago Press.

Wahlke, John W. 1971. "Policy Demands and System Support: The Role of the Represented." *British Journal of Political Science* 1:271–90.

Wahlke, John W., Heinz Eulau, William Buchanan, and LeRoy C. Ferguson. 1962. *The Legislative System*. New York: Wiley.

Weaver, R. Kent. 1988. *Automatic Government: The Politics of Indexation*. Washington, D.C.: Brookings Institution.

Weingast, Barry R. 1979. "A Rational Choice Perspective on Congressional Norms." *American Journal of Political Science* 23:245–62.

Wilkerson, John. 1991. *The Evolution of Strategy: A Case Study of Congressional Pay Raises*. Ph.d. Dissertation, University of Rochester.

Winneker, Craig. 1990. "Pay Raise Suddenly Becomes Red-Hot Issue in '90 Election." *Roll Call,* May 17, 1990, 8.

Zaller, John. 1992. *The Nature and Origins of Mass Opinion*. Cambridge: Cambridge University Press.

Author Index

Aldrich, John H., 59, 67n
Almond, Gabriel A., 40
Alston, Chuck, 4n
Arnold, R. Douglas, 14, 18, 21, 25, 27, 48, 71, 88, 97, 163
Austen-Smith, David, 39, 49, 52–53, 65n

Bach, Stanley, 87, 87n, 163
Banks, Jeffrey, 52, 177
Barber, James David, 61n
Baron, David, 35, 39
Bartels, Larry M., 31n, 36n, 65n
Bartlett, Robert V., 100, 113
Bennett, Charles, 87n
Berelson, Bernard R., 21
Bernstein, Robert A., 21, 65n
Bianco, William T., 32n, 67n
Black, Duncan, 31
Black, Gordon, 166n
Blondel, Jean, 22
Borgida, Eugene, 59
Buchanan, William, 21n, 23
Burke, Edmund, 23
Bush, George, 5

Calvert, Randall L., 40n
Canon, David T., 166n
Caro, Robert A., 147n
Carson, Richard T., 36n
Cho, In-Koo, 177
Clinton, Bill, 59n
Conover, Pamela Johnston, 59
Converse, Phillip E., 21
Cook, Karen Schweers, 40n

Dahl, Robert A., 21
Davidson, Roger H., 99, 105
Denzau, Arthur, 32–33
Dodd, Lawrence C., 161–63, 162n
Downs, Anthony, 13, 19n, 44, 88
Drew, Elizabeth, 20, 30, 161, 163
Duncan, Phil, 4n, 58, 187

Etcoff, Nancy L., 58
Enelow, James M., 65
Eulau, Heinz, 21, 26, 64n, 88

Feldman, Stanley, 59
Fenno, Richard F., 7, 12, 14, 25, 26–27, 29, 40, 48–53, 59, 61, 88, 110n, 151, 159n
Ferejohn, John A., 24, 25, 27, 27n, 28, 31n
Fiorina, Morris P., 13, 14, 67, 73, 166
Fisher, Louis, 99
Fiske, Susan T., 58, 59
Fund, John H., 165

Galvin, Thomas, 165n
Gelman, Andrew, 59
Gigerenzer, Gerd, 43
Gilligan, Thomas, 44n, 65
Goffman, Erving, 55–56
Grafstein, Robert, 40n

Hamilton, Lee, 58
Harrington, Joseph E., 52n
Harsanyi, John, 67
Hershey, Marjorie Randon, 60n
Herstein, John A., 43

Subject Index

Abdication hypothesis, 21
American Association of Retired Persons (AARP), 5, 128, 129
Asymmetric information, defined, 44

Beer and Quiche, game of, 56–57
Beliefs, defined, 44
Bounded rationality
  as critique of rational choice assumptions, 40–41
  defined, 39

Cheap talk, 51–53
Common interest
  defined, 75
  predictions about role in trust decisions, 76–79
Consistent point. *See* Induced ideal points
Constituent demands. *See* Constituents
Constituent opinions. *See* Constituents
Constituent trust. *See* Trust; Constituents
Constituents
  ability to control elected officials, 20–22, 30, 159–61
  ability to resolve uncertainties over time, 19
  assumptions about motives, 12–13, 72–73, 149
  beliefs (demands, opinions) about policy options, 16–19, 67–69, 72
  decisions about trust, 24
  predictions about trust, 74–79
  use of stereotypes, 59–62

Delegate. *See* Role orientation (legislator)

Electoral connection. *See also* Induced ideal points
  conventional wisdom, 30–37
  connection models, 155–59
  defined, 1–2
Ethics Act of 1989, 15, 16, 52, 96, 99, 151, 163n, chap. 5 passim
  described, 4
  constituent demands, 103–5
  legislator preferences regarding ethics provisions, 102–3
  legislator preferences regarding pay provisions, 101–2
  procedures used to vote on, 164
  reputational impact of votes, 118–21
  sources of trust, 106–11
  test of explanation hypothesis, 115–18
  test of leeway hypothesis, 111–14
  test of marginality hypothesis, 114–15
Evaluation game
  description of equilibria, 80–85, 178–84
  structure, 67–73, 171–78
  trust defined in terms of, 66
Explanations
  as cheap talk, 51–53
  defined, 49
  conventional wisdom about effects, 49
  how members of Congress view explanations, 49–53